Trout on a Nymph

Trout on a Nymph

John Roberts

The Crowood Press

First published in 1991 by
The Crowood Press Ltd
Ramsbury, Marlborough
Wiltshire SN8 2HR

British Library Cataloguing in Publication Data
Roberts, John, *1953–*
   Trout on a nymph : major tactics of the trout stream.
   1. Trout. Angling
   I. Title
   799.1755

   ISBN 1 85223 340 0

Black and white line drawings by Anthony Richards

Typeset by Acorn Bookwork, Salisbury, Wiltshire
Printed and bound in Great Britain by BPCC Hazell Books, Aylesbury

Contents

Dedication

To Roy Shaw, a master of the chalk stream and camera lens; Oliver Edwards, from whom no trout is safe; and Lars-Åke Olsson, fishing host of incomparable generosity.

Acknowledgements

I am indebted to Tony Richards for his line drawings and for the excellent painting used on the jacket.

My thanks to David Howden, Nick Bradley and especially to Oliver Edwards for reading and commenting on my manuscript drafts. But for them my errors would be many more. In fairness to the reputations of these gentlemen I must point out that none of the three agreed entirely with all I have written but gave me the benefit of their wisdom as we discussed fishing theory and practice.

The flies illustrated have been tied by Hans van Klinken, Oliver Edwards, Charles Jardine, Gary LaFontaine, Lars-Åke Olsson, John Goddard, Nick Bradley and myself. The nymphs tied by Frank Sawyer were supplied by Lars-Åke Olsson and those tied by Polly Rosborough and Charles Brooks were supplied by Charles Jardine. I am extremely grateful to Roy Darlington for providing access to the Abbotts Barton water of the Itchen; for his tireless but fruitless efforts to track down a genuine Skues-tied nymph and for allowing me to photograph his collection of Skues nymphs tied by the excellent Danish fly-tyer, Henrich Thomsen. My gratitude is also expressed to Lt.-Col. Charles Harcourt-Smith for giving access to the upper Avon where Frank Sawyer spent most of his life. I am grateful to Gary LaFontaine and Greycliffe Publishing for allowing me to quote from *The Dry Fly – New Angles*. Roy Shaw, Lars-Åke Olsson and Arthur Oglesby have kindly supplemented my own photographs. The colour plates of flies were photographed by Tony Pugh.

I imagine that all the anglers with whom I fish have influenced me over the years. Every one has taught me something, but more than that, has increased my enjoyment of fishing and of life. My special thanks go to David Howden, Richard I'Anson, Lars-Åke Olsson, Roy Shaw, Oliver Edwards and Nick Bradley.

I doubt if I shall ever have the chance to thank the following personally. I've never fished with any of them except as I've stood at their shoulder as they've written of their experiences of fact and fiction. All have two things in common; they have made me question why I fish the way I do and they have entertained me greatly, sometimes to the point of tears of laughter. With these men I've laughed at myself and after a fishless day I've learned to hear a trout laugh too. Thanks to David James Duncan for the *The River Why*, Nick Lyons, Don Zahner, Ed Zern and by no means least, G.E.M. Skues.

A NOTE ABOUT HOOKS

There are a number of manufacturers of high quality fly hooks. In my opinion one British company is outstanding in the quality of its products and in the suitability of their range to tying a wide range of trout flies. Partridge of Redditch Ltd also try to rationalize shank length and gape to produce some measure of standardization in their hooks. In giving the dressings of flies I have offered one or more hook styles from their extensive range. The code is given in each dressing.

1 Nymph Fishing – A Personal Philosophy

'I fish; therefore I am.'
Slogan on an American T-shirt.

I started out to write a book about nymph fishing on rivers and streams. In fact there are considerable grey areas in sub-surface fly fishing as to what exactly constitutes nymph fishing. Where do caddis larva and pupa imitations fit in and what of wet flies and North Country spider patterns? Almost inevitably I will not satisfy everyone's definition. For some readers this book will be a compromise; for others an overstatement.

There was once, I suspect, a fairly narrow definition of what was and what was not nymph fishing. My guess is that British nymph fishing was unduly influenced by the practitioners of their craft on the southern chalk streams. No doubt these waters offered the very best trout fishing and the writers who extolled the angling virtues and sang the entomological praises of these rivers gave the fly-fishing public, most of whom rarely saw a chalk stream, let alone cast a fly on one, a prejudiced opinion on fishing an imitation of the natural nymph. Their views were in some respects quite understandably and forgivably restricted to a style of fishing on a mere handful of streams in a relatively small area of the country. Their eloquent voices described limited methods of presentation of a type of artificial fly that was marvellously successful on clear chalk streams. Only once before had so many been influenced by so few.

Because Halford and his disciples propagated a gospel from Hampshire which had its effects the world over it was almost inevitable that any new age should have its inception in the heartland of the old order. G.E.M. Skues

and others of a later generation spoke up for the place of the sub-surface nymph imitation with conviction and sufficiently loud voice to ensure that their influence spread equally as far. Largely as a result of these reformers a new code developed and the chalk stream fishers confined nymph fishing to the upstream presentation of a usually quite small, sometimes weighted, imitation of an ephemeroptera nymph. Most would further restrict the presentation to visible trout only. The narrow definition that I alluded to in my opening remark still applies on some waters. Nymph fishing may have once been restricted to this and it may still apply on a few score miles of water today but in reality nymph fishing is very much more. We owe a great debt to Skues and later to Frank Sawyer because they influenced the whole course of fly fishing, of nymph design and presentation and more importantly, caused fly fishers to think about their imitation and its behaviour before they cast a fly.

Ninety-five per cent of the imitation of nymphs on running water takes place away from the chalk streams. We have developed a wider, more catholic code for the different and more diverse requirements of the freestone rivers. The range of fly life is broader, the water course more varied, the stream ecology so different that nymph fishing has become much more comprehensive in the fly patterns and methods of presentation. Some of the methods and flies I describe will not be accepted as nymph fishing by some fly fishers, a few of whom are good friends of mine. Here we agree to differ. If the flies and presentation styles I use are duping trout by convincing them that what they are feeding on is a nymph then what can I call the technique but nymph fishing? The term is broad and comprehensive; it covers the imitation of nymphs, however that is achieved. Wet-fly fishing is rather different for as I will discuss later, I doubt very much whether the flies used are taken as nymphs. I also consider the imitation of caddis larvae and pupae, midges and shrimps. They are not nymphs but their fishing styles are similar and are included for that reason. The purpose of this book is to re-examine the fly life and some of the other fauna of the stream with a view to presenting it to trout below the surface and to maximize the opportunities for taking trout with suitable imitations.

Nymph fishing is rarely easy. Do not be deluded by anything I may write. The sub-surface fly fisher works his imitation in a three dimensional world where a fourth variable, speed, also has a major influence. The dry-fly fisher escapes with two dimensions and the much less variable effect of speed on the surface fly. The nymph fisher has the problem of depth to solve. What depth should I fish? How should I get the imitation to sink there? How is its movement controlled, perhaps four feet below the surface? For most of the time the dry-fly fisher thinks only in terms of fishing in a dead-drift; such is the way the natural fly usually behaves. Upwinged and stonefly nymphs, caddis larvae and pupae, shrimp etc. all move at different speeds with different motions, at different times, in different parts of the river, at varying depths. They

Nymphing successfully in the style of Frank Sawyer on his home water near Netheravon.

drift, swim, crawl or dart downstream, upstream or across the stream, they swim to the surface and back to the weed or stream bed. The dead-drift works, but not all the time.

A rising trout is a friend indeed. Its lie is known, perhaps even what it is rising to. It feeds at the same depth every time: on the surface. The natural it takes is usually in our world – in the air not the water. For trout to surface-feed is all we could ask of them. When they don't feed on the surface, when there may not be a sign of a feeding fish anywhere in the river then it is the more difficult world below the meniscus that we are obliged to enter. We are forced to encounter the trout in its own territory, conceding ground all the way. We have to meet them on their terms, offering them what they want, in a manner they find acceptable. Perhaps it is true that nymph fishing is the last resort of the frustrated dry-fly fisher.

If there are no trout rising the most likely chance of success lies in a sub-surface imitation. For what proportion of the fishing day or the fishing season are trout actively surface-feeding on your river? If we are honest we will admit that for only a relatively short time during most days are fish concentrating on hatching flies, mated females or terrestrials. The rest of the time they are awaiting the hatch period or actively feeding below the surface. Some dry flies might bring a trout to the surface but the best bet is to offer something on their own level. Over the season the duration of surface-feeding activity varies from day to day. On the best hatch days perhaps the dry fly will work well for many hours, with the nymph required only during the lulls. At worst, not a sign of a fish will be seen all day and a sub-surface imitation is then the only course of action. Even if fishing the dry fly is the most pleasing way of fishing, it is not necessarily, over a season, the most effective way.

I have always felt that when faced with a feeding, yet uncooperative trout – they are confidently taking either a surface or sub-surface natural but never an imitation of the same – that the nymph fisher has a distinct advantage over the persistent dry-fly angler.

A trout that is concentrating on a nymph, pupae or emerger is much more likely to be duped by a sub-surface presentation than a dry fly. This of course goes without saying. But if the nymph fails, it is an exception for a floating pattern to work. However, if the rising trout feeding on the surface will not take an artificial dry fly it might fall for a sub-surface imitation. A trout which is concentrating its feeding below the surface is rarely lured to a dry fly. Even if a trout rises confidently to a dun or adult caddis and the artificial fails, an appropriate nymph or pupa just below or in the film will often work. *The nymph, or to be more accurate, the sub-surface fly fisher stands more chance of success in most difficult situations.*

I am wholeheartedly behind anyone who says he fishes the way he does because it gives him the most pleasure. It may not be the most productive way of doing things but as long as it's within the rules it's fine with me. I'm a born-again hedonist when it comes to fishing. The enjoyment I get from fly fishing is the only reason I go. My preferred style is a dry fly and I find the pleasure increases when a fish rises to it. But if I can't persuade a trout to rise to the scores of patterns I carry or the alternative presentations I might try, the pleasure wanes. The sub-surface approach has to be made. You might fish only with a nymph and rarely consider a floating fly. If that is what you enjoy (and if it's within the rules) go ahead. Measured over a season I think the sub-surface fly fisher will have more taking opportunities than the dry-fly fisher. I imagine most of the pleasure is derived simply from catching trout on an imitation of what they are feeding on.

My hope is that I might add to your knowledge of nymph and trout behaviour, thereby thrusting the rod firmly back into your casting hand, for the theory to be put into practice. The rest of this book explores some alternative nymphing styles and patterns, some of which I hope you will find successful on your rivers. Better still, I hope I set in motion a train of thought that inspires you to experiment further, resulting in a more effective presentation or pattern.

2 The Natural Nymph

'. . . to an entomological collector the rarity of a species enhances its value; to a fly-fisher on the other hand, the frequent occurrences of a species, and its being widely dispersed or found upon all waters, constitutes the strongest reason for preferring it, because the fish feed upon such species more readily.'

Alfred Ronalds *The Fly-Fisher's Entomology*

I have been surprised just how often – when I've been seining the river or participating in one of my favourite non-fishing river activities, stone turning – that a fellow fly fisherman has peered over my shoulder and gawped *'So that's what they look like!'* or even *'What on earth are those?'* You too have probably met his ilk; fly box by Fabérgé, Gucci waders and waistcoat by Yves St Laurent but a bit clueless when it comes to the business end of the leader. There is no excuse for ignorance in even only a moderately experienced trout fisher. If you want to catch trout with a fly you have to know what trout eat and how the natural fly behaves. This sounds just too logical to have to say but ignorance about stream entomology amongst some fly fishers constantly surprises me. We don't have to achieve entomologist status, merely an understanding of the basics. We are *fly* fishermen and more specifically *nymph* fishers. We have to know what the natural fly looks like and how it behaves. The angler who rakes the stream with a motley collection of patterns simply because they sometimes catch fish is enjoying his sport on a superficial level. At the other extreme, I've met some fly fishers who could happily converse with a passing Roman centurion, such is their fluency in Latin. Because he struggled to ingrain *Amo, Amas, Amat* into me my old classics master would despair if he could hear me trying to wrap my tongue around *Aphelocheirus montandoni*. Most trout speak English.

Scientists have a variety of names for the larval stage of the ephemeropeterans and nymphs, larvae, nymphules and naiads are all correct terms. As far as this book is concerned the immature nymphs are called larvae which, upon reaching maturity, i.e. displaying wing pads, are described as nymphs. It is at this stage they are imitated by the fly fisher. Strictly speaking, a nymph refers to the larval stage of the upwinged flies (ephemeroptera) or stoneflies (plecoptera) but so far as the fly fisher is concerned the term is rather loosely used to describe almost any subsurface food imitated by an artificial fly, except a small fish imitation. Larvae and pupae of other fly orders and other fauna are really not nymphs and are classified differently but the trout fisher is apt simply to claim he is nymph fishing when fishing below the surface.

UPWINGED OR MAYFLY NYMPHS (EPHEMEROPTERA)

The term mayfly is easily confused with the British and European species *Ephemera danica* and *E. vulgata* which are both specifically known as the mayfly. Therefore, in keeping with increasingly widespread practice, I have referred to ephemeroptera as upwingeds, although of course no nymphs have wings.

The upwingeds really are the fly fisher's flies. Much of the trout literature in the past has been devoted to writing about the fishing methods and imitations of the nymphs, duns and spinners of that order. We haven't ignored the stoneflies, caddis, midges, alders, smuts and the hundreds of assorted terrestrials but they have attracted less attention, at least by authors if not by trout. When writers of the English classics of nymph fishing mentioned nymphs they meant the nymphs of the upwingeds as being the true nymphs. We too start at this point.

Well-oxygenated water is the primary requirement for the habitat of ephemeropterans and it is no coincidence that the demand for unpolluted, well-oxygenated water is also shared by trout. It is unusual to find one without the other in the natural environment. Ephemeropterans thrive in water of high alkalinity although some of the more important species like the large dark olive (*Baetis rhodani*) are remarkably tolerant of slight acidic water. A stable temperature without the extremes of winter ice or intense summer heat is the most conducive to the survival and growth rates of all aquatic fauna. Although one temperature extreme may be tolerated it is the wide variation that proves unattractive and inhibits growth. The chalk streams and spring creeks, or American tailwaters below dams, provide a regular flow of highly alkaline, well-oxygenated water of a relatively stable temperature and are most favoured by aquatic flies. It is quite probable that streams able to produce two generations of a species in a year, as opposed to one generation elsewhere, are able to do so because of the stability of the water temperature.

Tiny larvae hatch out of the eggs that have adhered to stones, weed, rocks or obstructions along the river bed or bank side. Those eggs may have been deposited there by the subsurface-crawling female spinner some months previously or they drifted deeper and further downstream after the spinner had laid them at the surface. The eggs of a number of common species can develop parthenogenetically (i.e. without fertilization) although they may take longer before hatching, and in a few species produce only females. In a few *Baetis* species ovoviviparity (live birth of larvae after egg hatching within the female) rarely occurs.

Most upwingeds produce one generation of young per year and have a life cycle of approximately twelve months. Most of the eggs are laid in the summer months and they hatch out after a few weeks or months (some overwinter as eggs, others as larvae). They live as larvae or nymphs until maturity whereupon they emerge as duns, almost exactly 365 days later. After the final adult stage as a spinner the cycle is repeated. Other species produce two or more generations per year and at least one species, *Ephemera vulgata*, the true Mayfly, produces one generation every two or possibly three years.

The larvae or immature nymphs grow by a series of moults, each stage between moults being known as an instar. Most species experience twenty and thirty instars. Larval growth for some species is very slow during the first months but this is dependent upon a number of factors which influence the time interval between moults. During early larval life the moults occur with some frequency, sometimes only with a few days between each one. As they near maturity, usually 7–12 weeks before emergence, the wing pads appear on the dorsal side of the thorax. The final instar stage might last two weeks for a species that produces one generation per year. During the final instar gas builds up inside the nymph which aids the ascent to the surface and may help to split the nymphal skin. We are not able to say with certainty where the gas build-up originates but it may be produced by the nymph from dissolved gases in the water or by taking in air at the surface.

Temperature is the single most important variable, for those species which have been monitored. In a typical freestone stream, at winter temperatures the growth rate is almost nil but at warm summer temperatures a growth rate of 2–3 per cent per day has been observed in a number of species. The length of time spent from the egg hatching to adult emergence varies between species and between different rivers with lower and upper limits of two and thirty-six months. Other factors affecting growth rates are the available food and the chemical composition of the water.

It should be noted that because some species produce two generations a year mature nymphs will occur some months apart from each other. For species whose emergence is

Assorted nymphs: two stone-clingers, an agile-darter and a moss-creeper.

over some months through the season mature nymphs will be found throughout that period. Those with a two or three year life cycle will live throughout the trout season as nymphs in various stages of maturity with only the mature ones showing any inclination towards emergence.

Nymphs of the same species in different rivers sometimes vary quite significantly in their colouration. I have found this to be particularly so for the stone-clinging types, some of which have been almost black. Yet the same species from another stream might be much browner and considerably lighter. The variation might be due to different stages of maturity but it is more likely to be for reasons of survival. Many species in the animal kingdom are able to change their colouration to camouflage themselves from predators and blending in with the substratum is quite possible for nymphs. It would be particularly re-levant for the stone-clingers with the different shades and colours of stones etc. and less applicable to the moss- and weed-dwellers. This may in some way explain the variance in nymph colouring between rivers.

The nymphs of some of the different families within the order vary quite visibly in their body shape and size. Their general characteristics are similar and they share the same structure – an abdomen of ten segments with gills, a three-segment thorax, head, six legs, two antennae and three caudal filaments or tails. (Some European and North American species do not have the third middle tail but all British species do.) Accurate identification of nymphs is extremely difficult in many species and has to be left to experts. Family classification is, in most cases, easier but fly fishers group them by more practical criteria. Fortunately, trout identify them by their size, shape, colour, habitat and behaviour and beyond these characteristics we need go no further. For our own simple requirements we have classified them as agile-darters, stone-clingers, burrowers, moss-creepers, crawlers and laboured swimmers. Even at first glance it is possible to put most specimens into one of these categories. The body shape of nymphs varies between families, unlike those of the adults which are all very similar. The basic characteristics common to each type are summarized below.

Nymphs have adapted to their environment in a way that has influenced their body form and behaviour to cope with different water speeds, types of stream bed and the presence or absence of vegetation. Just as the physical characteristics of different trout rivers vary and as significant physical changes occur even within yards on the same stream then so those different environments attract different fly species. It is the micro-habitat of a few square feet that is important to the nymph. This knowledge is one of the basic tenets of the all-round nymph fisher. There are very good reasons why some rivers have certain species in abundance but will never play host to others.

The Agile-Darters

Families Baetidae (includes species of the genera *Centroptilum*, *Baetis*, *Cloeon* and *Procloeon*; *Callibaetis* (N. America)), Siphlonuridae and Isonychidae

This is probably the most important group of nymphs for many fishermen, especially those on the chalk streams, spring creeks and limestone streams in which the prolific Baetidae abound. They also figure prominently on many freestone rivers but not in the same numbers. For the most part when Skues, Sawyer and Kite were writing about nymph fishing this was the only group they were imitating. Chalk-stream nymphing had, and probably still has, a fairly narrow theology within the very much wider church of subaqueous fly fishing.

Most of these nymphs are strong swimmers and are capable of movement through the

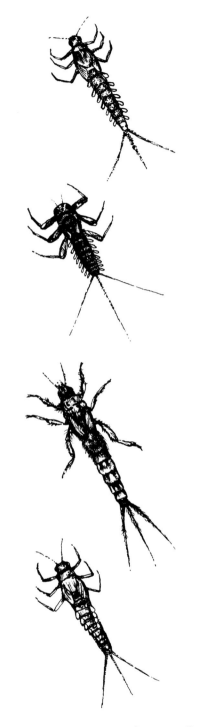

Fig 1   Four Ephemeroptera nymph types: agile-darter, stone-clinger, burrower and moss-creeper.

15

current to swim in search of food, to escape predation and to regain their safety after being dislodged from their habitat. All are capable of very sudden and rapid darting movements. Similar movement of the artificial is quite acceptable and sometimes necessary for satisfactory deception. The streamlined, slim, cylindrical body shape indicates their ability to move in a turbulent environment. In comparison with some of the other nymph types the tails are relatively long and hairy and are important in the swimming process. Many inhabit vegetation which can be found at all water levels from stream bed to the surface and so the nymphs may be expected at any depth.

Many *Baetis* are quite small, both as nymphs and adults. The size of a fly is generally quite irrelevant in their attraction as a trout food. It is the numbers of individuals available that is of more interest to the feeding fish. Many small flies, either as nymphs or duns will entice fish to feed more than a sprinkling of a larger species. It is their abundance of the *Baetis* species that makes them the centre of a trout's attention.

The Stone-Clingers

Family Heptageniidae (includes species of the genera *Heptagenia*, *Rhithrogena* and *Ecdyonurus* and N. American *Epeorus* and *Stenonema*)

Fast-swimming, agile-darting nymphs, typical of those that are the major nymph-type of chalk streams.

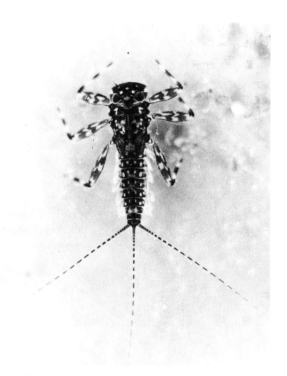

A well marked stone-clinging *Heptagenia* nymph.

As their name suggests the clingers attach to stones, rocks or any smooth surface near the river bed. Many can swim but they are quite ungainly in comparison to the agile-darters. The clingers are much less proficient and are rocked about in turbulent water. The bodies are wide, not very deep, and appear as though squashed or flattened and the eyes are on the dorsal side of the head. Their strong legs have large claws for gripping and holding themselves close to the substratum. Their shape enables them to hug stones in quite fast water. The gills of many species are quite large and serve to prevent water from getting between the nymph and the rock. Try prising these away from their stones and one realizes how efficient their structure is for holding on against force. It is probably impossible for trout to pick these off a smooth slippery surface. They are also very fast crawlers and although they venture on to the upper surfaces to feed they rapidly scurry to disappear down the tiniest crevices when predators approach.

Burrowers

Family Ephemeridae (includes species of the genus *Hexagenia* (N. America))

Mud, sand, silt and fine gravel attract the three British species better known collectively as mayflies. Twenty-seven North American species are burrowers. They rarely swim except to the surface to emerge and also during the days prior to emergence as they make hazardous exploratory journeys to the surface. Most are only of value to the nymph fisher in a hatch or pre-hatch situation or after a spate when the fine unstable substratum is disturbed and many of the nymphs swim in the opaque water just above the stream bed. At such times trout take them readily. The artificial mayfly nymph (*Ephemera danica, E. vulgata*) is a very effective fly on waters that experience good hatches of the naturals and

Ephemera danica, the mayfly nymph.

works well when trout are not fully geared up to their concentrated gluttony towards the duns. Few fly fishers express any qualms about matching the natural fly or nymph but Oliver Kite regarded the use of an imitation of the mayfly nymph as 'spiritual prostitution'. Perhaps only we British could make things more difficult for ourselves.

Stillwater and moderately paced currents are equally attractive but the slower the current the more likely is the build up of fine particles necessary for burrowing. The three British species are the largest of our upwinged nymphs (reaching one inch at maturity) but some of the American species are only a quarter of an inch long. The relatively long bodies and small heads are suited to tunnelling in the soft river bed. A U-shaped burrow houses each nymph. American studies have suggested that as many as 500 burrowing nymphs can inhabit one square foot of bed.

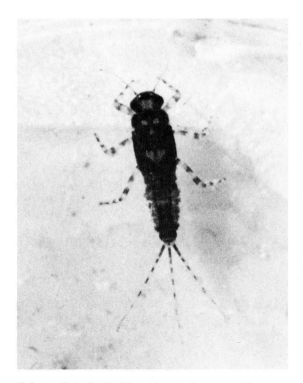

Ephemerella ignita; the blue-winged olive, one of the commonest nymphs on many streams. The barred legs and tails are very distinctive.

The gills are held over the back of the abdomen and aid the flow of water over the nymph whilst in its burrow.

Moss-Creepers and Crawlers

Family Ephemerellidae and Caenidae and N. American family Tricorythidae

The blue-winged olive (*Ephemerella ignita*) is one of the commonest British species. It is an important fly on many streams and is found in fast, medium-paced and sometimes slow currents. The moss-creepers live on moss and vegetable debris on the stream bed and crawl and occasionally swim in this vicinity. Some of the American species are quite different in shape from the two British species and more closely resemble the stone-clingers. It is the slow moving sections of rivers in which the build up of fine silt and mud accumulates that attracts the Caenidae and the American Tricorythidae. The bodies of these tiny slow-moving nymphs are covered with hairs to trap the fine silt particles that cover them and protect them from predators.

Laboured-Swimmers

Family Leptophlebiidae (includes species of the genera *Paraleptophlebia*, *Leptophlebia* and *Habrophlebia*)

The few species in this group are not very widespread in rivers. They have quite slim bodies and although they have long tails they are not equipped for fast propulsion as the tails lack the dense hair growth of the agile-darters. They crawl about the river bed among stones, pebbles, weed and decaying vegetation. In common with other poor swimmers, the imitations of these species are best fished in a dead drift.

Nymphal Movement

All nymphal movement is of relevance to the nymph fisher. Larvae and nymphs move in search of food and many are very efficient at free swimming. In addition to their restricted localized food search in weed or the stones of the river bed, nymphs also have other opportunities for movement.

A few species have noticeable horizontal and vertical movements through the substratum especially as they seek sanctuary in a spate. A few species are known to crawl ashore to moult from nymph to dun on dry land, and they are much more active during the days prior to emergence as they move laterally to and from the margins.

As might be expected in a flowing river there is some movement of nymphs and other fauna downstream. Freshwater biologists call this 'invertebrate drift'. It is a quite well researched field and some conclusions have been drawn. According to a standard work on nymphs, *Larvae of the British Ephemeroptera* by Elliot, Humpesch and Macan, there is clear

evidence of very much increased nocturnal activity which itself has peaks. Most species are more active at night as they search for food in relative safety from predators and many of these are caught up by the current. I know from my own observations of nymphal behaviour in my aquariums that they are much more active by night. Sometimes during the day there is little activity in the aquariums except for that of shrimps, but if I shine a light into the tanks at night scores of nymphs are on the upper surfaces of stones, and caddis larvae crawl about the bottom. Other research suggests that if food is scarce the nymphs may not be so passive about their entry into the downstream flow. Predation, pollution, temperature and current change may all encourage invertebrate drift. If nymphs are going to venture into the current it makes sense to do

Lars-Åke Olsson inspecting his window trap on the river Gim, northern Sweden. The night-hatching flies collide with the glass, stun themselves and fall into a tray of preserving fluid.

19

Scientific and Common Name	Distribution	Habitat	Months of Appearance of Full-grown Nymphs
STONE-CLINGERS: All require a substrata of small or large stones, rocks, pebbles or other smooth surfaces. They are able to swim.			
Rhithrogena semicolorata Olive upright	Mainly in the west of the country	Faster-flowing rivers, mainly riffles	April–September
Rhithrogena germanica March brown	Localized in Wales, North of England, Scotland	Faster-flowing rivers, mainly riffles	February–April
Ecdyonurus venosus Late March brown	Widespread, except south and east	Faster-flowing rivers, mainly riffles	April–June
Ecdyonurus torrentis Large brook dun	Widespread but localized	Smaller streams, mainly riffles	March–September, peak April–July
Ecdyonurus dispar August or autumn dun	North and west of England, South Wales	Mainly riffles but also in slower water	July–October, peak August-September
Ecdyonurus insignis Large green dun	North and west England, South Wales	Mainly riffles	May–October, peak July–August
Heptagenia sulphurea Yellow May dun	Widespread	Riffles, stony pools, weed stems	May–October, peak May–July
Heptagenia lateralis Dusky yellowstreak	West, south-west and north England, Scotland	Smaller rivers, riffles and margins	May–September
BURROWERS: All require a soft substrata of silt, mud or sand.			
Ephemera vulgata, E. danica Mayfly	Widespread, fast and slow rivers	Pools and margins	May–September, peak late May–June
MOSS-CREEPERS: All require a substrata of moss, aquatic vegetation or small stones. They are poor swimmers.			
Ephemerella ignita Blue-winged olive	Widespread	Throughout the river on vegetation and debris, mainly riffles	May–November
Ephemerella notata Yellow evening dun	Wales, north-west and south-west England	Moderately fast water	May–June

Table A   Characteristics of the Commoner British Ephemeroptera Nymphs

Approximate Time of Emergence	Place of Emergence	Size	Special Characteristics
Late afternoon and evening	Water surface	Medium	
Late morning and early afternoon	Water surface, often below riffles	Large 12–16mm	Nymph or emerger often preferred to the dun. Hatches sometimes concentrated over a short duration.
Late morning, early afternoon, dusk	Water surface, often below riffles, or in the margins	Large 12–16mm	Nearing maturity the nymphs sometimes move to shallower margins where they may emerge in the manner of a stonefly.
Daylight	Water surface	Large	Hatches often sparse but continuing through the day. Emergence also possible partly out of water on stones.
Daylight	Water surface	Medium to large	Mature nymphs also found in the margins. Emergence also possible partly out of the water on stones etc.
Afternoon and evening	Water surface	Medium	Hatches usually sparse.
Afternoon, evening and dusk	Water surface	Medium	Duns may possibly emerge below the surface in some instances. Research is inconclusive.
Evening and dusk	Water surface	Medium to large	Emergence takes place on stones below the surface.
Throughout daylight	Water surface	Very large upto 25mm	Lives in tunnels on the riverbed. Sometimes seen migrating to surface and back in days before a hatch. An active swimming ascent.
Mainly evening, also afternoon and dusk	Water surface, often below broken water	Varies from small to medium–large	Common and important fly. Possible high mortality rate at emergence. Emergers and floating nymphs work well. Nymphs inactive except at emergence.
Late evening and dusk	Water surface	Medium	Not found in small rivers. Nymphs inactive except at emergence.

Scientific and Common Name	Distribution	Habitat	Months of Appearance of Full-grown Nymphs
SILT-CRAWLERS: All require a habitat of fine sediment.			
Caenis spp. Caenis or broadwing	Widespread, most spp. prefer slow water	Upper layers of silt, mud moss in pools and margins	May–September
LABOURED-SWIMMERS/SPRAWLERS: All require a substrata of fine sediment or vegetation.			
Leptophlebia marginata Sepia dun	Slow-moving, slightly acidic rivers, often in the margins	Upper layers of silt, vegetation on the river bed, moss, stones	April–May
Leptophlebia vespertina Claret dun	Slow-moving, slightly acidic rivers, often in the margins	Silt and vegetation, moss and stones	May–July
Paraleptophlebia cincta Purple dun	North and west of England	Vegetation, silt and moss	May–August
AGILE-DARTERS: Found in fast-flowing and slower rivers; most prefer weedy alkaline water. All are strong swimmers.			
Baetis atrebatinus Dark olive	South, south-west and north of England, localized to alkaline water	Vegetation, moss and stones	April–May, September–October
Baetis niger, B. muticus Iron blue	Widely distributed except parts of the southeast	*B. niger* prefers vegetation. *B. muticus* found in stony rivers	April–November
Baetis rhodhani Large dark olive	Widespread, especially in faster rivers	Mainly in riffles on weed, moss and stones	Late February–May, September–November
Baetis tenax, B. vernus *B. buceratus* Medium olive	Widespread	Weed and stones	May–October, peak May–June
Baetis scambus Small dark olive	Widespread in alkaline rivers	Weed and gravel	March–November, peak May–August
Baetis fuscatus Pale watery	South of England, parts of Wales and the North	Weed and gravel	May–October
Centroptilum luteolum Small spurwing	Widespread on slow-moving rivers	Vegetation, sandy bottom	May–October, peak May–June
Centroptilum pennulatum Large spurwing	Localized in parts of Wales, south and north England	Weed, sandy bottom, slow-moving water	May–October, peak June
Procloëon bifidum Pale evening dun	Widespread in alkaline waters	Vegetation in slow-moving rivers	May–October, peak July–August

Approximate Time of Emergence	Place of Emergence	Size	Special Characteristics
Dawn, evening and dusk	Water surface	Very small 5.5–9mm body length	Imitation recommended only for use close to the surface during emergence. Nymphs otherwise inactive.
Daylight	Emerges via vegetation	Medium 10–11.5mm body length	Dark red-brown colour
Daylight	Water surface and via emergent vegetation	Medium, up to 11mm body length	Dark red-brown colour
Daylight	Water surface	Small–medium	Of localized importance only
Daylight and dusk	Water surface	Small–medium	Emergence often on cool windy days. Ascent often in a swim and rest, swim and rest motion.
Daylight	Water surface	Small	Known sometimes to make preliminary ascents to the surface by swimming or climbing.
Daylight, often late morning/early afternoon, dusk	Water surface	Medium–large	
Daylight, often late morning/early afternoon	Water surface	Small	
Daylight, usually afternoon and evening	Water surface	Very small, 7–8mm body length	
Daylight	Water surface	Small-medium, 9–11mm	Very fast swimmer
Daylight	Water surface	Small, 8–9mm	
Daylight	Water surface	Medium	Very fast swimmer. Often hatches alongside blue-winged olive.
Evening	Water surface	Medium	

so under cover of darkness. Studies of the large dark olive (*Baetis rhodani*) have shown that there are clear peaks at dusk and dawn and interestingly, the former period is when trout activity is high and the nymphs are open to predation.

It would seem that there needs to be some natural compensation for the downstream drift of nymphs or depopulation would occur. One suggestion is that the upstream flight of duns and spinners, known to be as much as two miles, provides the solution. The adults of some species actually fly downstream or are simply directed by the wind. Less well known is the upstream movement of some nymph species. This usually happens at night in the margins where the current is weaker, although the large dark olive is known to move upstream mid-current. As might be expected, upstream movement is generally less in distance and numbers than downstream movement. On average, less than a third of the number of those going down move upstream. From published studies it seems likely that most drifting nymphs travel between a half to three metres to a maximum of ten metres in a drift before returning to the stream bed. Upstream movement is much slower and not so far. It is doubtful whether any upwinged nymph can crawl upstream in a current speed greater than about one and a half feet per second.

In addition to the short excursions into the drift by the moss and stone-clinging nymphs and the short bursts of swimming by the agile-darters there is the most important period when nymphs leave their habitat: at emergence and in the days prior to the final ascent to the surface when their activity changes from nocturnal to diurnal. It is this movement with which the nymph fisher is primarily concerned.

Temperature change has a considerable influence on trout and insect behaviour. As water warms up from a lowish temperature it stimulates activity in both. The change may be on an hourly scale as the water warms during the day or on a seasonal scale as the average daily temperature increases from the early to mid or late season. If the extremes of very high

water temperatures are ignored it is a general rule that the warmer the water the more trout feed and the more active the insect life. It is not wholly true that trout feed solely because there is more insect activity but increased nymph activity obviously fulfils the trout's rising appetite. On a local scale the influence of temperature can sometimes be quite apparent. The shallows on the edge of the stream or pool warm more quickly than the rest of the river and on a sunny day it is there that sub-surface nymph and caddis activity first begins. In the early season when the rest of the river remains too cold for much insect movement it is in the sunny shallows that the fly life starts to move and the trout take advantage of this. A hatch may or may not result but the warmth makes the nymphs and caddis larvae more active, brings the stone-clingers on to the tops of stones, encourages the crawlers to crawl and the agile-darting nymphs to dart between the weed fronds. On many occasions I have fished early in the trout season and in midwinter for grayling when in the main food lane and other lies fish just haven't been bothered with my flies. The sun has come out and warmed the water at the margins and before long fish have been taken. They still haven't responded in the main lies where the depth is greater but only on the edge of the warmer shallows have they fed because the nymphal activity had begun. This isn't the only source of early season or midwinter food but it is one that is sometimes prompted by the sun's warming of the water.

Emergence

At the final instar the mature nymphs become agitated and restless and they can be observed being more adventurous in leaving their microhabitats. There is little doubt that the nymphs are unconsciously sensing factors in their environment that make it ideal for emergence. There comes a time when a nymph is physiologically equipped for the final moult to the sub-imago or dun stage but the trigger for emergence is awaited with others of its species for the conditions most suited to its survival. On rare occasions when

A close-up of the thorax and enlarged wingpads of a mature agile-darting nymph.

wading a clear stream I have seen quite sudden mass movements of nymphs. For a short time, no more than five or six minutes in my experience, it seemed as if hundreds of nymphs from a weed bed darted about frantically in the open water around the weed. Almost as quickly and as spontaneously as the activity began, it ceased. In each situation it was a mature agile-darting species. Such behaviour when nymphs act together *en masse* is attributed to impatience and frustration waiting for the hatch conditions.

As they wait, some species make preliminary ascents to the surface. It is thought that they do this to take in air that will eventually aid the splitting of the nymphal skin at the time of emergence. Other nymphs make preliminary excursions, crawling up stones or weed to the surface or into the margins. What is of no doubt is that during this movement they are relatively easy targets for feeding trout. On some days trout can be seen bulging and obviously feeding just below the surface without any hatch ever occurring. They may be taking tiny flies, midge larvae or smuts, but they might also be taking the non-emerging nymphs. *Trout actively feed on mature nymphs days before they emerge.* It is therefore extremely important for the nymph fisher to be aware of which species might be active in the stream at any time. There will be days when there is no

hatch is progress to betray which species is active and before every hatch there will be a period of nymph activity undetected at the surface. Knowing in what type of water, over what type of stream bed and when the mature nymphs will be preparing for emergence is a large part of successful nymph fishing.

The species that emerge at the surface ascend by swimming or floating. It should be remembered that except in water without any movement most ascending nymphs will be carried downstream a distance in proportion to the current speed. It is a downstream diagonal or zig-zag ascent. Blue-winged olive nymphs, (*Ephemerella ignita*) rise to the surface in a jerky undulating movement. Some species swim to the top without stopping, others swim and pause, being carried downstream in a horizontal dead drift at the whim of the current before swimming again. A few species appear merely to float to the surface with barely any movement at all. In slow-moving water nymphs may ascend almost vertically. Other species crawl to the bank at the water's edge or on to rocks that protrude through the surface to emerge on dry land.

Most nymphs make the final moult to adult form at the surface and it is these that require the fly fisher's attention. A few North American species emerge underwater and swim as winged adults to the surface, and this is

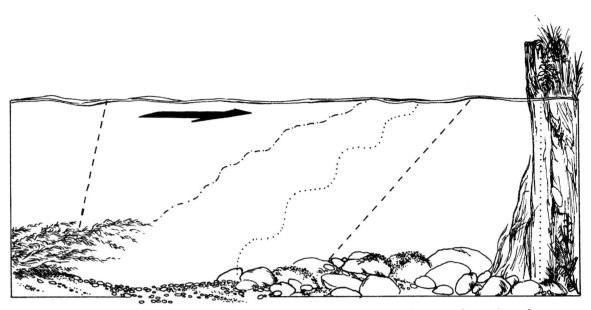

Fig 2 Nymphs ascend to emerge in different motions and at different angles depending upon the species and water speed. In slow water there will be an almost vertical ascent. Some nymphs make a steady unbroken ascent; others rise and pause, rise and pause; a few climb out of the water via stones and vegetation.

hatch in progress to betray which species is known to happen in Britain to the dusky yellowstreak (*Heptagenia lateralis*) and the yellow May dun (*Heptagenia sulphurea*). The other emergence point for a few species is by crawling out of the water as nymphs via the stony margins, rocks, plants, stakes or anything that will lead them from their habitat to air.

It is difficult to pin-point quite what the ideal conditions for emergence are. Scientists and anglers have found that water temperature or change in water temperature and light intensity are important factors but no foolproof basis for hatch prediction is available. What has become clear is that for the dun to moult to spinner it needs a certain amount of moisture retained within the insect body. If the air is too dry and the aridity means a significant loss of body moisture then the final moult cannot be achieved. This has meant that hatches during hot sunny days are frequently sparse and are usually delayed until evening. Delays in emergence because of unsuitable conditions leave the mature, eager-to-hatch, nymphs in an agitated state. If they are of a species that is normally a daytime emerger

then they may well be extremely active waiting for the necessary trigger. Nymph fishers should make the most of these opportunities; trout do.

The early season species are likely to respond to sunlight in addition to general air temperature. The sunny areas of the river will produce active nymphs and possibly a hatch. It often pays for fishing attention to be concentrated in these areas. As the season progresses the water temperature reaches the point at which hatches are more widely spread over the day. In the midsummer months it is the warm days with good cloud cover that provide the densest and longest hatches. The necessary water temperature or change in temperature is provided and there is sufficient light intensity to satisfy the hatch requirements but not an excess to prevent them. It is also probable that species that are primarily evening emergers will hatch earlier in the day on cloudy humid days. With few flies hatching during sunny summer days but with mature nymphs active it is not surprising that nymph fishing can be more effective than dry-fly fishing.

The nymph in the film takes on different characteristics from nymphs in their usual habitats. Beneath the nymphal skin is a fine layer of air around the body. The edges of the nymph become translucent and from a trout's perspective this is a highly noticeable feature when viewing the nymphs against a background of sky. It is not surprising that artificial emerger patterns that give a high priority to translucency are often more successful than those that do not.

The metamorphosis from nymph to sub-imago or dun, the first of the two adult stages of life cycle begins for most species when the nymph reaches the meniscus. The skin of the upper side of the thorax splits and then the skin over the nymph's head splits and the dun begins to emerge. The first sign of the wings is a crumpled clump which then becomes erected as blood is pumped through the wing veins and the adult pulls itself free of the nymphal skin (exuvia). The majority of trapped-wing and stillborn duns suffer their fate because they have been unable to break through the film and/or free themselves from the nymphal shuck.

In preparation for his book *The Dry Fly – New Angles*, Gary LaFontaine and a team of helpers undertook considerable research into what makes floating adults and emergers attractive. In particular Gary wanted to find out what were the characteristics of the natural fly at the emerging and adult stages that either triggered the rise or acted as confirmation to a wary fish that this really was food. This is what they discovered:

> The trait, one of the strongest secondary characteristics found in our work, only exists for ten to twenty seconds during the life of the mayfly. It so happens that this brief span coincides with the time frame of the trout's selection process.
>
> The trait was discovered by watching mayflies emerge in an aquarium. It was no ordinary aquarium, which is a limited tool for studying the appearance of an insect on the surface, but one with a partially mirrored bottom. The viewer, in our set-up, looks down at the mirror and sees the underside of the emerger.
>
> The hatching mayfly creates an aura, not a

brightness but a soft glow, as it climbs free of the nymphal skin. The way an insect breaks through the tough meniscus is by forming a meniscus, a concentration of molecules, of its own. It floats with its back pinioned in the film and the skin splits along the top of the thorax. Water doesn't rush in on top of the emerger because the edges of the skin are pulled out and by the tremendous forces of the newly created escape hole, or meniscus, spreading around it. The aura is this stretched, thin flange of skin, infused by light from the open sky and the reflection of air bubbles along inside the rim. From below it looks like the insect is wearing a halo.

The dressing for the Halo Emerger that Gary produced to incorporate the rim of diffused light can be found on page 147.

Surface tension works both ways and the emerging dun struggles to penetrate the film and shed itself of the nymphal shuck. The ease with which they break through varies. On some streams the mortality rate at this stage is relatively high and the floating still-born nymphs trapped in the film, and partially trapped duns are commonly found on

Fig 3   Emerging *Baetis* nymphs.

Heptagenia sulphurea, the nymph of the yellow May dun and an immature stonefly nymph.

the surface. This phenomenon also appears to vary between species. The blue-winged olive (*Ephemerella ignita*) is generally accepted as one that suffers a high mortality rate. Nature decrees that it is often at a major change in the life cycle of some creatures that a greater chance of mortality occurs and this cataclysmic transition from a nymph in a watery environment to a winged airborne adult is a transformation that takes its toll. Natural mortality, feeding fish and birds reduce the numbers of duns successfully leaving the surface. The life insurance premiums would be astronomic. The inch of water below the meniscus is the most dangerous for the fly and one of the most exciting for the fly fisher.

The difficulty with which nymphs struggle through the film varies between rivers. On a faster flowing river with a well-rippled surface I am inclined to believe the problem is rather easier than on a slow moving stream where the build-up of surface particles provides an additional barrier. This may be a reason why the stillborns and duns with wings trapped in the film seem much more commonplace on slower chalk streams and spring creeks than most freestone rivers. For the last sixteen seasons I have fished extensively on one small Yorkshire freestone stream. It is almost entirely free of pollution and because of its varying river bed enjoys many different upwinged nymph types. In the thousands of hours of my trout fishing on this water, most of which are spent actually wading rather than on the bank I doubt whether I've seen more than half a dozen stillborn flies. In contrast, I sometimes fish an equally small chalk stream that runs parallel just a half-dozen miles away. No-one suggests that the water there is pollution-free; a trout hatchery and the local sewage works see to that. Nevertheless the water quality is high and so is the surface tension. In the right light one can see what looks like a fine scummy surface film. In almost every hatch situation I have encountered, I have seen quite a number of stillborn and trapped flies. A closer examination of the surface shows a significant number of nymphs trapped in the film. Pollution of the sort that strengthens the surface film, on whatever type of river, inhibits successful emergence. On slow-moving rivers this becomes more of a problem as the fine particles are not dispersed by agitation.

STONEFLIES (PLECOPTERA)

In addition to the mature larvae of the up-wingeds the only other true nymphs are larvae of the stoneflies. They have attracted much less attention from fly fishers, principally I suggest because they do not naturally appear in midwater or higher in the stream in their emergence periods. The majority of writers about British nymph fishing have also almost exclusively restricted themselves to chalk streams where only a few small stoneflies are found. That small corner of the world in southern England defined nymph fishing very narrowly. The ninety-nine per cent of the rest of the world's trout streams enjoy varying stonefly populations. Trout feed readily on the nymphs, and despite what some respected English trout fishers have written in the past, the intelligent fly fisher will find great value in imitating them.

Stoneflies are widely distributed and as a general rule: the higher the altitude, the steeper the river gradient, the faster the water flow, the more stony the riverbed, and the greater will be the stonefly population. There are a few species like the willow fly (*Leuctra geniculata*) that prefer weedy lowland rivers but most prefer a faster, stony environment. Their micro-habitat is on the underside of stones and in moss. Of the thirty-two British species only about a dozen are of interest to the trout fisher, though rather more of the 400 North American species are of interest.

At first glance there is some similarity between the mature upwinged nymphs and the stoneflies. There is a strong resemblance in size and overall appearance of some species. All stoneflies have only two tails; all British ephemeropteran nymphs and the majority of North American upwinged nymphs have three. Here then is the easiest method of differentiating between the orders. The other easy confirmation lies in the position or absence of the tracheal gills. On the upwinged nymphs these are always along the sides or dorsal surface of the abdominal segments.

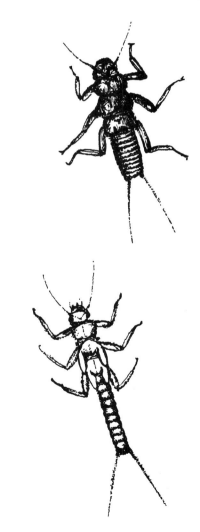

Fig 4   Two stonefly nymphs.

A large stonefly nymph (probably *Perla bipuncta*).

Some stonefly nymphs have no such gills or have them at the thorax, or more rarely, at the posterior end of the final abdominal segments. Despite some possible confusion in the names, no stoneflies are shaped like the stong-clinging upwinged nymphs. Each has two antennae, a head, three thoracic segments, ten abdominal segments and two tails.

The eggs hatch after a three to twelve week period. The nymphs live for about a year at this stage although a few large stonefly species live for three years and the largest of the American species for four years. All stonefly nymphs are ill-equipped for swimming and they move by crawling, which led to the large nymphs being given the common North Country name of creepers. The species vary in size but they all share the same relatively slim shape and there is no marked variation in behaviour as there is with the ephemeropterans.

The nymphs grow by a series of moults. The growth is more regular than in the ephemeroptera and even at low winter temperatures they grow steadily. Their movement is restricted to crawling around their micro-habitat although the larger species are known to crawl more widely up and down the riverbed. When the nymphs are fully mature the wing pads darken considerably until they become black and on some specimens in a very advanced state the folded wings can be seen under the wing pads.

When the time for emergence arrives the mature nymph of most species crawls through the margins and on to dry stones, gravel or occasionally vegetation at the water's edge. Where possible they seek shelter under stones or foliage. Here the upper side of the thorax splits for the winged adult to emerge. The duration of the metamorphosis can take some minutes and is much longer and less hazardous than the rapid transformation and almost simultaneous break through the meniscus of the upwingeds. Of the stoneflies I have watched go through this final moult I have not seen any that have died in the process. Many species do not leave the water until nightfall and dusk sees an increase in activity by the nymphs. The shoreward migration is not the quick swim to the surface of the upwingeds which might be completed in half a minute, but a slow crawl that will take many minutes on most streams and possibly hours on the largest rivers. This is a long time to be vulnerable to predation. A few American species emerge in open water and it may just be possible, if anglers' observations are anything to go by, that the British needle flies may also do the same.

Because the nymphs do not swim through open water to the surface, trout fishers have been apt to dismiss this migration as being of little relevance to nymph fishing. It should be pointed out that many of the old North Country spider patterns are stonefly imitations and these types of artificial have been used for centuries. The natural nymphs crawling along

Table B (*opposite*)   Characteristics of the Commoner British Stonefly Nymphs

Common and Scientific Name	Distribution	Months of Maturity	Size	General Characteristics
February red *Taeniopteryx nebulosa*	Localized in north and south-west England, Wales and Scotland	February–April	Small–medium, 8–12mm	Often found in slower rivers, on vegetation, moss or weeds.
Yellow sally *Isoperla grammatica*	Widespread except East Anglia and parts of the Midlands	April–May	Medium, 11–16mm	Often found in lowland rivers with gravel or sandy bottom. Adults have yellow body and greeny-yellow wings.
Small yellow sally *Chloroperla torrentium*	Widespread, prefers upland rivers	April–June	Small, 7–9mm	
Willow fly *Leuctra geniculata*	Widespread but localized	August–November	Small–medium, 8–11mm	Slim, grey-brown body. Often found in deep water in stones or gravel. One of the few chalk stream stoneflies.
Early brown *Protonemura meyeri*	Widespread and abundant	March–May	Small, 8–10mm	Overall a dark greeny-grey colour. Stony streams and on moss-covered stones.
Small brown *Nemoura cinera*	Widespread and abundant	March–July	Small, 6–10mm	Prefers slow-flowing water. Overall a dull brown colour.
Needle fly *Lectra fusca*	Widespread and abundant	August–October	Small, 7–9mm	Very slim; dark brown colour. Stony bottom required. Also in chalk streams.
Needle fly *Leuctra hippopus*	Widespread and abundant	February–April	Small, 6–8mm	Very slim; dark brown colour. Also found in chalk streams.
Medium stonefly *Diura bicaudata*	Localized in north-west England, Scotland and Wales	April–June	Medium, 9–17mm	Prefers small stony upland streams.
Large stonefly *Perlodes microcephala*	Fairly widespread	March–July, peak April–May	Large, 18–28mm	Brown and yellow colouring. Requires a stony river bed.
Large stonefly *Perla bipuncta*	Commonest in North, Not found in south, central and east England	May–June	Large, up to 33mm	Largest stonefly. Prefers faster water with bed of loose stones. Black or very dark brown with a bold yellow pattern.
Large stonefly *Perla cephalotes*	Fairly common and abundant except southwest	April–June	Large, up to 30mm	Prefers a firm river bed and moss-covered stones. Black or very dark brown with yellow markings

A large stonefly nymph, *Perlodes microcephala*.

Empty nymphal shucks after a stonefly hatch.

the substratum are an easy target for trout and grayling. This deep feeding may not be visible to the watching fly fisher and for that reason has become only a minor tactic in catching trout. However, during the period prior to a stonefly emergence this is an important food source and one that can be readily capitalized upon by the fly fisher. Some of my most successful fly fishing on northern rivers has been done in this way.

The Top and Bottom of It

I hope that one very relevant and important aspect of nymph behaviour is clear. *Except under specific circumstances, which are mentioned below, there is no great value in fishing a nymph midwater because the chances are there will be no natural nymphs there, and more importantly, there will be no trout either.*

Nymphs only appear midwater during their pre-hatch excursions to the surface, or during a hatch, or if they have been inadvertently dislodged from their weed bed home or the riverbed. The hatch, pre-hatch or dusk activity or any other accidental infringement into the current might draw trout into midwater but on most freestone streams at least, midwater is not a trout dining area. *In most freestone streams ninety per cent of the nymphal activity is in the foot above the river bed and the six inches below the surface.* However, on many days in the summer months there will be some mature nymphs of one or more species that will either be emerging or in the agitated pre-emergence state. Therefore it can be expected that there will be pockets of nymphal activity throughout the late morning, afternoon and evening which will in all probability attract trout attention.

In water less than thirty inches deep the midwater zone is never quite food-free. The currents lift the drifting fauna above the bottom and some will be carried a foot or so above the bed. This is midwater for this depth and it holds food. In a deeper run it would not be classified as midwater. It is obvious that in shallow water, up to about three feet deep, there is only a narrow relatively barren zone because the drift zone and the emerging zone represent a high percentage of the total. In water such as this a fish at the very bottom or in the drift zone will also be aware of food at the higher level. In deeper water the midwater zone is much wider and less likely to attract fish.

In much weedier streams agile-darting nymphs are dislodged from the weed beds and drift downstream midwater more regularly. Trout grub about at the rear of these beds mopping up the displaced fauna. The pre-emergence activity of the agile-darters can be quite frantic. In a chalk stream or other weedy limestone waters fish feed more widely from top to bottom.

The Amateur Entomologist

Part of the fascination of fly fishing is the study of the private lives of the natural insects that trout are so fond of and which we endeavour to imitate. If accurate representation of their characteristics and behaviour is sought by our artificials one of the best ways of learning about them is to collect and study specimens from the river. One or two home aquariums equipped with a bed of the river's substratum and water can provide a home for dozens of nymphs over a number of weeks. Each summer for five or six years I have sifted the weeds and turned the stones over in my local stream and brought home the stonefly

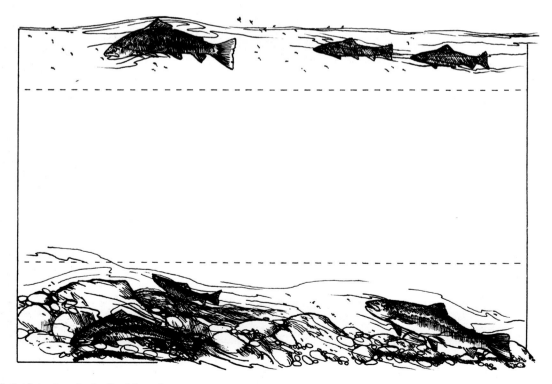

Fig 5   In water of a depth of three feet or more in a weedless stream there will be two distinct feeding zones; one just under the surface and the other in the bottom drift. There is very little food in the middle. In shallower water fish are prepared to move more widely to feed.

and upwinged nymphs, caddis and midge larvae. Some of the caddis and large stoneflies are carnivorous and will chase and eat the smaller species, so be aware that some species should not go together. Do not forget to provide a stone that sticks out of the water; this is the only way the stoneflies will ever emerge. Running water is preferable but by no means essential if the aquarium is kept well aerated with a small pump.

With such a window into their world one can study the different swimming motions of the various species, and most exciting of all, watch the emerging nymph metamorphose into the dun. Sometimes when there is a fine

surface film (relatively thick for the struggling insect) I suspect I've had a higher-than-natural mortality rate with stillborn and trapped duns. I've also noticed how half an hour's sunlight in an otherwise dull day can make the mature nymphs extremely active. Sometimes it prompts emergence; other times it does not. Nocturnal activity can also be observed. During the day there might be very little sign of some species but shine a light into a tank after an hour of darkness and it is a very different world. I keep a fine mesh net over the top of the tanks to prevent the duns flying away. It doesn't always work and I've found transposing spinners littered around the room. I guess

Roy Shaw on a weedy chalk stream where trout can be found more widely distributed from top to bottom.

that the room conditions are not as romantic as they should be; I've yet to persuade any to mate. Trying to produce a spinner swarm, still less get the mated female to return to the tanks is an impossible feat!

If you've never kept a nymph aquarium may I encourage you to do so. They are a source of great interest and will add another dimension to your fly fishing. Perhaps you've not even bothered to turn the stones over on the river or run a small net through the weed. Take those first steps and when your appetite has been whetted obtain a good identification guide to name your local species. Exact identification of some nymphs is impossible with-

out a low-powered microscope or magnifying glass. No trout can look that closely and for the purposes of imitation neither need we. But if you are keen, identification is easier in the duns and on the difficult species it is best left until this stage.

I strongly recommend two identification guides for British species: *Larvae of the British Ephemeroptera* (1988) by J.M. Elliott, U.H. Humpesch and T.T. Macan, and *Adults and Nymphs of British Stoneflies* (1977) edited by H.B.N. Hynes. Both are published by the Freshwater Biological Association. Some of the ecological studies from which I have quoted are referred to in these publications.

3 Trout and the Caddis

'As the dove to Noah, the sea to Xenophon or the shores of the homeland to the weary traveller, so is the first spring Grannom to the fly-fisher.'

David Jacques *Fisherman's Fly and Other Studies* (1965)

The caddis larvae and pupae are not nymphs in any sense except in the way they are fished. Because they are a subaqueous food source, the immature stage of an aquatic fly, the trout fisher represents these in a similar manner to the upwinged and stonefly nymphs. They fall within the scope of this book because it is only in their patterns and a variation in their presentation style that differs from true nymph fishing. Fishing the sub-surface caddis is a logical extension to nymph fishing.

Every trout stream abounds with caddis; the two are inseparable. Trout and grayling consume large quantities of the cased and free-swimming larvae, pupae and adults. Despite their regular and prolific appearance on the trout menu the specific imitation of caddis larvae and pupae was once fairly well ignored by most river fly fishers. With larval population densities that are known to reach into the thousands per square foot of river bed and with about 200 British and 800 North American species somebody was missing out and it wasn't the trout.

Surprisingly, it was 1977 before any author considered the lowly sedge and its imitation worthy of a book.

Larry Solomon and Eric Leiser's *The Caddis and the Angler* led the way, only to be superseded in 1981 by the excellent *Caddisflies* by Gary LaFontaine. It has proved to be a milestone in fishing literature. A sedge-starved fly fishing world at last had something of practical value. The British fly fisher has been rewarded with Taff Price's excellent book, *The Angler's Sedge* (1989).

THE NATURAL CADDIS (TRICHOPTERA)

The larvae are found on the river bed and more rarely amongst weeds. For purposes of imitation they can be divided into two categories; case-making species and free-living species. I confess that I am inexperienced in identifying individual species. Some of the families can be recognized by the construction of their larval cases but an angler's entomology need go no further than knowing what the larvae and pupae of the key species look like and how they behave. Common names have been given to the more important adult sedges but the larval forms are still simply referred to by a description of their case construction or the non case-makers by their colour. Some important species are recognized by their correct scientific name by a few fly fishers with an entomological bent but these are few in number.

Most caddis live for about a year and most of this time is spent below the surface as an egg, then a larva and the final sub-surface stage, the pupa, before emergence on the water surface as an adult.

Most larvae are slim, elongated and grub-like in appearance with soft segmented bodies and six short legs. The larvae of the majority of species build a case. From these the head and legs protrude but can be retracted quickly when danger threatens. To the uninformed a cased caddis is simply a cased caddis. On closer study one soon learns that there are scores of different case characteristics. Others are tube or purse-makers. The size, shape,

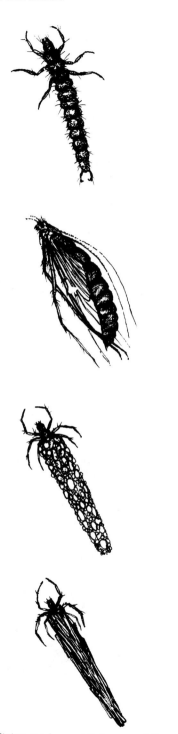

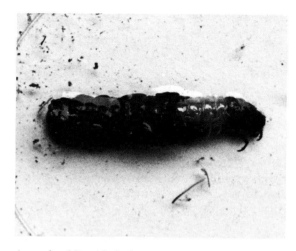

A cased caddis with the larva half out of its case.

Fig 6   Free-living caseless caddis larva, caddis pupa, and two cased larvae.

construction and the materials from which the cases are built are means by which families and genera can be identified. The size of the cases varies as much as the adults do; from just 2–3mm to 25mm or so in length. Some are straight or curved, some tapered, some round sectioned, square or highly irregular. They are made from materials of their environment, stones, sand, pebbles, sticks and plant segments. Some mix their materials, others use only one. These seemingly unappetizing and indigestible crunchy titbits are a favourite trout food. The high food value of the larva must make the unpalatable wrapping well worth while. Even the most unfavourable scientific studies of trout stomach contents give caddis larvae a highly significant place in trout diets. Studies I have seen vary but suggest the larvae represent between about twenty to sixty per cent of food consumed. They cannot be underestimated.

The cases (called shelters for the net-spinning species) are made by the larva sticking together the building materials with the aid of secreted silk. Over about eleven months approximately five instars are passed through by the larva and the case is extended each time to accommodate new growth. Some cases are anchored to the stream bed, from which the larvae of some species periodically emerge to collect food from spun nets. Other cases serve as mobile homes for the crawling larvae. There is considerable skill in the building of portable cases as the larva make them light enough to be carried but sufficiently heavy to remain on the bottom.

The free-living species (their name conjures up a picture of a Bohemian or hippy of the sixties) do not build cases but live amongst the stones of faster water, some collecting food by spinning nets between the stones and catching food from the currents. Others, like the characteristically green larvae of the Rhyacophilidae, also known as the green rock worm roam the stream bed, mostly on the underside of rocks and stones in search of food. They anchor themselves by their two anal claws to stones and spin a silken lifeline that allows them to regain their position if dislodged. These free-living species are very common on most faster freestone streams with many favouring the riffles. According to the American authority, Gary LaFontaine, some of these actually allow themselves to be lifted into the current. Their silken thread permits them to drift downstream and higher into the current. What a tantalizing sight for a hungry fish. I confess I've not heard of this phenomena in British species. My guess is that as a trout food they are more attractive than the case-makers. The imitation should be fished in a dead drift near the bottom. The natural larva suspended in such a way gives some credibility to the downstream presentation of a sub-surface fly as it hangs below the angler in the current. How better to represent the dangling larvae?

The vast majority of larvae do not swim. Some case-makers crawl very slowly on the river bed dragging their cases with them. As a result they are more difficult to imitate than the free-living types. Tying the imitation is straightforward but presenting it on the very bottom at an appropriately slow speed is very difficult. I have caught plenty of river trout on a cased caddis imitation but in my experience an imitation of the free-living species is much more successful. Selecting a larval imitation is no different from other fly-matching practice. One has to know what types of larva the river holds before going further. A two-inch brown cased caddis pattern won't catch anything if

the predominant larvae are covered in green vegetation or are free-living. The answer lies in getting your arms wet and searching the stream bed for examples. Don't forget to hold a mesh or net downstream of the stone-turning or weed-sifting as you may not find many free-living species clinging to the substratum. Although they can be firmly attached to stones some will be swept away and an inaccurate survey will be the reward.

There are differences in the feeding habits of different species of larvae. Some are herbivorous, some carnivorous and others omnivorous. In passing I'll mention that I am aware of a few complaints and suspicions from some fisheries which abound in the carnivorous species that their declining ephemeroptera stocks are due to the increasing abundance of carnivorous larvae. I'm afraid that I am ill-equipped to make a judgement about whether this could be possible.

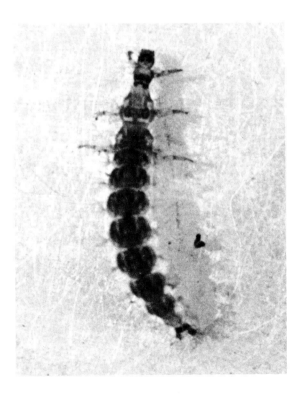

A free-swimming *Rhyacophila* larva.

Fig 7   Ascending caddis pupae.

At the end of their larval stage the cases are completely sealed and anchored to the stream bed. The free-living larvae build secure shelters on the substratum. Over the next fifteen to twenty days the larva begins its metamorphosis to the pupal state. Inside the pupal chamber the change is completed and under the pupal skin the adult develops. Wings and long antennae grow, a new abdomen is formed and the legs grow three-fold. Although the pupal skin still remains the fly inside has passed through its pupal stage and the pharate adult is ready to emerge. The angler continues to describe the insect which chews through its cocoon as a pupa even though it is in fact the adult enveloped in a loose, flexible and transparent sheath. The pupa is the insect at the stage between the end of the larval stage and the pharate adult during the time of its metamorphosis. I shall still continue to use the term pupa for the ascending stage as it has become common practice. The pharate adults of a few species, mainly the bigger case-makers, crawl ashore to emerge but the majority, and all those of interest to the fly fisher, emerge in open water.

The pharate adult or pupa releases gases within the sheath which aid its rise to the surface. As the sheathed adult leaves its cocoon it drifts downstream along the stream bed for a short while as it produces its buoyancy gases and co-ordinates its swimming. The distance of the downstream drift depends upon the current speed but distances of up to twenty feet are possible. Here they are vulnerable to predation by trout. The ascending pupa progresses to the surface. Some will be intercepted by trout in midwater but most take the rising insect at the surface. It is suggested that the adults rise to the surface like a balloon and burst through the surface at speed. Whatever the speed of their ascent they still have to penetrate the meniscus and its surface tension. Hanging below the surface the top of the sheath splits and the adult emerges. The act of freeing itself of the pupal shuck may take a few seconds and some of the most exciting caddis fishing takes place as trout concentrate on the emerger hanging in the film. In a sedge hatch when trout can become quite frenzied in their behaviour, rolling and jumping, it is invariably the emergers they are after and not the adults. Because the winged adults are completely dry there is no need to delay on the water and they take flight, often without even pausing on the surface. The pharate adults in their sheaths and emergers are taken in far greater numbers than the newly emerged adults.

It is therefore quite surprising that the artificial adult is so successful. The naturals are barely on the water for more than a few seconds at emergence and rather longer when they are egg laying, yet when fished intelligently a good adult imitation is a superb fly. For some reason trout find them attractive. The odds against a fish feeding on the adults in a hatch are fairly low and yet my fishing record shows I've caught a disproportionately high number of trout on adult patterns. The answer, as far as I'm concerned, is that many of the fish I've caught on an adult imitation have not been caught during a sedge hatch. Rather, because I wanted to fish dry I've used the fly as a search pattern when nothing has been moving. Because caddis can be expected at any time of day the imitation has been copying a natural fly that could well be anticipated. I use a pattern that is very lifelike and which can give the impression of movement; two very effective triggers to the rise.

The differences between species at the ascending pupa or sheathed adult stage are minimal and the only two of significance are size and colour. Many species are very similar. Of equal importance to the fly fisher is a key point of recognition which confirms to a trout the pupa's identity. This is translucency. The pupa at the surface is strongly backlit and the gas bubbles trapped beneath its fine semi-transparent sheath means that it is strongly translucent. I used to fish patterns with little translucency and they caught a fraction of the trout that have subsequently fallen to imitations designed with translucency as a priority. Incorporate size, silhouette and colour with translucency and you've got a winning formula.

Catching the ascending pupae to obtain examples from which to copy is far from easy. The stomach contents of trout will show examples but not live specimens in their colours and brightness. Stonefly and upwinged nymphs live for months but the swimming pharate adult might only be around for less than half a minute. A clue to the imitation is to visualize the adult enmeshed with folded wings inside its soft semi-transparent sheath. This will provide the size and muted colour. Then imitate the translucent sheath and you'll not go far wrong.

If sedges are popping off the water it is a pretty good bet that trout will be feeding off the sub-surface pupae. In slow water trout adopt feeding positions just below the surface. The current is such to allow them to stay there taking in a higher calorific value than they are expending. In a riffle or any fast water trout stay on the bottom in the slower current zone. They of course take the newly emerged pupae before ascending but they also watch the surface for the emergers below the film. They will traverse the current to intercept the fly and return to the stream bed. Any surface activity from fish in fast water has come from a fish that has a quieter lie in a zone of calm water, or from the very bottom.

The one other time sedges appear below the surface is when the females of those species that oviposit below the surface return. They often do so at dusk, a prime time for caddis emergence activity. Trout and grayling feed on the ascending pupae, the adults on the surface and the egg-laying females below. Some winged wet flies like the Invicta, Cinnamon and Gold etc. are successful at this time. A few patterns have been specifically devised to copy the sub-surface female.

I'm a big fan of the caddis; it provides so many fly fishing opportunities. They hatch throughout the season and can be expected at almost any time of day with evenings and dusk providing most surface activity. The dry fly is an excellent search pattern. Some species will continue hatching for months, possibly because there is more than one generation per year. Other species, typically the widespread and prolific grannom have their best hatches restricted to a few weeks. Caddis hatches of varying sizes can be seen almost all year. The larvae are permanently on the menu, 365 days each year, and the pupae and adults hatch almost every day of the trout season from the grannom of early spring to the caperer of late autumn.

FISHING THE LARVAL IMITATIONS

There are four keys to catching trout on any sub-surface flies. They are depth, movement or the lack of it, timing and pattern selection.

Depth

The primary feature in imitating the cased larvae is in presenting a suitable pattern on the very bottom. Anything higher in the flow than just inches above the stream bed will be viewed, in the manner of all unnatural presentations, with suspicion. It follows that the artificial has to be heavily weighted and might have to be fished on a sinking braided leader depending upon the water depth and current strength. The free-living species also require a deep presentation although the bottom-bouncing tactics are not so crucial to success.

Movement

Any dislodged heavy cased larvae drift very slowly along the bottom. To correctly match the behaviour of the naturals they must be fished more slowly than the speed of the current. If the free-living species are caught in the drift they will match the current speed. Some of the methods and tactics for the presentation of both larva types are considered in chapter seven.

Timing

Few fish will still be looking for food on the stream bed if flies are hatching at the surface and other trout are feeding on them. Fish go where the food is easiest to find and in most plentiful supply. If there is no sign of surface feeding – and this can represent a large part of the day – feeding attention will be diverted to the lower regions. On a weedless river all the food will be on the bottom and because larvae are present, usually in large numbers, on every day of the year the larval imitation is a good standby. On a weedier stream the chances of fish lying at higher levels is greater even though no hatch is in progress and using the deep sunk larva imitation is not as successful as a search pattern.

Pattern Selection

As in all fly fishing, pattern selection is a matter of matching the fly in the water. Copying the cased or free-living larva is still a question of matching the hatch or rather the non-hatch. You should discover just what types of caddis larvae live in your river. A stream bed survey should reveal many different species. On some rivers it is the free-living species and unattached mobile cased caddis that appear most in the diets of stomach-pumped trout; on other rivers the cased larvae predominate. The size, shape and construction materials of the cases vary between species and the imitation should be matched to the natural. Most free-living larvae are shades of green, from pale to very vivid green, beige or a dirty creamy colour.

I shall list some of the larval patterns that have been effective in my experience. One of the easiest ways of matching the cased caddis is to actually use sand, stones and vegetation from the stream bed. The result looks extremely natural, indeed it is almost impossible to differentiate between this and the real thing for the very good reason that on the outside, at least, it is the real thing! I confess I have never fished one of these natural caddis patterns. Firstly, I wonder whether the people who devise them mean them as a joke, and secondly, I have my doubts about their validity in fly fishing. I'm not normally one for ethical codes of doubtful value but I question the place of flies that have been constructed (certainly not tied) from the same materials as the natural. Why not glue an empty natural case on to the shank or impale a real larva on a hook? The *raison d'être* of fly fishing is imitation and not to use the genuine article – that is bait fishing. In my opinion, suitable materials to copy the natural case must be found.

Bradbury Caddis

Mottled contrasting feather fibres are very useful for producing a natural-looking imitation of the caddis case.

Carnill caddis larva.

Hook 12–18 long-shank Code H1A
Thread Brown
Underbody Fine lead wire
Case Golden Pheasant's tail feather fibres ribbed with fine gold wire for strength
Larva body Dubbed hare's ear fur
Legs One turn of brown partridge hackle
Head Peacock herl

Carnill Caddis
Hook 10–16 long-shank Code H1A
Thread Black
Underbody Wound lead wire
Case Two-toned fur from the leading edge of a hare's ear
Larva body White swan or goose herl
Legs Black hen wound sparsely
Head Black varnished thread tied quite large

LaFontaine Cased Caddis
Gary LaFontaine's exhaustive studies of caddis in their natural habitat show that as a cased larva drifts in the current it has its head, legs and front part of the body out of the case. The significant features are that as it wriggles there is a band of different body colour between the case and the head and because of the emerging larva the whole creature is elongated. To assist a more lifelike imitation Gary gives his hooks an upward bend and represents the case with clipped soft hackle feathers (speckled, mallard breast, lemon, wood duck, dark brown, grey grouse etc.) in a range of natural colours.

Hook 6–14 long-shank Code D4A or H1A. Bend upwards at 45 degrees the front third of the shank
Thread Brown nylon
Underbody Wound lead wire over the rear two-thirds of the shank
Case Soft gamebird hackle fibres wrapped together as far as the shank bend, and clipped to shape

Larva body Pale yellow chenille
Hackle Dark brown and grey grouse feather fibres tied underneath

Strawman Nymph

This is a simple dressing of a larva encased in a twig case. It was devised by American, Paul Young. The body needs weighting otherwise it is unsinkable.

Hook 10–14 long-shank Code H1A
Thread Strong brown
Underbody Lead or copper wire
Body Spun deer hair, roughly clipped and tapering to the rear
Rib (optional) Yellow thread

Caseless Larva (van Klinken)

Hook 12–14 Code H1A, E1A or K2A
Thread Black Sparton micro
Body Cream-coloured Body Gills (Traun River Products) or Furry Foam (Orvis) wound over an optional weighted underbody
Back Yellow Flexibody
Rib Clear mono
Wing-case Flexibody coloured black by waterproof pen
Thorax Mink body fur dubbed and well picked out

Latex Larva (Price)

Taff Price's comprehensive book *The Angler's Sedge*, (1989) lists this fine looking imitation of the free-living non-case-making species. A more durable alternative to latex is Swannundaze. Although weighting the larva isn't mentioned in the dressing I would recommend it as the naturals are all found close to the stream bed.

Hook 8–12 Code K2B
Thread Black or brown
Body Olive or green ostrich herl wound with cream or green latex so that the herl shows through as a rib
Thorax Brown seal's fur subs
Hackle Brown partridge

Green Caddis Worm (Olsson)

Apart from the obvious fish-catching capabili-

ties of this dressing it has the added advantage of being very easy to tie.

Hook 10–14 Code K4A, GRS6A, KB2 or GRS5B
Thread Olive
Body Four layers of copper wire or two layers of lead wire, covered by medium or dark olive-dyed fur. The front third of the body has a back of a dark brown or black feather
Rib Olive thread to form a segmented body and wound over the back feather

Free-Living Larva (Roberts)

I tie this pattern in green or beige to represent the *Rhyacophila* and *Hydropsyche* larvae. I can't remember how I came to tie them this way and if I've pinched someone else's dressing I apologize.

Hook 8–14 Code K4A or K2B
Thread Black
Abdomen Green or grey/beige dyed rabbit's fur, Orvis Antron/Hare blend or seal's fur subs over an underbody or lead wire or foil. Mark the upper sides of the front three segments with black indelible felt pen.
Rib Power Gum or clear mono
Thorax Dark green or dark brown seal's furs subs tied quite short
Legs Brown partridge tied as a throat hackle

FISHING THE PUPAL IMITATIONS

Depth

Trout feed on the pupae or pharate adult stage in two major and one minor dining zone. The principal areas are in the bottom drift and in the inches below the surface. The third zone is the variable expanse between the two across which the ascending pupae rise with some haste. Here the pupae are largely ignored but they are intercepted on the stream bed with ease and with even less effort at the surface. It is true that the rate of ascent varies between species with the general observation that the larger the species the slower the ascent; the smallest rise the fastest. It is a question of either weighting the imitation and using presentation techniques and line control to keep the fly down deep or ensuring that it fishes in or just below the surface film. The midwater presentation works in relatively shallow water, of say less than 2½ feet, where a trout has much less distance to move in order to feed.

Movement

One of the most attractive presentations when fishing a deep sunk pupa is the Leisenring lift (see page 131). This method allows the imitation to drift a little way along the bottom in a natural manner and then the fly is made to rise just like the natural pupa that has drifted downstream a few feet before heading for the surface. Any other variation that enables a drag-free natural deep drift to finish in a controlled rise will work very well. Fishing the weighted fly to give it a slack line dead-drift is also a fruitful method. An explanation of the methods and tactics for deep presentation are detailed in chapter seven.

Almost all pharate adults pause at the surface; very few are able to continue that ascend-ing movement straight through the meniscus. The length of time at the surface varies between species and is affected by the strength of the meniscus and possibly by the weather.

The emerger awash in the film should be fished in a dead drift without any movement. So too on most occasions should the struggling pupae below the film. Sometimes a more active presentation works, particularly if there is evidence of trout taking the natural pupae but the artificial one is refused. The answer might be to provide a feeding trigger and confirm to the trout that yours is a real one. This is done by imparting slight upstream movement to the pupa. It has been called the *stutter and drift* technique. Often it need be no more than a pause in the downstream drift rather than a positive upstream movement. The momentary pause is sufficient movement to represent the struggling adult trying to leave its pupal shuck and break through the meniscus. Just like the *twitch and drift* technique for the adult caddis the live presentation of the pupa can be deadly. Inevitably, any control of the fly that produces upstream or a slight sideways movement or a pause requires some degree of across or

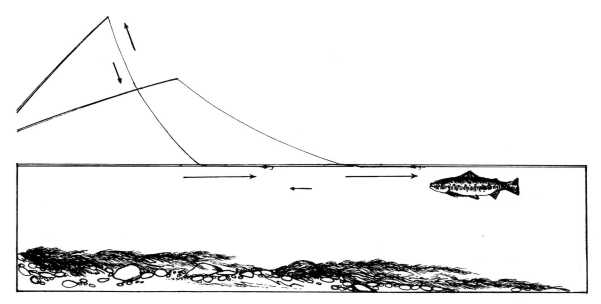

Fig 8   The stutter and drift technique. The pupa imitation just below the film is momentarily held against the flow or twitched very slightly before continuing its drift.

Fig 9   Presenting an arching rising pupa imitation downstream.

downstream presentation so that manipulation is possible. Casting upstream gives little chance of halting the downstream progress of the fly. If the fly is cast across the stream zealous line mending will produce the necessary movement. Cast downstream, the fly's drift can be interrupted and allowed to continue as line is fed out. The drift can be completed with one or more stutters as the drift is fished out. It is very effective where a trout is holding its position and visibly feeding regularly. The fly can be controlled to pause in its drift 12–18 inches above the fish and then allowed to continue. The life-imparting movement can make all the difference.

Dusk is a prime time for the emerging caddis and just when the light fails there is an easy way of fishing the pupa. Cast across or across and downstream with some slack line. As the line tightens the pupa begins to arc and this dramatic sideways movement can prompt some savage takes. For this reason hold the rod tip high so that there is a belly of line hanging between it and the surface – tight line may mean being broken on the take. It isn't particularly difficult but it is effective. It is less effective in the full light of day but at dusk trout and grayling are more forgiving. My experience in Lapland where there was but forty-five minutes of a very light night and a couple of hours of twilight and dawn was that from the late evening through to the early hours of the next day trout and grayling would take the pupa. Even when no hatch occurred they still took the pupa imitation and they always took it in preference to the adults when the hatch was on.

Timing

Fishing the pupal imitations is obviously most effective when the adults are emerging on the surface. Sometimes they work when there is no evidence of the adult but generally the pupa is not rated highly as a search fly. Trout seem enthusiastic about it when the naturals are ascending but when they are not there's not much interest expressed. My experience of its use on rivers leads me to believe that it takes the number that constitutes a hatch to attract trout attention. But when that attention is gained they really do concentrate on them. On the river Kaitum in Lapland I fished the caddis pupa imitation without any adults ever being seen and fish were happy to take them. I imagine on rivers like these where caddis are a majority food source which hatches twenty-four hours a day the pupa is more readily accepted.

If the species are those that drift down along the stream bed after chewing through their cases or it is moderate to fast water then the deep presentation works well, especially in moderate to faster water where the current will move anything that isn't swimming in another direction. Even when trout are feeding at the surface there may still be some deeper fish – taking drifting pupae from the bottom. If trout are not already at the surface at the beginning of the hatch period the activity will be centred on the bottom before trout get wise to the pupae pausing at the meniscus. Therefore the deep imitation may be fished early on in the hatch or when the emergence period is under way but few fish will take the pupae just below the surface.

Trout feeding on the pupae just below the surface and on the emergers usually betray their presence by a rise-form or water displacement that indicates their activity. It is an obvious time to try a suitable pattern especially if caddis are emerging. But pay attention; unless you are watching carefully caddis hatches can be overlooked and missed com-

Dusk on the river Kaitum, Tjuonajokk fishing camp, Swedish Lapland where the natural caddis abounds and the pupa imitation excels. This is the land of jumping grayling where a two-pounder can be expected to jump half a dozen times.

47

pletely. The adults are on the water for so little time, if at all, that they pass unnoticed by the angler. Sometimes they stay on the water a little while but in my experience most caddis move off pretty quickly. Some of the rise-forms can be misleading. Sometimes the surface is broken in a splashy rise which would normally suggest that a surface fly has been taken. Often it is because trout take the pupae so enthusiastically that they break the surface. If the pupa has risen fairly quickly trout will snap it up because they've seen its speed. Occasionally a trout will follow a fast-hatching pupa and leap into the air. In all these cases it is the pupae that trout are after. Presentation styles for fishing just under the film will be found in chapter nine.

Pattern Selection

As fly fishers began to realize the importance of the caddis hatches in recent years, some excellent pupal imitations have been devised. Twenty years ago the stream angler would have been hard pressed to produce an imitation from his fly box that was tied specifically to match the pupa. Now we are spoilt for

A sparkle caddis pupa under water. The translucent sheath is clearly seen to copy the same feature in the natural pupa.

choice. Many of the soft-hackle North Country spider flies have been used at least since the last century fished in and just below the film for a sedge hatch. They are still as effective and some of the dressings are found in chapter twelve. Most are very simple to tie and are no more than a dubbed fur body with a turn or two of a soft hackle. T.E. Pritt wrote of the pupal imitation with spider-type flies 'Trout undoubtedly take a hackled fly for the insect just rising from the pupa in a half-drowned state; and the opening and closing of the fibres give it an appearance of vitality.' Almost a hundred years later Carl Richards felt confident enough to proclaim that 'the soft-hackled fly is the best imitation of emerging caddis, from a size 6 orange to a 22 black.'

Below is a representative range of modern patterns.

Deep Sparkle Pupa

I believe that I am correct in suggesting that Gary LaFontaine's Deep Sparkle Pupa was the first pattern devised specifically to represent the newly emerged pupa on the stream bed. Other fly dressers devised a single pattern for both deep and sub-surface presentation. Usually patterns for fishing deep are merely weighted general pupal imitations. The Deep Sparkle Pupa is extremely successful and in Gary's hands has accounted for some fantastic catches.

Many of Gary LaFontaine's patterns use Antron as their main ingredient. He takes the credit for discovering the usefulness of this material when representing a translucent natural underwater. The original fibres were trilobal and are now in square cross-section. Each nylon filament is translucent *and* reflects light. It also has the properties and shape that attract and hold air bubbles. How better to represent the natural pupa with its gas bubbles in a translucent sheath? Appropriately coloured materials should be used to match the natural pupae. The Sparkle Yarn overbody should be tied in at the rear above and below the shank and combed out. This is then brought forward and tied in at the front of the body to cover the body in a sparse envelope.

Hatching Sedge Pupa (Roberts). A good pattern when fish are taking the pupae in the film.

Hook 10–14 Code A, G3A, CS7 or GRS2A with a weight of wound lead or copper wire
Underbody Mixed coloured Sparkle Yarn (Antron) sometimes mixed with natural fur
Overbody Coloured Sparkle Yarn (Antron)
Hackle Soft hackle or other feather fibres
Head Wound coloured marabou fibres or dubbed fur

A simplified version is also tied without the overbody.
Body Dubbed Sparkle Yarn (Antron)
Hackle Soft hackle or feather fibres
Head Wound coloured marabou fibres

Goldhead Pupa

In recent years this continental pattern has become popular in Britain. The weighted head means that the pupa is fished deep. Under water the bright head is dulled and is suggestive of the gaseous sheath surrounding the natural. It is an excellent autumn grayling pattern.

Hook 12–14 Code L2A
Thread Black
Body Dyed rabbit fur, coloured Antron, Erezi-dub, Body Gills or Furry Foam
Head Gold or brass bead

Hatching Sedge Pupa (Roberts)

I originally devised this style for stillwater fishing but the smaller sizes have also worked well on rivers, particularly in the riffles. The muddler-style head ensures it hangs in the surface film. The original patterns used coloured seal's fur for the body as this is translucent and is available in a wide range of colours. I also now tie them with dubbed Antron because of its additional qualities. The deer hair head need not be densely packed nor all the fibres trimmed to the same length.

Hook 10–22 sedge hook Code K12ST or K2B
Thread To match the body colour
Body Orange, green, brown or beige seal's fur or Antron
Rib Fine gold tinsel or wire on the seal's fur version only
Hackle Brown partridge tied as a rear-sloping collar
Head Natural deer hair spun in muddler style and roughly clipped

Latex Pupa

One way of achieving a translucent body is to use coloured or natural latex. A ribbed effect is produced which might look fine on a nymph imitation but does little to enhance a pupal imitation. Often the micro-caddis species are overlooked by trout fishers when puzzling over fish feeding on an unidentifiable food. This style of dressing is most suitable for such an imitation. A fluorescent floss underbody is also a useful variation. The latex should be ribbed under tension from the bend, relaxing towards the eye. The green and cream versions are also fair imitations of the free-living larvae.

Hook 12–20 Code K2B or G3A
Body Coloured or fluorescent floss wound with natural or coloured latex
Legs (Optional) Brown partridge tied either as a rear-sloping collar or on the underside only
Thorax Dark brown fur or peacock herl

Gongi Sedge

Hans van Klinken produced this variant on the latex body theme. It is primarily a pupal dressing but the clipped palmer hackle also makes it a good imitation of the free-swimming larva. I decline to explain the derivation of the pattern's name.

Hook 10–14 Code CS7, K4A or K2B
Body Wound latex
Rib Light ginger cock feather palmered and trimmed
Thorax Dark green seal's fur
Wings Bunched brown hackle fibres each side of the body

Mono Pupa

This achieves translucency through the wound monofilament body over a coloured floss or thread underbody. Its effect and use are similar to the Latex Pupa.

Hook 12–16 Code A, L2A, K4A or CS7
Thread Brown, green, orange or white (optionally fluorescent)
Body Tying thread overlaid with clear colourless mono tapering to the rear
Legs Partridge hackle tied as a rear-sloping collar
Head Brown fur or peacock herl

Emergent Sparkle Pupa

In this, Gary LaFontaine has produced his best pattern. Maximizing the unique properties of Antron the pattern represents the pharate adult hanging below the film on the very point of emergence. Even the loosening sheath is represented by the Antron fibres trailing to the rear. The colour of the materials should match the natural. As an alternative wing I use a bunch of cock hackle fibres the colour of the adult's wing. It works well and has taken many fish in slow clear water, always the most difficult of circumstances.

Hook 10–14 Code A, L2A or CS7
Underbody Mixed dubbed Sparkle Yarn (Antron) and natural fur
Overbody Sparkle Yarn (Antron) tied in above and below the shank at the rear and brought forward to cover the underbody in a sparse envelope. Some fibres should trail to the rear
Wing Natural or black deer hair tips
Head Coloured marabou fibres

A simplified version was later devised:
Body Dubbed Sparkle Yarn (Antron)
Wing Deer hair
Head Coloured marabou fibres

Caddis Pupa

This style of dressing with minor variations is listed by a number of authorities. I doubt if any can claim sole credit for the style and this is a hybrid, as are most of the others. It can be weighted for fishing at an appropriate depth. The many variants are very successful patterns.

Hook 10–16 Code K4A, A, CS7 or L2A
Thread Brown
Abdomen Naturally coloured dubbed seal's fur or substitute, or other natural fur or Antron
Rib (Optional) Fine gold wire, strong coloured thread, mono or translucent power gum
Thorax Mixed guard hair and/or natural fur
Legs Dark partridge on the underside only or as a rear-sloping collar
Wing-cases (Optional) Dark grey or brown wing quill sections sprayed with clear fixative for durability
Head Tying thread

Edwards' Ascending Sedge
Oliver Edwards has produced this excellent imitation of some of those species that are predominantly green. The drooping wing cases are also imitated by the raffene which

produces an accurate silhouette. It can be weighted with an underbody of lead wire as required.

Hook 12–14 Code K4A, A, L2A or CS7
Thread Brown
Abdomen Light green Fly-Rite poly dubbing or same colour Antron
Abdomen back Olive-green dyed swan shoulder fibres
Rib Fine gold wire
Wing-cases A loop of dark brown or near-black raffene either side of the thorax
Thorax Mixed sepia and chestnut brown seal's fur subs
Legs Cock pheasant tail fibres (crumpled for effect) with the butts wrapped as the head
Antennae Wood duck fibres or dyed mallard breast fibres

Klinkhamer Special
My friend Hans van Klinken, the creator of this unusual fly assures me he tied it with the emerging caddis in mind. Although to my mind it looks a poor representation of a caddis

Klinkhamer Special. In the author's opinion this is probably the best river trout and grayling fly to be devised in the last ten years.

it works extremely well in a sedge hatch. It fishes like an iceberg with eighty-five per cent under water. However, the highly visible upright wing is well above the surface and for that reason it could fall within the category of a dry fly. I apologize for including it in a book on sub-surface fishing but its body is below the surface and only fifteen per cent remains dry so perhaps I can be forgiven. The only reason I offer for its inclusion is the best one – it is a superb trout and grayling fly on freestone streams and has caught hundreds of fish for me. It is best fished in the riffles and at the neck of a pool. It isn't a slow water fly. Don't let the size put you off; the riffle-inhabiting fish really find it a mouthful. It is one of those rare patterns that works when others won't. I can tell stories of how, time after time, this has been the best pattern by a long way.

Hook   12–22 Code K4A or K12ST
Thread   Brown
Body   Light tan Fly-Rite poly dubbing
Thorax   Peacock herl
Wing   White polypropelene yarn tied upright
Hackle   Chestnut brown cock in parachute style round the wing base

Edwards' Emerging Adult Sedge (Post Ovipositing Female)
Many of the sedges return below the water to lay their eggs and in the course of ovipositing or struggling to return through the meniscus they are taken by trout. Oliver Edwards ties this very realistic imitation. The thorax and legs are made of a dubbing devised by Roman Moser tied in with the aid of a dubbing loop.

Hook   10–16 Code K4A
Thread   Pre-waxed olive or brown Danvilles Flymaster or equivalent
Underbody   Lead foil; just sufficient to prevent the fly skating
Abdomen   Fine synthetic dubbing to match the natural's colouring, about two-thirds body length
Rib   Fine gold wire
Thorax and legs   Moser sedge dubbing comprising 70 per cent deer/elk hair trimmings mixed with 30 per cent fine poly dubbing for one-third body length. Deer fibres roughly picked out underneath and tied sloping back
Wings   Pale brown raffene, doubled then folded to produce 4 wings about 1/8in (3–4mm) wide and extending about one and a half times the shank length and trimmed to shape
Head   Tying silk

Moser Emerger (Caddis and upwinged sp.)
This is a Roman Moser devised emerger to represent both caddis and upwinged species. Its size and colour should be varied to match the naturals. The example illustrated is tied by Charles Jardine.

Hook   12–18 Code E6A or other lightweight hook
Thread   Hot orange or olive
Tail   Spade hackle from a jungle cock cape or soft grizzle hen
Body   Dubbed mixed deer hair of various shades to match the natural
Wing   Smokey blue dun/grey Antron fibres
Hackle   One and a half turns cul de cunard and clipped short if necessary

4 The Trout and its World

'Ah, trout. Let other people boast about salmon – gross oily stupid fellows with that blind urge to swim upstream which makes for easy fishing. All you need are big boots and a strong arm and a clever gillie. But the trout – oh, the trout – he's the real king of fish.'

Graham Greene, *The Human Factor* (1978)

Nature has decreed that some animals are hunters. Most river trout rarely have to hunt. They may scavenge, scouring the stream bed or weeds, but for the most part they live in a food factory that does home deliveries in a big way. Rarely does a trout have to venture much further than on to its own doorstep to collect its meal. Most trout take up their stations around the principle production line – the food lane which is the main current. Eventually any food item on or below the surface will end up there. Trout live within easy access of the food lane and will adopt lies that give sight of its contents or take up positions in a lesser food lane like a back eddy. It is true that every part of the river produces something edible at some stage in the season or time of the day but wild trout learn where these times and places are and move their positions in a river accordingly.

Unless you know where the fish are you don't stand much chance of catching them. This isn't dry-fly fishing; nothing is that easy in nymph fishing. Sometimes on a clear chalk stream or spring creek, or more rarely on a freestone stream individual fish may be spotted, stalked and cast to but most river nymphing involves casting an artificial to trout you cannot see. Trout do all they can to help the dry-fly fisher. It doesn't need the skills of Frank Sawyer to spot a rising fish when a myopic octogenarian can see them a field away. Nymphing fish offer few clues as to their habitats and behaviour. Therefore it is the knowlege of trout lies and the observational skill of the angler that determines whether he is going to be casting to fish or merely fishing in hope. I am reminded of the story about the well-heeled and expensively-equipped fly fisher whom the river keeper had chaperoned, guided and instructed along the bank of a clear chalk stream. With infinite patience the keeper had pointed out numerous fish amongst the weeds and gravel. Nothing had risen; it was just one of those days. This angler hadn't even seen a trout let alone caught one. *'You must be the world's worst keeper,'* he complained. *'No, I don't think so,'* replied the keeper, *'That would be too much of a coincidence.'*

Every wild trout adopts a lie that offers easy access to food and, as a secondary consideration, protection from predators. The hatchery fish has never faced man as a predator, rather the opposite, when for as long as its memory can recall the human form on the edge of its window was the herald of manna from heaven. Until the weeks of its basic education pass it may live in open water with little regard for its safety. The fisherman is the catalyst in speeding up the learning process. The wild trout has survived the attention of bigger hungry fish, the lightning strike of the heron's beak, the explosive behaviour of that strange looking nymph it once took a fancy to, and has become extremely wary of any shadow falling on the water. All wild fish and, given time, introduced hatchery trout, adopt lies of food access, ease and finally, safety.

Few fishing skills are achieved other than by fishing and reading the water so that you can say with some certainty where fish can be expected. Walking the river and studying its bed, current course and surface will be an insight into where trout take up their positions. If in your mind you can go below the surface and begin to think as a trout would think, in terms of as much food and protection as possible for the minimum energy expenditure, then you will begin to get an idea as to where trout may lie.

Even on a freestone river where trout lies are usually in and around the principle food lane, the main current may be divided over a wide area with smaller lanes running alongside each other. In a more slowly moving chalk stream or other well-weeded stream there is less likely to be a single main food lane; the current is more widely dispersed across the river and particularly between the weed beds. The chalk stream and spring creek

are more likely to be of a uniform depth without the wide variation of fast shallow riffles and slow deep pools that can be found in just a short length of freestone river. Because of the differences between the two, trout lies in each will vary. In a weedy river much of the water's area will provide food. Extensive weed growth provides massive amounts of food at varying depths, whereas in an almost weedless stream all the food sources (with the exception of falling terrestrials) will come from the very bottom. Because there is far more area for food in a weedy stream there will be proportionately more fly life. Here trout lies should be thought of in terms of depth as much as positions on an aerial plan.

When fishing to visible trout or invisible trout in a prime lie the ability to assess the

The scum lane along the far bank is a collecting point for half-emerged and trapped flies. Oliver Edwards fishing the Ure.

54

depth of the fish in conjunction with the current speed is of paramount importance. The chapters on nymph presentation will emphasize that if the simple maths of depth, water speed and the sinking rate of an artificial are wrongly computed then failure is the only outcome.

It is a relatively easy task to assess the speed of the water at the surface and to see how it varies considerably across the width of the river. Less obvious is the water speed at various depths. If water were being carried along a perfectly smooth stream bed without any variation in the river width and depth there would be almost no variation in water speed across the surface or at different depths. But every river is on a gradient, or more accurately, it experiences varying gradients. It flows over different substrata of very uneven depth which, along with the river bank produces varying amounts of friction to slow down parts of the stream. Because water looks uncomfortably fast at the surface it does not rule out the presence of trout in the slower water at the river bed or in the calm pockets eroded in the substratum where dead spots of almost no current at all are possible. The deeper the water the greater the variation in current speed from top to bottom. Fig 10 illustrates diagrammatically how the water speed varies.

Depth assessment is extremely important but there has to be some practical consideration. As Oliver Edwards comments 'We can't go round humping huge fly boxes with rows of one lead-wrap nymphs, three lead-wrap nymphs, five lead-wrap nymphs etc. The mind boggles at all the permutations. I would need a ghillie just to carry my flies! *Pass me the five lead-wrap Paraleptophlebia Smithers; this little gulley is 0.97 metres deep and my flow meter tells me the water speed is 1.01 metres per second; now divide that by 0.21 friction factor . . .'*

PRIME LIES

Given a good lie, room service for a trout should be a 5-star affair with a regular and adequate food supply. Except to spawn, trout might hold the best lies all the year round, day in day out, twenty-four hours a day. Why move? Find the prime lies that offer protection, comfort and food and you will invariably find better than average trout.

In almost any stream good lies are found where two current speeds merge or run very close together. The faster water is more likely to carry food picked up and swept into the current and the calmer water will hold trout watching for food in the faster water. Wherever calm water can be found which offers an

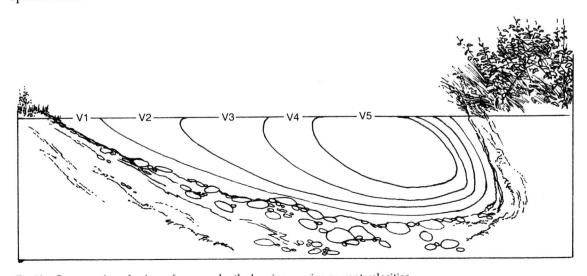

Fig 10   Cross-section of a river of uneven depth showing varying current velocities.

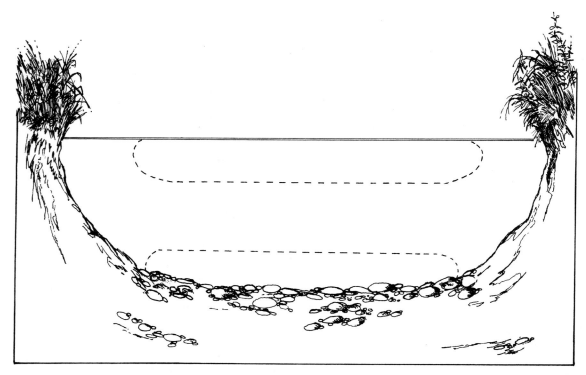

Fig 11   Cross-section of a weedless river showing the principal feeding areas.

easy entry into a food lane, there will be a prime lie. Along these boundaries between the two current speeds trout will invariably take up position if other factors such as sufficient depth and cover are also present. These places are too numerous and variable to mention. On every river and pool the currents and depths are different. Anything that causes a break in the current will create a holding lie. It is the water-reading skills of the angler that determine whether the lies are spotted.

Trout think of cover in terms of more than overhanging banks and branches. A rippled surface effectively draws the shutters over the trout's window and obscures its view of the surface and beyond. This isn't cover in the obvious sense but trout must have learnt that if they cannot see out of the water then neither can anything else see in. It is a pretty effective shelter.

Some of the major lies are described below. The exact configuration of the suggested lies varies between streams. No two pieces of

flowing water can ever be quite alike with different current strengths and substrata producing a million unique habitats. The difference in scale should also be considered. The riffle on one of my local streams is never longer than six feet and rarely wider than eight feet; if your local stream is the Madison the first break in the riffle could be twenty-five miles in either direction. Each of the lies must be adapted from stream to stream. Thankfully no two lengths of river are alike.

The height of the water and current strength is a major influence on the attraction of most lies. Differing water levels can wipe out good lies or create new ones. In low water some of the pocket water might disappear; there is just too little flow or cover. In high water trout will take refuge in the calmer bankside eddies and backwaters which, when the river drops, are left dry or too shallow.

My fly fishing education began and still continues on some relatively small rivers and streams. They are an excellent place to start because caution and stealth are required in approaching a lie or trout soon disappear. On a bigger river it doesn't take as long for them to adopt their lies again and begin feeding but on a small stream they are much more wary and are put down for longer. In a narrow stream no fish tolerates the clumsy angler. The second major benefit of the smaller waters is that they are simply the bigger rivers in miniature. It is easier to study the lies in the smaller stream and once they have been understood it is just a matter of scaling them up to match the larger river. A big river can be a daunting prospect to the uninitiated and visualizing the lies in the vast subsurface world can be difficult. Scale up the small stream and the problem is eased.

Lastly, my caveat is this: If there is an unwritten rule about trout lies it is: *expect the unexpected*. Trout have never read this chapter. You'll find them in the most unlikely places. On one of my earliest visits as a guest on a fine chalk stream, I had entered the river to wade. I quietly approached at the tail of a pool with the shallow water lapping round my ankles. My eyes were fixed on a rising fish thirty or so feet upstream. Ten minutes of concentrated but unsuccessful casting and recasting passed by. As I turned down to tie on another fly I saw a heart-stopping brown trout of at least three pounds inching its way up through the shallows a mere six feet to the side of me. It must have seen me; it probably heard what I uttered beneath my breath but it made no sign of being disturbed. Although it was aware of me it continued its slow journey through open water which barely covered its back. It just shouldn't have been there. What chance did I have? Too numerous and embar-

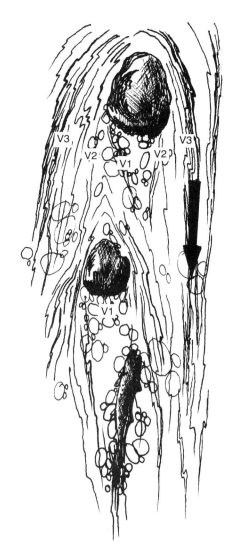

Fig 12   Current velocity. Trout rest in zones where the current speed is slowest but offers quick access to faster water which carries food.

Fig 13   Trout adopt lies to take advantage of the variation in current velocity.

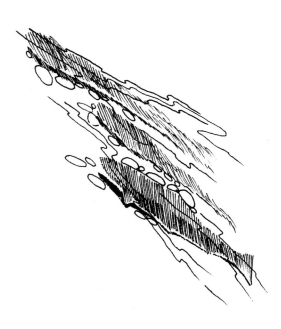

Fig 14 Spotting trout. Is it a fish or is it weed?

rassing to mention are the dozens, even scores of times I confess to missing trout in unexpected lies, particularly in very shallow water in the shade right under the bank.

Riffles

The faster water bouncing over a stony bottom is apt to be passed by rather quickly in the belief that the current pace is too fast to hold fish. The truth is that within the riffle there will be dozens of depressions in the stream and slightly larger stones creating lies just big enough to hold a fish. Especially if there is a couple of feet or more depth then the riffles provide good lies. Trout have to hit drifting food hard and fast in this water. They respond to the initial stimulus if the pattern and presentation are acceptable and take the food or fly without a second thought. If they hesitate the opportunity has passed by. It is possible to see the change in the water surface produced by larger stones and rocks below. The obstruction causes the water to be forced around and above it.

Many stone-clinging and moss-creeping nymph species, caddis larvae and other food items live amongst the stones of the fast water and provide a continuous line of food as they are picked up by the current. Many upwingeds and caddis, when ready to emerge, begin their ascent from the riffle area. There is probably no area of the river where nymph tactics are so successful. At dawn and dusk there are peaks in nymphal activity. Trout feed avidly on them and trout in the riffles become very active. Because of the choppy surface the whole area offers adequate cover.

Even within the riffle there may be one or more stronger currents. Fish take up positions in the calmer water along the edges or in the eye at the head of the current. Reading the surface of the riffles is by no means easy and only comes with observation and practice. As with all water reading there is no better time than during low water for studying the stream bed and becoming familiar with its varying depths, obstructions and current lanes.

In low water especially if coupled with

A long broad riffle on the River Kaitum, Swedish Lapland, good holding water for both trout and grayling.

Robinson Creek, Idaho. The current has divided either side of the large obstruction to provide two good food lanes. Trout could be found anywhere in these lanes, around the obstruction and rocks right under the far bank.

Fast flowing, rocky water that creates trout-holding zones around every rock and below every ledge. This type of water is fished out with quick casts with a short drift into the likely lies.

Fig 15

bright sunlight it is in the riffles that many trout and grayling take refuge from the heat. The shelter, the cooling effect of flowing water and the possibility of additional dissolved oxygen make the riffles attractive.

Rocks and Obstructions

Natural or man-made obstructions provide excellent lies. Because the current is broken there is a zone of much calmer water behind the obstruction and in the cushioned area in front of it. The size and shape of these zones depend upon the characteristics of the obstruction. Nearly every obstruction will cause a break in the current and be a potential lie. In a strong current the water immediately behind a rock might be too turbulent to hold trout; water comes round the rock from both sides and makes life too difficult. The rock size and shape and water speed determine whether trout will take up such a position. Even if it is unattractive there will still be a lie a yard or so downstream.

Pocket Water

Picking the pockets of water between riffles and rocks is very productive. In the quiet calm water trout are able to feed on items swept into the pocket or they can make quick temporary forays into the current to capture food. In a deep pocket a fish finds safety, food, well-oxygenated water and an easy lie that requires little energy expenditure. It may hold that lie all year, only leaving it to spawn. Fishing a nymph in the pockets presents its own problems and techniques that are considered later (*see* page 95).

Weed Beds

Aquatic vegetation of all types holds a wide range of food of which shrimp, agile-darting nymphs and snails are the most important. Fish take up position in between the weeds where food is brought along in the current. They also lie under the weed especially at the tail of the concave flowing fronds. A lie under the weed offers cover from bright sunlight,

Fig 16

Fig 17

the surface. They can be observed moving slightly to one side to intercept food or rising to inspect a surface fly. Even the movements of the mouth can be seen when no other indication of feeding is visible.

The streams between the weed beds are attractive feeding lies as each current between the weeds carries food. If alerted to danger there is ready cover very close at hand. During the hatch or pre-hatch period trout move to the upper water levels; if there is no nymphal activity trout will stay much deeper.

One should also be aware of the different substrata between the weed beds. Where there is silt and sandy mud this will be the habitat of burrowing and silt-crawling nymph species. During their emergence these nymphs as well as the agile-darters will be found in the water between the weeds.

Overhanging Banks

A good rule of thumb on at least one smaller stream I fish is: if it's grayling you want, fish

easy pickings from the weed itself and a clear view of passing food in the current. I have seen some of the biggest fish in a stream at the upper end of the weed cover. Sometimes trout lie over weeds in the cushion of water above. Trout appearing here, usually quite high in the water and without any overhead cover may be feeding on dislodged immature nymphs, but more likely on ascending mature nymphs, or taking surface food. Such fish are easy to watch because most are fairly close to

Fig 18

Fig 19

The moment of the take. Lars-Åke Olsson takes a fish tucked right into the bank of the upper Avon in Wiltshire.

Fig 20

the main stream, if it's trout, then fish the margins. Strong currents on the outside of a bend or on streams subject to spate undercut the banks to produce lies that offer cover and an easy access to the food lane. Water flowing close to a bank is slowed down by friction and a calm pocket is produced next to the bank. If these pockets are under an overhanging bank it is only likely that trout can be taken if a nymph were to drift right into the lie.

There is often a line of fish to be found fairly close to the bank along the outside of a bend. The current is pushed to the margins and if it is of a moderate pace trout take up station in Indian file at regular intervals. In a hatch or during the pre-hatch activity they will move nearer the surface; for the rest of the time they adopt deeper positions.

Shelves

On many freestone streams the river bed is shaped so that quite sudden changes in depth occur (*see* fig 20). These are usually the result of a gradual erosion of a softer part of the substratum by the current. They can be found anywhere on a stream but invariably along the course of the main food lane and its edges. Wherever such a shelf occurs there will be a change in current speed and, taking advantage of the calmer water, a trout will be lying close to the river bed. After close examination of some shelves I have noticed that below the lip of the shelf the current on the stream bed actually moves in an upstream direction. Matter suspended in the water and loose debris in the bed drift back towards the shelf. This clearly illustrates how the current at the bed can vary dramatically from that at the surface.

In the Eye of a Pool

The eye of the pool (*see* fig 16) is the area of calm water at one or both sides of the faster water entering at the pool's head. This is one of the major lies for better than average fish. It offers first sight of sub-surface food and any ascending nymphs arriving from the faster riffly water. Even if trout adopt a position near the surface they can quickly melt into the

Fig 21

much deeper water of the pool. A backwater or reverse current might develop at the eye and this will result in trout facing into the reverse current in a down-river direction. This lesser current carries sufficient floating and sub-surface food from the main food lane.

If the pool is on a bend or the main current only on one side of the river then perhaps only one eye will be produced. If the current is in the middle of the river and particularly if there are rocks or other features that force the current through a narrower channel an eye will result on both sides of the flow. Trout take up position in the calm area right on the edge of the fast water and a nymph should be presented in the faster water as near as possible to the boundary with the calm waters of the eye.

Water tumbling in at the head of a pool produces deeper water just below the head which invariably holds fish.

The Head of a Pool

There is often a prime lie on the stream bed at the upper end of the pool where it shelves into deeper water and the current surges over the lip of the shelf. There used to be an attractive small pool on the River Costa in North Yorkshire that held a number of excellent trout who ventured into the turbulent water at the pool's head. Alas, the pool has now silted up like much of this once-great stream. The interesting feature of this pool was that a bridge crossed at its neck and the angler could watch the trout (some up to 3lb) taking up their positions. If I am not actually fishing then fish-watching must run a close second to stone-turning. Bridges are useful observatories of fish behaviour. At the very head trout stay close to the bed in the calmer water in the lee of a shelf. As the current speed slows further

down the pool they are more willing to take up positions mid-water. Those at the head of the Costa pool did not stay there permanently but perhaps spent five minutes there, then dropped down to the pool centre or to the eye. At the head the water was fast and a nymph had to be fished right on the trout's level. It's an entertaining challenge particularly if a partner crouches unseen on the bridge calling out the trout's reactions to the nymph. Only in such a way does one learn just how many takes go undetected by the angler.

The Centre of a Pool

Pool-dwelling trout are travellers around the pool taking up different positions within the pool according to the food supply, temperature and water height. The centre of the pool is often its most deepest part and for that reason it is an attractive winter lie because it is warmer, and a summer lie because it is cooler. Its depth offers the necessary cover and the main feeding positions will be in the current if it is not too strong or along the edges of a strong current. Towards the tail of the centre where the current is slower trout are more likely to be found feeding in the upper levels. Ascending nymphs reach the surface by the centre of the pool and might have emerged as duns. Consequently, before and during a hatch, trout move into the upper levels of this part of the pool and it becomes excellent nymphing water, particularly for fishing the top inch or so of the stream. Generally, fish found in these positions are feeding or on the lookout for surface or sub-surface food and they have an excellent opportunity for a leisurely close examination of both food and the artificial fly. It is an excellent mid- to late-evening and dusk lie.

The very slow-moving deep pools are also good lies because of the security and refuge from bright sunlight that they offer. Food does not arrive as frequently and trout have to be willing to search. It is an excellent dusk feeding zone.

The Tail of a Pool

Under the cover of dusk trout are found midstream in this relatively shallow water. There is little cover and under normal circumstances only a few fish venture here. The late evening draws them here to mop up spinners that have oviposited further up the pool. The margins under the banks at the tail hold the occasional fish but a more likely lie is in the cushion of water in front of a lip into the next pool or riffle.

Depressions in the Stream Bed

Whatever the water type there will be depressions in the stream bed that hold trout. The current speed is slower at the bed than at the surface anyway, but if there is a lie further into the bed then this will enjoy even calmer water. Trout in these positions feed almost exclusively on nymphs, caddis larvae and other bottom food. They will rise into the drift level above the bottom to intercept food but they need not move very far.

SPOTTING FISH

Even when one knows where to expect to find trout, actually seeing them is another matter. Often it is just a matter of having faith in the likely lies and of having sufficient belief in your water-reading abilities. If it looks like a trout lie I'll fish it through with a dry fly or nymph, whichever I feel appropriate. Unless the water and light conditions are ideal most fishing is done blind in areas where you suspect there may be trout activity. So it is on most freestone waters.

It is on the clearer chalk streams and spring creeks that the stalking of individual fish is more common. Conditions here give a better opportunity for fish spotting and for human

Fig 22

spotting by trout. With the aid of glasses my eyesight is perfect and with an excellent pair of polarized lenses I can see fairly well into the water but even so, making out fish in a darker alien environment is rarely easy. Incidentally, Oliver Kite never used polarized lenses. If he couldn't catch trout without them, he didn't consider himself competent to discuss nymph fishing. Would you enter a boxing match with one arm tied behind your back? Neither would I. Kite's eyesight was no better than mine; but his understanding of what he saw made the difference. I never fished with Frank Sawyer but those who did, speak of his trout-spotting and take-detection capabilities so as to make him legendary. Both Kite and Sawyer did much of their fishing on a single stream and came to know a relatively small piece of water extremely well. Perhaps the source of

some of their success in fish-spotting lay in their considerable experience of where trout had been caught in the past. Trout invariably fill an empty lie. The half-blind G.E.M. Skues also had the uncanny knack of good water vision. In an era when fellow fly fishers were watching the surface for a rise Skues turned his attention below it. There is a saying that in the world of the blind, the one-eyed man is king; it took the one-eyed Skues to show the chalk-stream fishing world what was happening below the surface.

In addition to a broad-rimmed hat or long-peaked cap and polarized glasses the angler needs the well-practised skill of observation. A cursory glance over the water may reveal no fish or only obvious individuals lying over light patches of gravel but by patiently studying the underwater world other tell-tale signs

Gary LaFontaine playing a trout in a fast pool. The water surface indicates just how uneven the stream bed is and trout lie in calmer pockets around stones and in depressions.

The stealthy approach to the river will always pay off. This angler on the Derbyshire Wye is using the bush as cover; he keeps low and six feet back from the edge; he is also equipped with polarized glasses and a broad-brimmed hat to aid fish-spotting.

will be unveiled. The ability to spot trout is more of a fishing skill than fly-tying or accurate casting and is closer to its 'man against the animal' hunting origins. It should be a basic fishing skill on clear water streams.

Any approach to the water should be made extremely slowly. It is possible to get quite close to fish if you don't enter their field of vision suddenly. Hatchery trout are remarkably tolerant of man but wild fish really have to be stalked. You should make use of bankside foliage to mask your approach. The higher the position above the surface the easier it is to see below as there is much less reflected light. If you do have to stand within the trout's cone of vision make sure you are obscured by bushes etc. Use the sun to your advantage and not the trout's. By having the sun behind you your own line of sight follows the sun's light into the stream and illuminates it with little being reflected back. Avoid letting a shadow fall on the water. If the water being searched is directly between the angler and the sun then there is little chance of seeing into the water as most of the sun's light is reflected towards the angler.

Total concentration is required. The dry-fly fisher is accustomed to studying the surface for signs of a rise but when trying to spot trout on a clear stream this should be avoided and one should try to get used to automatically looking into the water for signs of trout. I say 'signs of trout' with good reason for most fish don't show all of themselves but just give clues as to their presence. Recognizing the clues is the key:

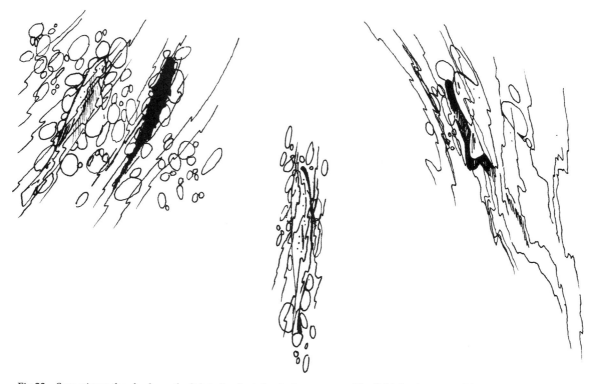

Fig 23   Sometimes the shadow of a fish is the first clue to its presence. The fish's back may well be camouflaged; only the darker shadow is obvious.

This fly fisher wades carefully and uses the tree cover to stalk a fish on the river Costa.

Movement

Except for the moving water and flowing weed the only other sub-surface movement will be from fish. I've been duped by weed a few times as it has swayed gently on the stream bed. Fruitlessly casting a deep nymph in the hope it will be taken has always left me a bit embarrassed as I have looked over my shoulder hoping I've not been observed. One obvious clue is the flash of light from a trout's side as it has turned to feed. Even then the fish might not be visible but the flash has betrayed its presence. The pulse-like movement of the trout's tail or the fluttering of its fins as it holds position in the current can also be spotted. Trout move slowly and in leisurely fashion unless scared and it is only by taking time to unhurriedly watch the under-surface without interruption that the barely discernible movements will be seen. Any movement below the surface is likely to be a sign of fish.

Light and Shadow

A dark fish shape over a patch of gravel or light-coloured river bed is not uncommon. It could well be a trout but it might not. On sunny days trout cast shadows on the stream bed. If the bed is light-coloured the shadow shows up well. Try to determine whether it is the fish or its shadow. Remember not to cast to the shadow but assess where the trout will have to be in relation to the sun for it to cast such a shadow. The fish itself might be impossible to see because it blends in with the stream bed. Grayling are particularly difficult

to see because they generally lie deeper than trout and offer only a dark grey upper surface which blends in with the ill-lit depths. Their French name *l'ombre*, the shadow, seems appropriate.

Shape

It is the nature of the way we see into the water which means that often only the silhouettes or shapes of objects are visible. A trout at the rear of a waving weedbed has the habit of leaving its tail or more of its back in the open water. Because there is cover above their head they probably think they are out of view. The 'head in the sand' attitude prevails. Trout in such a position can be seen by the break in the line of the rear of the weed. Trout on the edge of weeds similarly disclose their position by the broken line along the weed edge.

The Problems of Refraction

Every angler is familiar with the bending of light rays as they enter and leave the water. Our line of sight into the water is bent or refracted so that when we see fish in the water they will always appear further away and nearer the surface than they actually are. Every fish spotted will be deeper and nearer than it appears. Refraction also occurs in trout vision too and makes objects on the bank appear much higher in the sky. This refraction causes a blind zone for fish and anything lower than about ten degrees from the surface is unseen. Refraction is a problem for the nymph fisher as he considers where to cast his

Fig 24

nymph so that it drifts on to a trout's nose. It is a question of remembering just what refraction does and taking it into account.

READING THE SIGNS

I have already made the point that spotting individual fish for the nymph fisher is doubly difficult when compared with the amount of co-operation trout give the dry-fly fisher. There is little excuse for missing the disturbance created by the break in the surface as trout take food off the top. The dry-fly fisher is even given clues as to the type of natural fly being consumed by the different rise-forms produced by the variation in water displacement. There are a few surface disturbances that expose the nymphing behaviour of trout, but not many.

The Head-and-Tail Rise

To the angler this appears as the most leisurely feeding behaviour. When a big trout cares to show itself in this way it is the rise that brings on coronaries for the faint-hearted and dizzy spells for the weak-limbed. There are few sights more exciting for the fly fisher than the sight of the back and tail of a good fish breaking the surface. Such fish are almost always found in slow water (it is of course a

common stillwater rise-form) and trout can take their time in picking out the food. The speed of the rise also suggests that there is either a lot of food to choose from or that it won't escape. Struggling or trapped emergers, spent *Baetis* spinners or midge pupae are the target.

The Nearly-Rise or Sub-Surface Rise

When a trout takes a fly from the surface it takes in a mouthful of air which it expels through its gills and thus always leaves a small bubble of air. When a fly has been taken from just below the surface, even though the water displacement looks similar there will be no betraying bubble. It is the sub-surface rise that misleads us so often. These fish are feeding on ascending nymphs and pupae just below the film and an artificial has to be presented just below the surface or a floating nymph that offers a similar silhouette will often work.

I recall one lunchtime caddis hatch on the West Beck, a chalk stream near Driffield. At the head and in the middle of the pool trout were rising to the steady stream of sedges coming off the water. The rise looked as though they were taking the fly off the surface but it wasn't until the hatch had all but finished that I realized it was the emerging pupae just below the film that was attracting

Fig 25   The head and tail rise-form.

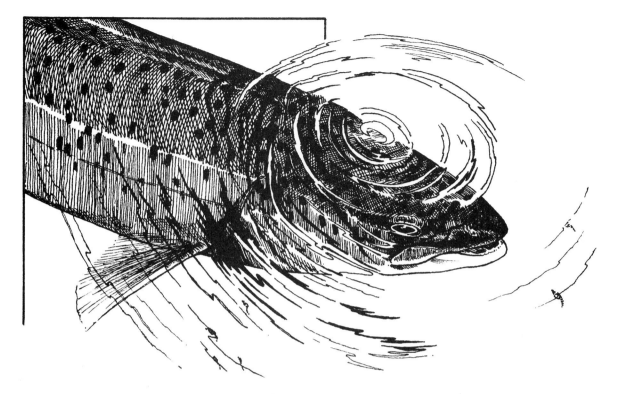

Fig 26   The nearly-rise or sub-surface rise.

their attention. The characteristics of the water displacement were so similar to the plain surface rise that the missing air bubble hadn't been noticed. What finally gave their game away was that my fishing partner changed position to view the fish and rise-form from a different angle. I had been fishing to them directly across the stream standing on the bank two feet higher than the water, making my eyes eight feet above the fish. My colleague moved directly behind them nearer to their level and from there it was easy to see that the trout didn't actually break the surface. So you might not be as dumb as I was but I just want to emphasize that what looks like a rise to a surface fly is not always so.

The Bulge 1

This bulge rise-form is very similar to the nearly-rise or sub-surface rise. It is the same action of the trout which is completed an inch

or so lower in the water. Less water is displaced and all that is produced is a bulge of water to show the rapid movement of the fish just below. Trout are taking the ascending nymphs, pupae or sunk spinners in the top six inches of water.

The Bulge 2

I regard this surface indication of trout activity as being distinct from the behaviour described in the last paragraph. Other authors refer to it as a bulge but it is quite unlike that described above. It is largely the result of water displacement by a fish deeper in the stream. As it moves to feed a less obvious change occurs in the water surface. If the water is calm a very slight bulge results but on a rippled surface a flat spot appears where the water looks calmer. Whatever the surface is like the trout behaviour produces a contrary effect to reveal itself.

73

Fig 27   The bulge rise-form.

Tailing Trout

When trout feed on shrimp and nymphs on the bottom in shallow water they do so in two distinct ways. Why they do this in two ways I offer no answer. The first is to lie as they normally do almost parallel with the stream bed and tilt slightly to take their food. There is no tell-tale rise-form although it might be possible to see the feeding trout. The second method is to tilt more dramatically so that the top of the tail breaks the surface. Sometimes it is very difficult to spot because of the surface currents and because just a small part of the tail is visible. I have never seen the latter behaviour on a freestone stream but it is relatively commonplace in the shallows of chalk streams and spring creeks. Some of my most dramatic sightings have been while autumn grayling fishing and a shoal of between forty and sixty fish have moved into the shallows. Sometimes as many as half a dozen full tails and an inch or two of body are waving out the water at one time. They are on the feed but I sometimes wonder if they knew I was there and they were just reacting in the way a group of teenage girls do to a passing truck driver.

The tailing grayling remind me of an inci-dent my friend Roy Shaw once witnessed. Roy is a keen observer of wildlife and has the patience and skill required to capture the unusual with a camera. Grayling are a particu-lar fascination for him and on this occasion he stood in his local chalk stream rooted to one spot for three hours while he observed the behaviour of a shoal of grayling just a few feet away in about a foot of gin-clear water. He stood in the shadow of a large bush and didn't move. They just went about their business not expressing any interest in feeding or anything else. They held their position in the stream. Well into the late afternoon their attitude suddenly changed. They started to look for food. It wasn't being provided by the stream. Instead they all began to move the pebbles and gravel on the river bed with their snouts and to feed on the dislodged shrimps. For about twenty minutes they fed in this way, grubbing and lifting stones until satisfied, and then as suddenly and with the same unison they stopped. Roy's patience had been well rewarded with such a rare sight. How keen a fishing naturalist are you? Would you stand for three hours to see this at such close quar-ters? I'd like to think that I would stand there knowing the grayling would perform for me

74

Fig 28 Tailing trout feeding off the bottom in shallow water.

eventually, but I'm afraid I don't think I could wait three hours without any idea how the fish would behave. Perhaps one day I'll have reached that stage. One of the purposes of the illustration is to show that sometimes fish don't just rely on the big food factory they live in but become more positive about finding food. Just why they waited so long before feeding and why they decided as one to so behave are unanswered.

Whether or not you subscribe to the view that nymphs or other sub-surface food make up the majority of the diet of many trout, most trout position themselves to take maximum advantage of such nymph availability as there is. Writing of the chalk streams, Frank Sawyer commented that with each passing year he 'became more convinced that when trout take up a feeding position during the summer months it is with the primary intention of intercepting nymphs'. If that is so and even if there is only an element of truth in it on the freestone streams it is of the greatest significance and serves to highlight that for the nymph fisherman the ability to read the water and understand where trout might lie is of the highest priority.

5 The Trout and the Nymph

'But I will lay aside my Discourse of Rivers, and tell you some things of the Monsters, or Fish, call them what you will, that they breed and feed in them . . .'

Izaak Walton

THE STREAM-WISE TROUT

There is no doubt that recently released hatchery trout behave more recklessly than the truly wild fish or even one that has been in the river a couple of months. Thankfully, there are still some rivers and lakes in Britain that provide wild brown trout fishing, where the fish are the result of hundreds of years of breeding and struggling for survival. Indigenous fish like these are hardy and stream-wise and don't hang around for introductions when a human form appears in the window. Hatchery fish have been used to seeing man as the provider of food; initially they don't scare so easily. Neither have they had to feed in the wild. Every day at specific times food has arrived with no effort on the trout's part to find it. Also they haven't been accustomed to the behaviour and life cycle of the stream's fly life. At one extreme, a dry fly might be taken simply because it looks edible and all the food at the hatchery came from up there, whereas the stream-wise fish won't give it a second look if it is an unnatural pattern or fished at the wrong time, and may become agitated and wary. Similarly it will be some weeks before they know one nymph type from another and know when the naturals will be active. Give them half a season and they will have begun to be wiser. Until then they are a lot of fun but hardly a test of fly-fishing skill.

As stocked fish begin to acclimatize and are assimilated into the real world they absorb the natural way of survival. However, the influence is not all a one-way affair. Wild fish can be influenced by hatchery trout. Wild brown trout are not by nature social feeders and without outside influence they prefer to decide for themselves when and how to feed. Hatchery fish have been used to doing everything together; such was life on the farm and on occasion for some time after their release they will feed together, most noticeably on the surface. If hatchery fish begin to feed in concert it can spark off the wild trout into an unnatural feeding frenzy.

I am inclined to believe that the more a stream is like the hatchery the longer the education of the introduced fish takes. The trout farm provided clear water, only a moderate current and regular feeding period. A slow spring creek or chalk stream offers clear water, often only a moderate current and where they still exist, regular fly hatches and plenty of other sub-surface food. In most freestone rivers the acclimatization is quicker. The currents vary more widely, the flow and temperature are more subject to fluctuation and the probability is of less regular or prolific fly hatches. Life is generally tougher.

Perhaps man is the ultimate catalyst in a trout's education, making it wiser each time it is pricked or caught. Certainly some individuals become more wary, but I've also caught other individuals time after time without any evidence of memory being shown. The more experience I've gained over the years edges me further towards doubting much of the ability we give trout to make 'thinking' judgements. I wrote elsewhere that trout intelligence is the fly fisher's greatest invention. I still have no reason to doubt it. Intelligence should not be confused with a

76

The Derbyshire Wye; one of the few places in Britain where one can fish for truly wild rainbow trout.

wild trout's natural survival instinct that tells it to be suspicious of anything unnatural. No doubt we've all got our own stories of stupid trout. Mine concerns a rainbow trout that I noticed just two feet beyond the tip of my seven foot rod. Quite incredibly it rose six times to my dry fly; four times I hooked it and twice I lost it at my feet. Each time it returned to its lie content to continue rising. Here was a fish that had neither intelligence nor the ability to absorb an education.

TROUT REACTION TO NYMPHS

It is quite possible to fish for some hours with excellent nymph or caddis imitations, at the correct depth, in a lifelike presentation and not have a trout to show for the effort. If you are fishing to visible fish there is little as frustrating as changing patterns, sizes and presentations, to no avail. Then a trout lifts its

head and another moves a few inches to one side. The movement of the fins quickens and before you've had time to realize what is happening fish have begun to feed. The feeding trigger has been activated. It was never the artificial constantly bombarding them from every angle but the natural stimulus of not one or two mature nymphs but a trickle and then a surge of nymphal activity. One artificial will rarely convince them that emergence time has arrived but the sight of dozens of nymphs on the move will. If you are fishing blind into the likely lies the blank hours can be desperate. You worry over the choice of pattern, its depth and movement, you begin to question the stocking policy, query the taper on the leader, the colour of fly line and wonder whether the rod licence is out of date. Worst of all is the self-doubt; there are trout in the stream and I can't catch them. What am I doing wrong?

The periods of trout inactivity are commoner on streams with excellent regular fly hatches, be they caddis or upwinged. Wild trout haven't lived in the river for three or four or more years without realizing that these tasty little wrigglers hiding in the weed have to come out some time and that emergence can be anticipated at certain times of the day. I emphasize I am referring to streams with regular prolific hatches. Trout in such streams are less inclined to feed on the odd titbit that drifts their way; they don't need to because they know what's coming in the main course. Momma nature taught them not to eat between meals, it's hardly worth the effort so they don't. When they do feed they often do so simultaneously. From lazily ignoring food they move in unison to the silent sound of an imaginary dinner bell. It is the quantity which triggers the feeding mechanism.

The same is less true for the majority of rivers wherein trout feed throughout the day with periods of varying intensity. Even though there may be no hatch in progress or any pre-hatch activity many trout feed on the dislodged nymphs, shrimps, caddis larvae or fallen terrestrials coming their way, or they actively grub along the bottom or weeds, and they respond accordingly to the artificial. They have learned to feed on more or less everything that comes their way. Trout can be taken during all the daylight hours but it is during their concentrated feeding in the pre-hatch, hatch and egg-laying female fall that the excitement really begins. For me, and I imagine for all committed fly fishers the visual stimulation of trout nymphing just inches below the surface is an exhilarating thrill that I hope will never wane. If the sight of a pool the surface of which is broken by the backs and tails of feeding fish does nothing to lift your spirits then sell the rods and take up golf.

A trout that is maintaining its position in the current has to work to hold its ground against the flow. Such a fish that is committed to holding its height and position is on the look-out for food; there's no point in spending energy if there is little being replaced. If you are fortunate enough to fish a stream where individual trout can be stalked you will be aware that trout display small physical clues as to their interest in drifting food. A quickening of the fins, a lift of the head, the white of the opening jaws which Skues so aptly described as 'a wink underwater' or other, tiny body movements betray the feeding trout. Some fish might move a yard to intercept food but unless they are observed very carefully others don't appear to move at all. The opening and closing of the jaws is a very quick movement that is easily missed. Often the tell-tale white flash is the only clue that food or a nymph has been taken.

As a general rule the deeper a fish is lying the further it is prepared to move to intercept food. Trout adopting a position just below the surface are usually looking to the few inches below the surface or on the surface for their food. Their eyes are concentrating on the upper reaches of the water and usually only within a fairly narrow feeding lane. Such trout, locked into feeding on a steady flow of nymphs, frequently ignore surface food even though it is passing only inches away. They also ignore food passing on a lower level; trout have gone to the upper levels because they have been attracted by nymphal activity or they expect to see nymphs or other food there and thus they are unlikely to react to food at a slightly lower level. Midwater and deeper fish are more inclined to look more closely at lower food but be aware that a trout cannot see objects on a much lower level unless it tilts its body or unless the object is some distance away. The bottom-hugging fish is expecting nymphs, caddis larvae and pupae from the stream bed, so it concentrates its search on its own level and below. The midwater trout is only common on weedy streams where there is a more reliable food supply at this level. It spreads its field of interest more widely and might be prepared to move up or down or a yard or more horizontally to feed.

It is the pre-hatch activity that first excites trout. The agitated mature nymphs crawl, swim and dart about around the stream bed or weeds. Some might make the journey to the surface and back again. All this stimulates trout feeding and they adopt positions to take the nymphs at all levels and will feed wherever the nymphs are found. The movement is progressive from bottom to top and eventually when the hatch proper starts they may feed exclusively on the duns on the surface. Between the nymph and the dun there is the critical emerging period that creates the most exciting inch of fly fishing. Here the half dun, half nymph, so aptly named the 'flymph' by Vernon Hidy, particularly attracts trout attention. Even when trout concentrate on the duns the nymph fisher always has the consolation that there is much more chance that a surface-feeding trout may be induced to take a nymph than the nymphing trout be persuaded to surface feed. Oliver Kite regarded the use of the dry fly over a nymphing trout as 'unethical' and 'unnecessary' on the basis that it was pointlessly worrying a living creature and also adding to the trout's education. I believe Frank Sawyer also considered it unfair. Failing to apply any train of logic behind their reasoning they had no such doubts about using a nymph on a rising fish. I've never looked upon the dry fly to a nymphing fish as unethical; not very successful it may be but never unfair. As for adding to a trout's education, most wild fish that are fished for frequently are fairly stream-wise anyway and the hatchery fish need all the education they can get. My bet is that there are very, very few trout so wised up they won't surface feed because a dun imitation sometimes appears above it when the nymph activity begins. Duns on the surface are a direct and consequential result of the latter.

The length of time duns spend on the surface before becoming airborne varies from virtually no time at all to a minute or two or more; rarely considerably longer. The variation is probably entirely due to the speed in which the wings of the dun dry, and therefore

The home of modern chalk stream nymph fishing. Lars-Åke Olsson tightens into a trout on the upper Avon, the water Frank Sawyer keepered.

Fig 29

sunlight, air temperature and wind influence the time the duns remain on the river. The longer the duns drift the more their vulnerability increases and the greater the trout's interest in them. However, if the duns are taking flight quite quickly there is little opportunity for trout attention. Trout soon learn that the flies are disappearing quickly so why bother expending precious energy trying to catch them; it is far better and more efficient to miss out the duns and concentrate on the nymphs. That is why when there might be a good dun hatch during a summer day the duns are on the water for little more than a second or two and why the nymphs are taken in preference. Trout obviously concentrate on the nymphs and the nymph fisher has a clear advantage over the dry-fly fisher.

If, in a hatch situation, a trout is feeding on a food source, it picks out that food from any other fauna that might be coming its way. To a greater or lesser extent it adopts some measure of selectivity. It follows then that a naturally presented accurate imitation of the preferred species is more likely to be taken at this time than in a no-hatch situation. An imitation of the active species will be viewed by the trout with much less suspicion than an artificial, even a quite lifelike one when there are no naturals about.

Trout can exercise selectivity over nymphs just as much as over duns. Like all trout selectivity it is more frequently practised, and to a higher degree, on streams with abundant

fly life and prolific and simultaneous hatches. The nymph fisher who restricts himself to a single pattern adopts the same philosophy as the one fly dry-fly fisher. If a trout is able to exercise some measure of nymph-type selection I suggest there is probably only one good reason why the one pattern nymph fisher succeeds and that is because the streams being fished primarily hold only one type of nymph. (I don't mean only one species but one nymph-type.) In the chalk streams the agile-darting nymphs predominate. The shape, colour and behaviour of most of these is very similar; in the right hands one good pattern might suffice for much of the time. It is why the Pheasant Tail Nymph was rarely off Frank Sawyer's leader.

Tactics like these won't work as well on rivers which enjoy a wider spread of nymph types. Trout selectivity ensures that in a surface migration of stone-clinging nymphs it is the artificial which incorporates their characteristics that catches the most fish. Although many freestone streams don't experience the volume of fly life enjoyed by the best chalk streams or spring creeks they do benefit from the very wide range of nymph types. My local stream has burrowers, moss-clingers, agile-darters and stone-clingers; sometimes trout demand a pattern-type that represents the characteristics of each. Or if they don't demand it, they are often more readily duped by an imitation with these features.

One final thought – although a negative one – about trout reactions to a nymph, concerns the mirrored undersurface. The mirror reflects the sub-surface world and in theory nymphs closing down on a fish holding a position midwater and above will be reflected in the mirror. However, the mirror is usually so distorted and rippled as to make any clear reflected view of a nymph impossible. The body of an emerger hanging in the film is more easily noticed than the reflection of a nymph below the surface. On a bright flat calm the nymph in the mirror may be spotted but such conditions are rare in river fishing.

6 Streamside Strategy

'The character of the stream and its fish always establishes the best pattern of fly and the best manner of fishing it, not the fisherman.'

Vincent Marinaro

If trout are rising cover them with a dry fly; it's what they are after; it's a relatively easy way of fishing and it's a lot of fun. If a suitable artificial fails with a consistently good presentation check that the fish are definitely taking surface flies and not emergers or sub-surface nymphs or pupae. The rise-form will offer a clue, as will the insect on the water. If, after studying the rise there is any difficulty determining the feeding zone I offer this advice. Does the river generally, or this stretch of water particularly, have a slow current flow where the film is stronger and the meniscus might be harder to break through? Or is it a faster, more rippled current which might offer an easier emergence for insects? Answering this might give a pointer as to whether the adult fly or an emerger or sub-surface nymph or pupa is the target. If winged flies are emerging and the adult imitation fails there is a strong probability that emerging nymphs or pupae are the attraction. If trout are not taking the adults they may move on to them later in the hatch period but they may not. They may never get further than gorging themselves below the surface; a sub-surface imitation is needed.

It may be that feeding trout can be seen quite easily and that their behaviour in taking near the surface can be watched to judge what is happening. Often the rise-form is visible but because of the way we've approached the trout the fish cannot be seen because of reflections off the surface or because of the distance. I have often found on smaller rivers that I have been able to get out of the river if I've been wading, and move with some stealth along the river bank to a position that offers a better view with more favourable lighting so that the rise-form can be studied more clearly, or better still the trout itself can be observed. Now it might be possible to assess what is actually happening. The adult flies coming off the water will provide the species to be imitated and an appropriate pattern should be presented on, in or just below the surface.

When confronted with a rising trout or one feeding visibly below the surface the temptation is to continue to present pattern after pattern in the hope that you'll stumble over the solution. This may well work. With stream experience, educated guesswork and detection the answer might be found very quickly. If it is slow in coming or if you want to do something that we could all spend far more time doing then forget about fishing for five minutes and try and get in a position where you can observe the feeding behaviour of the trout without it seeing you. Some rivers may never afford such opportunities but if you have the luxury of fishing a stream with clear water then indulge in a little further education. Time spent in such observation will be repaid many times over. Not only will you become wiser about trout behaviour, their manner in taking insects at different depths, their varying reactions to different nymphs, pupae and emergers but you will probably, like me, never cease to be thrilled by simply watching fish. Observation is a critical key to successful fly fishing. As I have studied the river and its lies, fly life and the behaviour of wild or stream-wise trout and grayling I've learned more about the application of fly

Surveying the water to be fished and trying to spot individual fish on the Itchen.

fishing skill than I would have done in hundreds of hours of fishing carried out without having first seen what I was trying to imitate and the trout's reaction to it.

When trout are not feeding on the surface it is a matter of personal preference whether to approach the problem with a floating or sub-surface fly. It doesn't require the application of a scientific mind or advanced logic to determine that in most situations the latter is the most successful. During high summer days of bright sunlight trout seek out shade until the evening hatches begin but some will be found in full sunlight under a well-rippled surface. Under such bright conditions their fixed-aperture eyes will not be searching the surface for food but will be directed below the surface where light conditions are easier. If they feed at all it will be on their own level and on a food source drifting past their noses. On sunny days, with the exception of the short day hatches, terrestrial falls, evening hatches and

spinner falls most fish will be most easily duped by a nymph. At the other end of the weather scale, rain inevitably means few fly hatches and if the weather is warm and rain falls it is a probability that the activity of mature nymphs is high as they await ideal emergence conditions. A nymph is the ideal line of approach.

ORGANIZING AN EFFECTIVE STRATEGY

I apologize to the fly fisher who knows the basics of sub-surface river fishing but the ground rules have to be explained or the new-comer will accuse me of jumping the gun. Rarely will the experienced fly fisher consider each of these steps individually but, as he selects a pattern and presentation and makes the cast he has, in effect, worked out the answers to these five problems:

1. Where are the trout lies and at what depth will fish be found? If the stream is of the type, or water conditions are such, that spotting individual fish is impossible, the section on trout lies answers the first part of the question. Their likely depth is assessed in conjunction with water depth and river type; whether it is a weedy stream, consideration of water temperature, sunlight and time of the day.
2. Once the likely lies are determined it is then a question of assessing the current speed and selecting a suitable presentation that will enable the nymph to be fished as near to the trout as possible, in the most natural manner. The chapters on fishing deep, midwater and just below the surface offer some alternative methods.
3. What will trout be feeding on? The fly fisher should know what common species of fly inhabit the river and which could reasonably be expected to be active when he is fishing. In addition to the fly life, is the river one with a significant shrimp population? It also follows that the fly fisher needs to know what natural flies, nymphs and pupae his artificials represent or at least under what circumstances they work.
4. Know the effective sinking rate of the artificial fly, nymph or bug and the same for a braided leader and the fly line if they are not floaters.
5. Ensure that takes can be detected. Only if necessary and appropriate to the water-type use take indicators. Keep a close control over the nymph.

If spotting and stalking individual fish is not possible it will be the water reading skill of knowing where the lies are that will determine any success. It is a matter of fishing a nymph or a team of flies into the holding areas at an appropriate depth. Fishing blind requires a degree of confidence in your ability to read the river, to know the depth at which trout will be lying and to make a judgement on the food source being consumed. When fishing like this you never know just how successful you have been because what isn't known is how many fish you have or haven't covered and how they were feeding. Neither do you know

whether the three trout from a riffle is an excellent or pathetic result. Unless someone else is also fishing there is no yardstick to measure against. If trout can be seen and cast to the success rate is accurately measured. When fishing blind I can invent a hundred and one excuses for failure but when a stalked trout turns tail there is usually only one reason and that's me. The reasons for failure are the same in both situations, it's just that because I can't see the fish I can delude myself why nothing is happening but I cannot escape the reality when I can see exactly what a fish thinks of my nymph and its presentation.

Like every other angler I know I would rather not fish blind and where possible I much prefer to have sight of the trout because of the greater excitement and enjoyment in watching its reaction. Also the chances of catching it are greatly increased. The tactics for a sighted fish compared to those when fishing blind into the lies are similar to a .45 calibre rifle compared with buckshot. The rifle is designed for maximum effect at a specific target; in this case with a tactic to exploit the trout's greatest vulnerability. By comparison buckshot is usually less effective, relying more upon chance hits, albeit targeted into likely water. The element of the hunt, which is a significant part of my fishing pleasure is much enhanced when the individual fish can be spotted and stalked. It is the nature of most freestone rivers that on many waters sight-fishing is often impossible and the majority of sub-surface fishing has to be done blind in conjunction with informed, educated guesswork.

In W.H. Lawrie's much undervalued *The Book of the Rough Stream Nymph* (1947), he writes 'If, therefore, "fishing the water" is justifiable in the case of the dry fly, there does not seem to be any justification for condemnation of similar practice with the nymph, for the only distinction seems to be that the latter requires by far greater skill and knowledge.' Even from a totally different branch of fly fishing came this comment from John Waller Hills in *A Summer on the Test* (1924), 'Fishing the sunk fly is as exciting and entrancing an art as fishing the dry; in fact I am not sure that fishing it upstream when you cannot see your fish is not the highest art of all.' Seventy years on, a lot of fly fishers agree with him.

Fishing the water is not unskilled nor should it be simply randomly raking the stream. Rather, when it is carried out correctly it is a searching technique that is both selective and highly profitable. It demands the application of knowledge of local entomology, trout behaviour and fishing ability. It involves being able to determine from the study of a river, its surface, current flow, depth and type of bottom, the principle lies and presenting an artificial that satisfactorily represents an indigenous sub-surface insect in a natural manner. A skilled exponent avoids fishing water that usually holds no fish. Whatever presentation technique is used few casts should be wasted but all should cover potential holding water, or at least that is the theory. Practice is less than perfect for trout are sometimes found in the daftest places and for unfathomable reasons they ignore the most obvious lies.

I'm aware that searching the lies with a nymph has its drawbacks and that trout and grayling may be put down by the fly line over them or by their mouthing and rejection of an artificial that goes undetected. This may of course add to their education but whether this is a good or bad thing depends upon how stream-wise they are and how easy you want your future fishing to be.

Only when casting a nymph or dry fly to a sighted fish are you able to see what reaction the pattern or presentation receives. How fortunate is the angler who enjoys most of his fishing in clear water. There is none of the hit and miss business of where to find the trout, none of the casting in faith and hope, no exhaustively covering a range of lies and water types at different depths in search of an elusive and invisible quarry. I can think of a score of reasons why I'd rather fish to visible trout and grayling and none of them are outweighed by the only disadvantage: that fish have an equally clear view of me and my errors of presentation. I am not denying the thrill in using water-reading skills to assess a trout lie and in the successful presentation of a nymph to an 'invisible' fish I suspected was there. In fact there's nothing quite like it for building or restoring my confidence in my understanding of trout behaviour. However it

Concentrated effort on a specific lie will usually pay dividends. This knee-deep water holds fish but around the boulders are the more obvious lies.

Open water with no bankside cover necessitates a very careful approach on this northern chalk stream. The rippled surface helps the fisherman but obscures a good view into the water.

doesn't match the excitement of the hunt as the stealthy approach is made in preparation for a patient observation of the stream. Fishing blind involves reading the water surface and trying to visualize the topography and trout behaviour below. Clear-water fishing means a careful study of the visible world below the surface and watching for the tell-tale signs of fish before they see you.

Because a trout can be seen its position in the water should be clear and its attitude to food, how far it is willing to move to feed and sometimes what it is feeding on can be assessed. With the requisite skill a very accurate presentation can be achieved if the depth and currents can be mastered. The artificial can be controlled and guided into position and, if required, be manipulated to copy the movement of a natural at the critical time. All this can be done to unseen fish but never with the same accuracy. The climax of observation, presentation and manipulation comes as the nymph closes down near to the trout. Will it or won't it be taken? Will there be a savage lunge to intercept it, a natural acceptance, apathetic indifference or a startled bolt into the closest weed bed? Whatever happens a full view is given to the fly fisher; fishing blind you might be no wiser about any of the alternatives as a trout can take and reject a nymph without the slightest indication on the surface.

Sometimes it is not possible to trace the path

of the artificial and the behaviour of the fish has to be watched very carefully for a sign of the take. Watching the greased leader on the surface is just one indication of the take but is not a very reliable guide. Only by watching the fish do you discover just how many takes never register on the surface. Because both the participants (fish and nymph) and the variables (current and trout behaviour) are visible a much better hooking ratio is achieved than when one is fishing to unsighted fish. True, in the latter instance you may think the ratio is acceptable but, I suggest, only until you have the chance to see what is really going on. Even on a clear stream it is rare to have the luxury or the thrill of seeing a tiny nymph disappear between the opening jaws of a trout but other signs have to be monitored; a sudden dart forward or to one side, a tilt of the body, the opening and closing of the mouth or merely the convulsion of the gills. The flash of white as the mouth opens is sometimes quite visible even if the rest of the fish is only fairly vague. In the second before any movement it may quicken the pace of its fins; a sure sign that it is preparing for action. Unless the nymph can be clearly seen to be untouched by the trout any of these movements warrant a response from the angler. Tighten on any of these signs. An indication on the surface may be too late or may never happen. My advice is to concentrate on watching the fish.

One of the most exciting ways of fishing is to fish as a team with a friend. One acts as the eyes going ahead of the fishing partner crawling through the undergrowth like a Sioux Indian. Fish can be spotted and directions given to the fisherman. It is more productive when dry-fly fishing because the takes are obvious. When nymph fishing you will never be able to communicate to your partner at the required speed to inform him of the trout's interest and the take. What it is better for is enabling the angler to place a nymph with great accuracy and advising the time for imparting movement to it and relaying the trout's attitude towards it. The stalking partner is the one who learns the most as he watches the trout or grayling's attitude towards the artificial as it approaches. In this way you can learn how casually they take real nymphs and how successful the artificial is in copying the natural's behaviour. Is the fish taking without a second thought? Only in this way do I realize the speed a fish can take and reject a nymph without the angler ever being aware of it. I'm sure that there is no more educational or informative way of improving my fly fishing than watching fish's attitudes to the artificial. If we are any good at all at assessing trout lies then I would suggest that the flies or nymphs on perhaps half our casts are seen by trout – but how many are taken? You will go a long way to discovering why the fish never take them by observing reaction to the artificial and its behaviour. Fishing as a team is also a lot of fun.

The reality is that more often than not nymph or any sub-surface fishing is all about casting a fly or flies to trout that can't be seen. Perhaps there is nothing rising and there are no signs of feeding just below the surface. No clues are given as to where trout are or what they are taking. Water-reading skills and a little entomology for pattern selection are the first two requirements. Finally, make a choice of a style of presentation. A cast up or across the stream with a dead-drift is a standard choice. It often works well but with a little thought one of the subtle changes in presentation may bring more success. Consider whether some of the alternatives are appropriate. They may offer the opportunity of fishing deeper, slower or faster or, in effect, just the chance to fish the artificial in a more natural manner in a way trout expect to see real nymphs behave.

In all but the slowest of streams there may be a marked difference in the current speed at the surface and on the bottom. Two to three times faster at the surface is quite possible. This has great significance for the sub-surface fly fisher who wants to fish midwater and on the stream bed. Unless there is sufficient slack leader between the nymph and the fly line on the surface when the nymph first enters the water the drag from the line will reduce the sinking rate and also cause the nymph to move faster than its surrounding water speed when it reaches the bottom zone.

Line Control

It is the control of the nymph or team of flies that is probably the lynchpin upon which success or failure depends. The behaviour of the artificial is ultimately dictated by the control of the line; master this and more than half the battle is won. The aim should be to present the fly so that it moves very slowly. Only then is it able to be speeded up, twitched or lifted. The angler needs to ensure that it is *he* that is fishing the nymph and not the nymph and current dictating terms to the angler. Only with great difficulty can you slow down a moving nymph once control has been lost.

When the cast has been made immediate control of the line is critical. If the current is allowed to take the line and leader without any control or even any contact being maintained by the angler there will be no hope of tightening on any takes. You may not even be aware of the fish taking. How the line is controlled depends very much on the type of presentation being made, whether it is upstream, downstream or across the current. Control is maintained with both hands; one looking after the rod and the other the fly line. As a general rule more line can be controlled with a longer rod than a shorter one. Mending techniques, lifting of line clear of intervening currents, and the control of slack line to enable drag-free drifts are all better executed with longer rods. The line-holding hand, the left for a right-handed angler, can play as important a part as the rod hand. In many presentations it governs the rate and style of retrieve and in an upstream cast it strips back line to maintain close contact with the line on the water. One retrieving style involves figure-of-eighting quickly as the rod is raised taking up

Fishing across the stream. A long rod held high lifts the line free of intervening currents.

87

slack line but allowing enough snaked line on the stream still to permit a free drift. When a fish takes the fly the left hand draws back the line as the right hand raises the rod so using both hands to tighten on the fish and thereby speed up the strike.

NYMPHING THE STREAM

I carefully considered the most appropriate ways to describe nymphing tactics in different parts of the river and at different depths. I decided that the best way to approach the problem is to consider nymphing techniques in terms of depth and so the next three chapters discuss deep- and midwater methods, nymphing in the upper layers and in the film. In the following sections I suggest a number of ways of nymphing in specific parts of the river. It is inevitable that there is some overlap. Some of the techniques are not elaborated because they are more fully described in the chapter appropriate to the fishing depth.

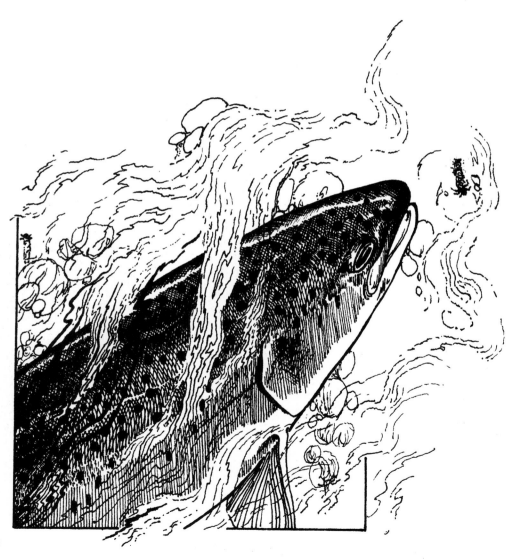

Fig 30

Fishing the Riffles and Stickles

There is no doubt that the nymph and caddis populations are at their most dense on the stream bed in the riffle of most freestone rivers. It is here that the nymphs of many upwinged species begin their ascent to the surface and emerge. Stonefly and nearly all ephemeroptera nymph types can be found there. It is why dry-fly fishing in the lower and middle riffle is invariably productive right up to within a few feet of the head of the riffle. With so much nymph and caddis activity the whole of the riffle is a primary feeding zone and an important one for the fly fisher. Agile-darters, stone-clingers, moss-creepers and stoneflies are all found on the substratum. Many caddis species and particularly the free-living species also abound in the riffles. In the absence of a fly hatch it is the imitation of these nymphs, larvae and pupae that are the most successful.

When there is no hatch in progress and there is no other surface activity my pattern selection revolves round the free-swimming green *Rhyacophilidae* or grey *Hydropsychidae* larvae, a large or medium stonefly nymph, and when all else fails in high water I'll be tempted to tumble a Leadhead nymph in a dead-drift. If trout are feeding at the surface on emerging nymphs or caddis pupae then more appropriate patterns should be used. The best riffle or fast water fly I've ever used is the Klinkhamer Special, an emerger of sorts which has its body below the surface but hackle and wing above. My experience of low water fishing has been increasing rapidly in the last few years and in these difficult conditions during the day I recommend the use of a heavily weighted olive or stone-clinging nymph. Fish will be staying close to the bottom and a nymph on this level, even when there is low water and bright sunshine, will still catch fish. Use a pattern that matches the

A fast riffle over a very uneven rocky river bed. This is excellent nymphing water. Sometimes a strike indicator might be necessary; other times trout hit nymphs and caddis imitations so hard the line movement is dramatic.

Fig 31

predominating nymph type. Trout will inhabit the smallest stickle so long as there is some moving water and a rippled surface above. Casting a small weighted nymph into these zones will bring its reward even if it is only a single fish from each stickle.

Some anglers have commented that bigger than average fish are rarely caught in the riffles. I would have to disagree; my experience is that you are just as likely to find them here as anywhere else. The biggest fish might not take up residence but they will move into the riffle when a hatch is in progress. There are usually plenty of calmer pockets in the well-oxygenated water that prove to be attractive lies.

Before stepping into the water or making the first casts, study the riffle and decide how to fish it effectively and assess the best approach. A good area where many trout lie is the part that deepens near the head of the pool at the rear of the riffle. The deeper water offers a calmer zone with easy access to the drifting nymphs.

I prefer to fish the riffles directly upstream or with some degree of across with a natural drift downstream. Down and across the stream can be successful but because of the speed of the current a nymph holding position in the flow or swimming upstream is unnatural except in a pretty slow flow by riffle standards. A straight drift is more natural. This can be achieved with one of the drag-free presentations described later. Often a downstream arc in wet-fly fashion brings too many plucks and not enough firm takes. Fish may also be hugging the bottom making the most of the calmer water and feeding where most of the food is. Unless the downstream flies are heavily weighted they will be arcing just below the surface. One of the best downstream techniques in the riffle is during a caddis hatch when a swinging pupa or emerger can often work well. Cast across the stream and mend the line a couple of times, perhaps throwing some extra slack, and allow the fly to get down. As the line tightens the fly lifts and swings to the surface in a very lifelike manner. Trout can hit these really hard (just look at the way they slash at the natural pupae) and takes are usually easy to detect with many fish hooking themselves.

Lars-Åke Olsson fishing directly across the stream and allowing the fly to lift drag-free. As the line tightens the fly lifts and takes are either felt or seen by line movement.

It makes sense in any sort of fishing to cover the water nearest to you first with short casts before you put down the fish with the line or by wading through them. If I start at the rear of the riffle I'll work my way up casting upstream and across. A fast retrieve of the line with the non-casting hand is essential if you are going to keep close contact with the nymph as the current brings it rapidly downstream. Casting across the current will involve some measure of mending the line to enable a drag-free drift. Takes will be seen by movement on the line or leader or from the strike indicator which is a very useful addition in the poor surface visibility of the riffle. How high you hold the rod depends upon how much line you are trying to keep clear of intervening faster water.

If I've entered the stream half way up or at the top of the riffle I'll fish it down with a drag-free presentation across the current. Takes will be registered by line or indicator movement, by the tell-tale flash of a trout's side or water displacement if the nymph is being fished shallow. You may even feel a firm tug on the line but don't wait for this. Fishing by braille, even downstream, will result in few takes ever registering at the hand. One consolation and aid to detection is that trout and grayling in the riffles have to make up their minds pretty quickly about food drifting past them, so they hit it hard.

If you want to fish in the down-and-across style it sometimes pays to jiggle the rod tip to impart some action to the arcing fly or team of flies. I'm not too sure how lifelike this be-

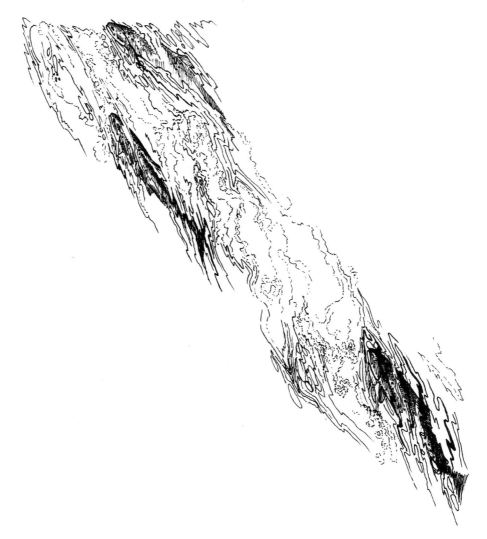

Fig 32

haviour is as it seems to represent an exaggerated movement of an emerging fly but it can produce spectacular results, particularly in a dusk caddis hatch. Keep the jiggling movement to a minimum, a two-inch variation in the rod tip is sufficient and anything else far too exaggerated.

Unless flies are hatching and trout are feeding on them trout will stay close to the stream bed in the calmer water. Artificials have to be presented as close to this level as possible. A well-weighted nymph, larva or pupa is the answer. Anything too lightweight will be swept along in the current and never get down to a fishable level. A sinking braided leader can assist this. In this water a heavy nymph can usually be fished below a large buoyant bite indicator without the latter scaring fish. The line between the two is relatively free from slack and gives an immediate response on the surface to any takes below. Fishing fairly deep over an uneven bottom inevitably means that the fly will snag on debris and stones. Every sign of a fish has to be hit quickly. It might mean that only one in three dips on the indicator is a fish but there is only one way to find out which is the real thing.

Even quite shallow stickles and riffles will hold fish. Stickles up to knee depth can provide good lies and are prime nymphing water at the appropriate time. Fishing the correct depth is not so much of a problem at this water level. If the imitation is lightly leaded it will sink to midwater and fish need the minimum of effort to move to it. Of all river fishing situations I find riffles and stickles the most absorbing, partly because a lot of time can be spent fishing a relatively small area but also because they provide a lot of fish and for that reason give me the most fun.

The riffles should be fished very hard; they hold fish for ninety-five per cent of the time but they might be scattered over a very wide area. The whole area should be thoroughly searched. Generally speaking it calls for shotgun tactics rather than target rifle marksmanship. However, with careful study of a riffle

lies will be spotted and these can be concentrated on with greater effort.

If a pattern or presentation technique isn't working try something else; the reason for failure is unlikely to be the absence of trout. These are noisy turbulent waters. Fish cannot see very far nor detect the vibration of an approaching angler until he is very close or being careless. It is relatively easy to fish upstream with a short line without scaring fish. If you wade carefully don't be surprised to find fish rising in a radius of less than ten feet.

It is probably most appropriate in the section dealing with fishing the riffle to mention the various floating aids which indicate a fish's take below. I know of anglers who criticize their use, likening it to float fishing. I agree that it is unsightly and out of place where a good view of the leader or line end is

Across and downstream at the head of a broad stickle. The line is held clear of intervening currents to achieve 20–30 degrees of free drift.

available. It is inappropriate in slow or clear water where an additional aid should be unnecessary. It is also absolutely useless where trout have a clear view of the indicator. However, on a faster turbulent riffle a floating mono leader is soon lost in the wavelets and light and shadow. Unless all the leader sinks and takes are clearly shown on the line an additional float may be required. An alternative is to use a line like the Cortland Nymph Tip line which has a fluorescent final few feet of line but this is only of use when all the leader sinks. In addition to being a guide to a trout's take the indicator also helps the nymph to be fished at a fairly consistent depth or drift line. Continental fly fishers use short sections of brightly coloured floating fly line placed on the leader. The core of the line is removed and the mono pushed through the centre and if necessary looped through the same hole a second time to keep the float in place. It can be moved up and down the leader relatively easily.

Perhaps the most skilled and most satisfying method of monitoring the takes is watching the floating fly line. As Oliver Edwards describes it, it is one long continuous strike indicator, whether one watches the line end or the belly in the line from the rod tip to the water. Line movement is often very obvious especially in moderate to faster water in stickles and riffles. It may be more appropriate in slower water to watch the leader but whether line or leader are the clues to takes it is a truer, dare I say purer, form of fly fishing.

In recent years the tackle industry, ever eager to capitalize on our need to buy every gadget we think will increase our catches, has

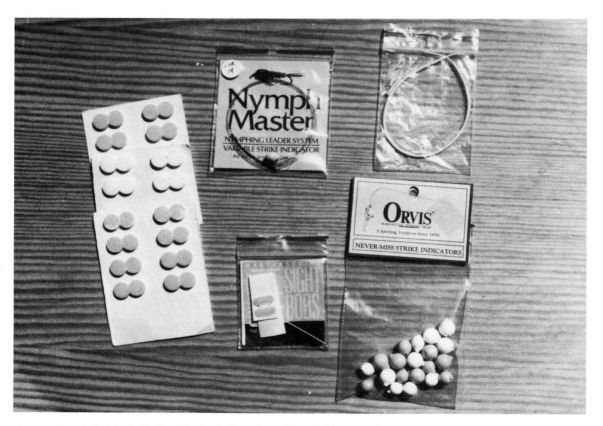

An assortment of strike indicators: Orvis pinch-on foam, Nymph Master strike indicator, orange fly line, Orvis Never-Miss indicators and Masterline Strike Bobs.

marketed purpose-made indicators in the form of pinch-on adhesive coloured foam, buoyant plastic or cork. These work very well. For many years I have used a strand of coloured wool or poly yarn soaked in floatant, looped or tied on to the leader. The advantage of the loop method or the pinch-on foam is that they can be easily moved up and down the leader to change the fishing depth. The Nymph Master and Orvis Never-Miss systems are easy to see and have the benefit of being able to change depths within seconds. I still use the poly yarn or wool tag unless a very heavy nymph is fished; the interference with the casting process is nil with the wool but with other indicators it may call for some amendment. My advice is to use indicators wisely, where you really think you need some additional benefit or where it makes take detection possible when it would otherwise be almost impossible. Don't fish them a rod's length away or on a water surface on which a competent fly fisher should be able to read the takes without a further aid. Over-use of strike indicators on water where they shouldn't really be used will make you a lazy nymph fisher.

One other indicator remains: a well-hackled dry fly on a dropper. Not only is this effective as a register but also in attracting fish itself. Particularly on the faster water where a clear view of the fly is obscured it catches fish on its own account. I'm all for increasing my chances of success. Its only drawback is that the position of the dropper is fixed. It makes sense to fish an imitation of a species likely to be emerging or an attractor pattern.

Picking the Pockets

Pocket water appears in rocky, boulder-strewn riffles where the calmer breaks in the flow between the rocks are designated pockets. They may be so small as to only just house a single fish. Even the fastest streams will produce pockets of calm water around rocks which become attractive lies. Trout expect to see food on the edge of the main current and they will make a quick dart into the current to intercept a nymph. Consequently the best

place to fish a nymph is in the zone where the two water-speeds meet, on the edge of both the pocket and the current. It also pays to put the nymph right into the centre of the pocket although a sinking nymph here is much less natural. You will achieve only a few seconds of drag-free fishing before the line is ripped away by the current, so if the nymph has to sink to any depth it has to be heavy to get there quickly.

I've found fishing *upstream* into the pockets more difficult than a directly downstream approach. The problem is mainly one of achieving a drift of the nymph at sufficient depth at an acceptable speed as the intervening currents make the approach from below the pocket or across the stream more precarious. It can be done but it isn't easy. Close contact with the nymph is essential and so a close control must be maintained by minimizing the slack between the line control hand and the nymph. A strike indicator works well in the area where the two current speeds meet but I think it less effective in the pocket itself. I feel that the indicator on the surface is distracting to the trout and in some cases puts it down completely. The calmer surface will often permit a clear view of the leader.

A close approach is often possible with the result that you need to cast only a very short line, often not much more than a few feet of line beyond the rod tip. After making the cast into the edge of the slower water at a point sufficiently upstream to allow the nymph to be at a fishable depth at the right time, you can either strip line back through the rings or simply raise the rod to keep contact with the nymph. Such is the speed with which a trout dashes into the current and back to its lie that you will quite probably feel the take or see the movement of the line. Like most nymph fishing it is a matter of trying to keep an eye on the fly, the trout, the leader, the line and feel for a take all at the same time. Sometimes it pays to twitch and lift the nymph through the lie with the extra movement convincing the trout of its authenticity. With this sort of control the takes rarely pass unnoticed. You might fail to hook the fish but you won't be mistaken as to whether it took the fly or not. A

Superb nymphing water. Trout stay down deep and a nymph searching the lies within this stickle, short pool and around the rocks is a very productive tactic.

Tuck Cast (*see* chapter seven) provides a quick entry for the nymph and gives some slack to be taken up as it sinks to the required depth.

The *downstream* approach offers even more control of the nymph, mainly because the short line techniques allow a manipulation of the line, leader and fly that is impossible with longer casts or when fishing upstream. Fishing downstream it is probably easier to steer the nymph through a lie and to regulate its depth. One of the most enjoyable aspects of picking the pockets is that you can get very close to a lie behind a rock or boulder by keeping low and using the obstruction as a shield to keep out of view of fish in the pocket. The nymph can be cast, drifted or simply swung into position no more than a few feet away. Keep the rod tip high to keep the line clear of intervening currents. Such close ac-

tion is always great fun. Close control is possible as you allow the nymph to move through the lie at a pace accurately controlled from your upstream position. It can be fished dead-drift, with a drift and pause, drift and lift, a slow upstream retrieve or with an across current arc into the pocket like a natural escaping from the flow into a calm haven. Gaining control of the nymph is a key feature of successful nymph fishing and in this situation fishing downstrem with a long rod offers the most control. The fly can be slowed down and steered much more effectively from above. A heavily weighted nymph is essential unless fish can be seen feeding near the surface.

Nymphing the Pools

A pool has a shape that looks as though it has been scooped out of the river bed. It shelves

Two agile-darting nymphs (actual length about 10mm).

Frank Sawyer fishing the Upper Avon.

Oliver Edwards fishes one of his nymphs in the kneeling pool on the River Wharfe.

Poetry in motion as Lars-Åke Olsson crouches low to cast on the Derbyshire Wye.

The moment of the take for Lars-Åke Olsson on the Upper Avon.

Mike Mee nets a nymph-caught trout on the River Test.

An Itchen trout comes to the net.

An underwater perspective of the trout's world. A brown trout in the shallows.

The Swedish River Gim at Gimdalen; an excellent clear water dry-fly and nymph fishery. A long rod is in use with a team of North Country spiders.

Lars-Åke Olsson nymphing the tail of a run.

Hans van Klinken battles with a fish on a North Yorkshire stream.

It doesn't need to be a chalk stream before fish spotting is possible. Stealth and a slow, low approach is made. With the aid of a sun-shield and polarized glasses individual fish can be stalked on many freestone rivers.

The West Beck, East Yorkshire and Roy Shaw nymphing a slow moving pool. The angler's slightly elevated position gives a clear view of every fish in the water.

Twelve nymph patterns of G.E.M. Skues tied in his style with original materials by Henrich Thomsen.

A stone-clinging nymph, an immature and a large stonefly nymph.

Two stone-clinging nymphs.

Two midge pupae amongst the larvae and nymphs; the stomach contents of a trout.

Cased caddis larvae of a species that builds cases from vegetation.

A recently caught rainbow trout reveals its gluttony for shrimps, so often the major food source on the chalk streams.

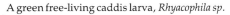

A green free-living caddis larva, *Rhyacophila sp.*

off to become suddenly deeper at the head and gradually becomes shallower downstream to a very much shallower tail or it merges into a run or glide. Its shape has been made by the force of the water entering at the head. In low water there may only be a trickle flowing in to produce large areas of dead water at the sides but it is the flood water that has carved out its contours. The lies within the pool are described on pages 65–7.

If there is an area of faster water above the head of the pool it will be a prime nymph and caddis habitat. Therefore the water entering the top of the pool will hold ascending nymphs and pupae, emergers and adults on the surface. Some of the biggest fish in the pool will be at its upper end or in calmer lies around the eye from where they can enter the main food lane. Here they can take ascending nymphs as they are brought into the pool. Nymphs also live on the bed of the pool itself and in its weeds, and trout will take up positions to feed on these. If the stream bed is uneven shallow lies may be created by the swirling currents and unless there is nymphal movement or another cause for surface activity trout and grayling will be staying close to the bottom.

The most difficult problem to solve is one of depth. Very often the water pouring in at the head has made the upper middle of the pool comparatively deep. This is found mainly in freestone rivers but also in chalk streams where sills and weirs create their own pools. Chapter seven looks in detail at the different methods of nymphing on the bottom. Much depends upon the size of the pool and its depth as to which presentation style is most effective and minimizes scaring fish. Perhaps the most straightforward approach is up and slightly across stream using a floating line with a braided leader and a heavy fly. I've used fourteen feet leaders for deep water. Coupled to a heavy fly this doesn't make casting easy at short range but it might be the only way of getting to a fishable depth and giving an effective presentation.

If a hatch is in progress and fish are feeding close to the surface it makes no difference whether you are fishing over eighteen inches or eighteen feet of water; trout will adopt positions in the very upper layers and the methods of taking them are very similar. Chapter nine covers the relevant presentations and patterns.

Slow Water Nymphing

Most people's concept of nymph fishing in medium to slow paced streams is one of a sedate, clear chalk stream flowing between rippling weed beds. This might be the most challenging of all slow water fishing but it is hardly a river type that provides the major proportion of nymphing in this manner, and for many it can only be a Utopian concept. There are very many areas on most freestone rivers that offer slow water nymphing, and after a dry summer there may be rather more slow water than we want. I spent many evenings of a recent season when the levels were exceptionally low, fishing in water with almost no flow at all. It was like fishing a series of small lakes and I used tactics to match. Even at normal levels there are many areas in which there is very little current.

Stillwater tactics are not inappropriate for slow, deep pools. Here trout often behave like stillwater fish; moving about during the day, cruising, often in a predictable path. This seems particularly so for bigger fish or maybe it is just that they are easier to spot on the move. They cruise because the main current that once delivered food at a steady pace has all but stopped and now they must search for it. Sometimes they cruise close to the surface where they can be spotted or they betray themselves when they rise to take surface food – often a fallen terrestrial when there is no hatch or spinner fall. Even when there is surface food or nymphal activity they still search for it in a very slow current because they realize it won't come to them.

Some nymph and caddis species prefer slow water so their activity can be expected, if not anticipated. Some of the agile-darting types, the large and small spurwings and pale evening duns will be found in slower alkaline streams and some of the olives in the slower parts of most rivers. Slow water allows settle-

On a small stream it is rarely possible to fish other than straight up or downstream. Here the angler uses the cover of bushes to fish a short line upstream. This is a small rain-fed river where fishing to visible wild trout creates a challenge.

ment of any suspended matter and the sub-strata is often sand or mud even on otherwise stony streams. This provides the habitat for the silt and mud-dwellers and the mayfly and *Caenis* burrow here. When the nymphs of these species ascend to the surface many do so in relatively slow-moving water. Caddis live in all sorts of water speeds and there will be plenty on the river bed so the larvae and pupae can be imitated. Midges are highly important on some rivers and they also prefer slow water.

On a very slow stream there is little point in merely fishing in a dead drift except when representing an emerger in the film. Almost every sub-surface insect, and all those we want to imitate are able to swim across or upstream against a slow flow. Movement of the nymph or pupae is expected; it also catches the attention of a cruising fish. An insect moving only in a dead-drift in a slow

current is probably a dead one. The agile-darting nymphs move very fast in short spurts and the artificial should do the same by using some of the induced takes or the Live Nymph technique described on page 111 for when fishing deep. My most successful presentation for slow water is a simple sink and draw style. With a floating line I cast across and upstream. When the nymph, which may or may not be weighted has sunk to the depth to be fished the rod tip is raised to gently draw the line back a foot or two and as the rod is lowered the line hand takes in the slack. This is repeated as the line drifts slowly down-stream. In a very slow flow or none at all the cast can be made across the pool or down-stream. Unless you can see the fish the only sign will be a movement of the leader.

Here I'd like to sidetrack slightly and mention the use of polaroid sunglasses to help reduce glare from the water surface and to

Fishing in very slow and clear water where stillwater tactics are required.

Grayling fishing on a northern chalk stream. With the aid of polaroid glasses individual fish can be stalked in the clear water.

improve vision below the surface. They can be of immense value in fish-spotting and in monitoring their behaviour and attitude towards a nymph. If I'm watching a trout for evidence of the take then polaroid glasses are essential. However, if the leader on the surface is being monitored as the only clue to the take the reflected light on the water, if it is not too bright, is an excellent background for the mono. Leader movement is more visible against the glare than on a surface where the glare has been removed. Polaroids sometimes hinder the observation of fine leader movements on the surface.

The best fishing in these circumstances is when trout are feeding in the upper layers on emerging nymphs and pupae. Often the fish are clearly visible and accurate casting is possible. A good caddis pupae pattern is an excellent standby for this situation and for a number of years I have relied upon a simple Gold-Ribbed Hare's Ear fished in the film or at no deeper than six inches. Few flies are easier to tie than a cylindrical hare's ear body ribbed with gold wire or tinsel, and I have found none that are as widely effective. If flies are hatching you will be able to determine which nymphs or pupae should be fished. If no obvious flies are hatching fish might be taking spent spinners under the surface or midges and appropriate patterns should then be tried.

7 Presentation Techniques for the Deep Nymph

'Since that's where the trout are most of the time, deep-drifting nymphs are probably the single most effective way of taking trout'.

Lee Wulff

The deep-sunk nymph is a very important tactic on all rivers. At some stage in the season there will be a time, for one of a number of possible reasons, why every fish in the river will be lying deep on the bottom – and I mean deep when referring to the deep-sunk nymph; I am not talking about a foot below the surface or midwater. I refer to the four inches above the bed. Skues expounded the use of a nymph just sub-surface as Sawyer later explored mid-water patterns and presentation. No-one has given the bottom-scraping nymph such exposure. Considering the amount of time trout and grayling spend there and the vast larder of food it harbours the reason for this omission escapes me.

Depth is relative because rivers vary. Deep tactics on one stream might mean one foot in a slow glide, at the other extreme it could be six feet in a turbulent pool. A different method should be applied to each and to the wide range in between.

Extremes of cold or bright sunlight, high or coloured water or just the absence of food elsewhere will drive trout deep. In the early season when the water is still cold the stream bed will be the principal feeding area when surface-feeding excursions are infrequent and short-lived. If during any time of the season there is nothing hatching or there are no egg-layers or terrestrials arriving at the surface trout will generally be lying well below the

A medium-paced pool on the Yellowstone river, Wyoming. The depth is 3–5 feet. Most of these anglers were fishing 20 yards away and searching the water with the aid of strike indicators.

upper layers. In a weedy stream they might adopt midwater positions taking errant agile-darting nymphs and shrimps. In a weedless river they are more likely to be lying deeper still, even hugging the bottom. The stream bed is the ultimate source of all except airborne food. The cold water of early spring means a minimum of fly activity so trout stay deep. Their metabolism is slower and they are less willing to move far to feed. A summer of low water and bright sunlight will also find trout either seeking deeper, cooler water during most of the day or in the well-oxygenated water of the riffles.

Getting a nymph or caddis down to the bottom means additional weight of some sort. This will mean including weight in the dressing, a sinking braided leader or additional weight in the form of split shot on the leader, or a full sinking line. Just one of these options might suffice but you may need two or more in combination. For the sake of a few lost flies and broken tippets I would rather risk the occasional snag on the bottom than be fishing too shallow to be effective. The few inches above the stream bed is the primary holding area for trout and is a major dining area. Charles Brooks was convinced: 'I do not believe this particular point can be overemphasized, especially since I firmly believe that all that separates the average wet-fly angler from the very good one, in most cases is the *depth at which the fly is fished*.'

THE BROOKS METHOD

Charles Brooks was one of western America's foremost fly fishers and probably its best known exponent of nymph fishing tactics for the big western rivers. Not only are his methods and patterns superbly efficient on their home waters they also have much to offer any nymph fisher with an enquiring mind. Arnold Gingrich commented that 'You may not agree with everything Charlie Brooks says, but it's next-to-guaranteed that he will in several places prod you into thinking fresh new thoughts of your own.' Brooks was an eloquent and lucid ambassador for the very

big nymph fished very deep in fast water. Even if you never fish larger than size 14 on a placid chalk trickle Brooks will shed light into previously dimly lit and poorly fished waters. His methods are anathema to many brought up with a more traditional approach to nymph fishing. Take this example: 'I know a few fishermen who claim to be serious nymph fishers, who use nothing but a floating line – these people are kidding themselves.' Such was the Brooks and one Western USA philosophy. If it does nothing else it makes you question why you fish in the style you do; at best Brooks will have you trying some of his tactics for yourself in parts of the river you had previously left well alone. I will summarize his methods in the hope that more nymph fishers will experiment with them and catch trout from where they had never caught them before. I did.

The technique is used in deep channels where the current runs fast, as fast as three metres per second. The faster riffles are too fast to hold fish except around large rocks or pockets in the stream bed and a few fish will be found in these isolated lies. All trout in these channels hug the bottom where the current is slower and the nymph has to be fished right down there. Food going past at that speed has to be presented very close to the trout or else it means the fish chasing a rapidly disappearing fly in a turbulent current. It may be that no artificial nymph will get down on the trout's nose and that the fish has to take food from the nearest part of the current. When it does react to food from here it has to enter a moving wall of water and is momentarily carried downstream before returning to the lie. The method is also used at the head of a pool where the water pours in, often over a shelf or lip. It is here in the fast, deep water that until the development of fast-sinking braided leaders the Brooks method was probably the *only* way to present a nymph on the trout's level.

There are three aspects to consider for effective presentation: the pattern and its size, depth and behaviour. The method demands that a very heavy fly, a short leader and a truly fast-sinking line get the fly to the bottom and

Fig 33

just as importantly, keep it there. In some ways the nymph movement achieved is similar to the Leisenring Lift. The intention and result are similar; the manner of achieving it is different. As in many deep presentations the cast is made *upstream* but by the time the nymph is being fished at the correct depth and with the necessary movement it is *downstream* of the angler. The time taken for the cast and nymph to come downstream allows it sufficient time to get it to the bottom where it can be controlled and fishing begin.

The equipment should not be lightweight; this is not a delicate or even a relaxed method of fishing. Some would barely acknowledge it as fly fishing. However, it is a case of 'horses for courses' and if you want to fish deep in fast water the options are few. Brooks took a lot of big fish in this way and his tackle was suitably beefed up to cope with them and their surroundings. To quote Brooks 'Such fishing requires a rod of eight or nine feet to control

the drift, and with enough backbone to raise thirty feet of deeply sunken line and a weighted nymph and hurl it back upstream without false casting. False casting a heavily weighted nymph is a form of Russian roulette with eyes and ears as stakes.' I have yet to find a British rod of less than nine feet with sufficient power and in practice I have found a nine and half foot or ten foot rod offers the right power and gives more control. The fast-sinking line is essential but had Brooks lived to see the introduction of very fast-sinking braided leaders I'm sure he would have been using one in this presentation. Other Western fly fishers use a home-made rig of five or six feet of lead-core line spliced to fluorescent orange shooting line. Big flies are fished on short, stout leaders for big trout. Perhaps it is just my casting technique but this amendment sounds like a recipe for an expensive or painful disaster. Back to the Brooks method, the leader is between four and six feet, tapering

103

down to 1X or 0X, between seven to ten pounds breaking strain. Using a longer leader prohibits the deep presentation as the mono is buoyed up by the upwelling current. In this situation a longer leader means less control.

You are probably reacting now in one of two ways: either this is leaving you fuming, going against all you have ever accepted as nymph fishing and you are vowing never to invite the likes of Brooks or his method on to your river, or you've realized that at last here might be a method that will have a chance of catching those big fish safely in previously unfishable water. The bigger freestone rivers of Britain, which are usually associated more with salmon than trout, and similarly sized rivers of Scandinavia are crying out to be fished in such a way. Those big brown trout and grayling will fall for this method.

The first part of the performance means casting only about twenty feet of line upstream and across so that the fly lands in the parallel lane which flows about six feet to the angler's side. Keep the rod tip low and aim it at the point where the line enters the water. As it moves downstream, during which time the heavily weighted fly and line are sinking pretty quickly, the intention is that the fly should be on the bottom by the time it is opposite the angler. The distance between fly and angler is minimal but much more line is beyond the rod tip. It is imperative that the rod tip does two things during the drift to the point opposite. Firstly, it should move downstream slightly ahead of the point where the line enters the water. Secondly, it should be simultaneously raised to maintain some control over the slack line. Because the water

Autumn grayling fishing often means bouncing a bug or nymph along the stream bed. This trio which topped six pounds were all caught on Sawyer's Grayling Bug.

speed at the surface is faster than at the bottom the accumulating line at the top would otherwise develop a downstream bow pulling the nymph downstream faster than the bottom current. The surplus line must be lifted clear of the surface. On the first twenty-foot cast the rod tip will be no higher than about four feet from the water but on a thirty-five foot cast the rod will be held high over your head and there is nothing you can do if a trout takes here. If it does, Brooks comments that the only way to hook it is to fall over backwards, and anyway you have miscalculated the trout lie because you should have started fishing further upstream.

Now we've reached the critical part of the method; the dead drift on the bottom and the swing of the nymph. The second part of the technique is almost a reversal of the first half. As the line goes below you, pivot downstream to face the line as it travels away from you. Keep the rod tip aimed above the point where the line enters the water and as it drifts downstream lower the rod keeping only a slight droop in the line. Too much slack will mean missed takes but too tight a line will make the fly move too soon. The nymph drifts naturally until the rod is lowered or the current gives the line too much of a downstream bow. Continue to fish out the drift as the fly and line swing directly downstream. The inevitable bow in the line causes the fly to move down and across the current in a tantalizing rising arc.

The takes come in four parts of the cast: in the dead drift downstream from a point below the angler to the end of the drift; as the nymph lifts off the bottom; as it is swinging across the stream, and depending upon the type of water the angler is standing in, on the dangle directly below him, especially if the fly is tweaked upstream. Trout have to hit the fly hard in the fast water and the take is usually unmistakable. There is great current pressure on the line and an inevitable amount of slack so trout and grayling have to be firmly hooked with a solid strike of the rod and a downward pull of the line hand.

Brooks maintains that you should not false cast for very good reasons of safety. I have yet

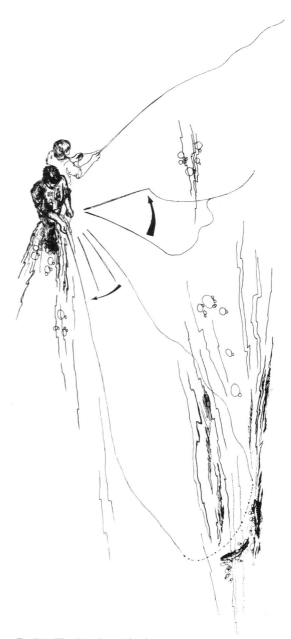

Fig 34   The Brooks method.

to master the technique that allows me to lift from a downstream position twenty feet or more of fast-sink line with a lead bullet on the end and place it accurately upstream with a single movement of the rod. I just have to live dangerously.

105

After the first drift has been fished through, repeat it a few times and then make further casts progressively lengthening the line one or two feet at a time. The line is cast further upstream each time and not further across the current. When the limit of the line control is reached, then move position.

I have used the method to good effect on spring trout, and when winter grayling fishing if I've needed to achieve depth in fast water. I've caught many fish that I think I would not have caught but for the Brooks method. In the last few years I've changed my opinion about the value of sinking lines on rivers. I now use a floating line in conjunction with sinking braided leaders of varying sink speeds. I believe these offer a more effective presentation, more sensitive take detection and are considerably more pleasurable to fish with. Therefore, for me, the Brooks method has been superseded because of the advance in tackle development. Fast-sinking braided leaders have made the full sinking line almost superfluous in river trout fishing. The fastest-sinking braided leader is the Airflo Extra Super Fast Sinking LSR24 which is claimed to go down three feet in three seconds. I find this leader too cumbersome and so heavy it pulls down the fly line but with leaders to cover the intervening speeds who needs a sinking line?

Artificial nymphs, of course, must represent some natural food source. The western rivers that Brooks fished hold huge stonefly nymphs, some of which are twice the size of the biggest European species. With some credibility he could fish nymphs tied on a size 4 with 4X long shanks. Needless to say, you can pack a lot of lead around such a hook. 'There is nothing subtle about a western fly' said Brooks. The type of river that requires these techniques usually means good stonefly and caddis populations and it is imitations of these two that are required. Each artificial must be heavily weighted. In addition to the patterns described at the end of the chapter the cased or free-swimming caddis is excellent for this fishing style. One other fly which has proved to be the most successful nymph I have come across in recent years is the Leadhead Nymph which belongs to Dutchman Hans van

Klinken, and is ideally suited to fishing in the Brooks method. I further recommend a suitably weighted Hare's Ear Goldhead or similar, almost any large stonefly dressing and good caddis larva patterns, and in particular, imitations of the free-swimming species are excellent bottom-bouncers.

Brooks contended, and I do not doubt his observation, that whether they are swimming or drifting, natural nymphs always stay the right way up when in their natural environment. If bottom-dwelling fish only ever see the backs of nymphs there is no need to imitate the different colouring of the underside. For midwater or higher there may be some value in such imitation but in the deep patterns Brooks only tied nymphs 'in the round' so there is no difference in the sides, back or underside. Neither did he tie flattened nymphs. The turbulent current causes an artificial fly to be turned, bounced and spun as the water force wills. If the artificial is tied other than in the round a gyrating two-coloured nymph appears very unnatural. Brooks's own Montana Stone listed at the end of the chapter is tied in this way, as is the very successful Woolly Worm.

My alternative to the Brooks method is to use a fast-sinking braided leader with a floating line or the Cortland nymph line. The tippet is 2–3ft of level mono of 5lb breaking strain. The cast is made upstream and across. In fast water you should wade out as close as possible to the area to be fished. In rough water the noise of the current and imperfect visibility mean that you can approach much closer without alerting fish. I've caught trout less than six feet away. A tuck cast can be incorporated to aid a rapid entry of the fly. On the final forward stroke of the cast and as the line goes out horizontally stop abruptly in the 11 o'clock position or check the rod and give a little jerk backwards. This will catapult the nymph forward, 'tucking' it under and allowing it to drop into the water at the end of the fly line. The fast-sink leader rapidly follows it to the bottom. The sinking speed of the heavily weighted nymph and braided leader ensures that it reaches the fishing depth very quickly. The rod is held high as the line comes down-

Fig 35 An alternative to the Brooks method using a fast-sinking braided leader.

Fig 36   The upstream dead-drift.

stream. As much line as possible is held clear of the intervening currents. Pivot to face the line as it moves downstream and lower the rod to allow the drift to continue. It is possible to feed further slack line to extend the drift. Takes are registered by line movement, hence the value of the Cortland specialist line. Strike indicators have a value here depending upon the density of the braided leader. Some of the fastest-sinking leaders drag down the top of the floating line and with it any bite indicator. Leaders with less dramatic sinking rates are used where the fishing depth is less or the water speed slower and with these, bite indicators are more effective.

The technique can be used on fast water; perhaps even on water where previously only the Brooks Method would have been successful. It has the advantage of being much easier to master than the Brooks Method and is a much more pleasurable and relaxing way of fishing. It is an excellent searching technique in water that is often ignored as being too difficult to fish effectively. This is one area where the relatively recent development of fast-sink braided leaders has opened up new fish-taking opportunities.

THE UPSTREAM DEAD-DRIFT

Perhaps this is the most widely used nymph presentation across the whole range of river and water types, from riffles to deep pools and genteel chalk streams. A wide range of patterns is used from heavily weighted bottom-bouncers to tiny emergers in the film. Because of its universal application many variations have inevitably evolved.

There are three areas where nymphs naturally drift in the current. Firstly, in the film as they hesitate at emergence. Secondly, as they pause, as some do in their migration to the surface, or as they drift after being dislodged from weeds. Thirdly, in the inches above the stream bed as they are caught up by the current or as they voluntarily enter the flow to move downstream. The dead-drift is a totally natural presentation and whereas one of the keys to successful nymph fishing is the correct movement of the nymph, in this instance the natural movement is no movement at all except at the direction and pace of the current.

As in all sub-surface presentations it is the reading of the water speed and depth that will determine how accurately the cast is made. Where will the fish be lying? What is the current speed? How deep is the water? What sinking speed of leader should be used? How heavy is the fly or any additional weight on the leader? How long does the leader need to be? Assessing all these aspects the cast is made so that the nymph sinks to the correct depth just upstream of the trout's lie. Make the type of cast that gives the longest drag-free drift. By casting across the currents some line mending will be necessary.

For the deep presentation with this method it is usually only practical to use a floating line. A weighted nymph, caddis or shrimp, is cast either directly upstream in the same current lane or usually across to some degree to pre-

vent the line spooking fish in the same lane. In practice the nymph is taken at any time – from hitting the water to its final deep position – but the intention is to fish the nymph back towards the angler at a constant depth just inches off the bottom. The fly line has to be taken up to take care of the slack in the same manner of keeping track of an upstream dry fly. Too fast a retrieve of the line will nullify the dead-drift presentation although it might catch a few trout. Too much slack line may mean a take is not converted into a firm hooking or is not even registered. One thing is sure, it is fairly unusual to be able to cast to and monitor trout lying deep and take detection may be quite difficult depending upon the surface and light conditions. In slow water fish may mouth the nymph and reject it without you having the slightest clue about what is happening. Watching the leader or line in fast water for the tell-tale pause or dip may be equally unsatisfactory as a guide to what is happening a little way below. Some other

The river Ure in winter: an excellent grayling water where if fish are not in the mood for surface-feeding they have to be taken from the very bottom.

indication might be advised. The different aids to sensing takes are discussed on page 94. Without any such aid it is a method of fishing that demands total concentration as you try to read reactions in the line or leader. In anything but a slow-moving stream constant casting and close scrutiny of the surface makes very tiring, but rewarding fishing.

There are a number of casting styles that improve the rapid entry and sink of the nymph with this type of up and across stream presentation with a floating line. The tuck cast is probably the most widely used.

Roman Moser developed his own style for fishing deep on the river Traun. He uses an indicator tied to the end of the floating line and a fast-sink braided leader with a weighted free-swimming caddis larva but other patterns can be used. The casting technique has been described as a parachute roll-cast. Facing up and across stream a roll-cast is made and the power stroke continued through to end up almost parallel to the surface. A large loop is created with the effect that the fly drops into the water with the leader all very close together at the end of the line. The cast is rather like a lazy, poorly executed roll-cast and contrary to how the leader should roll out in the standard roll-cast. Because both fly and leader are weighted and the former sinks unrestricted by tension from the latter it gets down quickly even in quite fast water. The presentation is a dead-drift so the line must be mended, either up- or downstream, to prevent drag. The coloured tip of a Cortland nymph line is useful but a bite indicator is a better guide.

THE DOWNSTREAM DEAD-DRIFT

Usually one thinks of the deep dead-drift as being an upstream presentation; how else can the nymph be freed from the restrictions of being attached to a line and leader? However, there is a little-used tactic of fishing downstream. In the normal course of events when fishing down or across the stream the current lifts the leader and prevents the dead-drift. In

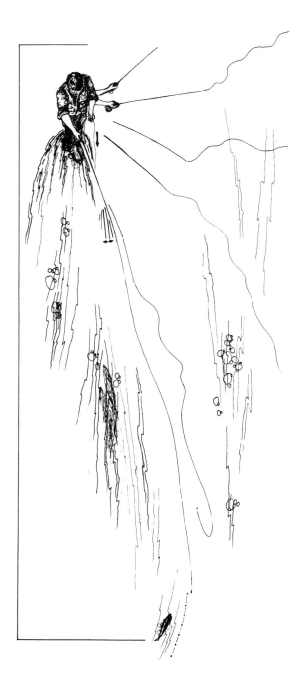

Fig 37 The downstream dead-drift.

addition to the reach and lean cast and line mending there is at least one further solution that permits a deep downstream dead-drift.

A floating line is required with a clearly visible end to the line or with a bite indicator positioned on the leader. A sinking braided leader is a useful inclusion. Cast the weighted artificial diagonally upstream into a parallel current lane. Any form of cast that drops the leader in a pile of slack coils at the end of the line is an advantage. With the rod tip, follow the nymph to a point just below where you are standing, mending the line as necessary to prevent drag. At the moment the line tightens under the current and the nymph is caused to rise (a marvellous tactic in itself) pause briefly, then pay out more line as near as possible into the lane directly above the line. The amount of tension on the line is critical. The line at the surface will be travelling faster than the trailing nymph following the fly line. The brief pause before paying out line allows the nymph to catch up and lead the rest of the line and leader downstream. Firm hooking is more likely. The trick is to pay out line at the same pace as the current so as to maintain enough contact to firmly hook a trout when it hits the fly. My method is to pull about three feet of line off the reel and shake it through the top ring. When this is taken up repeat the line-feeding procedure. The deep dead-drift can be continued for some distance. The important part is to keep a minimum of slack line beyond the tip. Takes are registered on the end of the fly line or on the floating indicator. A long rod offers better control than a short one and takes can be hit more quickly as the line is picked up off the surface. The technique is not easy and takes some practice. It might be a minor tactic but it may be the only way of fishing some parts of the river.

THE LIVE NYMPH TECHNIQUE

I dislike the name of this method; it implies that other methods are something else. Other than imitating the stillborns on the surface all techniques should represent the natural be-haviour of the living nymph. No one sets out to do anything else. For very good reasons the deep dead nymph technique has yet to be invented. What the phrase is trying to convey is that it is not a dead-drift presentation.

The question to be answered is how do nymphs move on the stream bed and in the slower couple of inches above the bottom? The answer is that different nymph types move in different ways, usually by swimming or crawling and the imitations should be fished with the appropriate movement. The trouble with most techniques on the bottom is that the rig needed to get the nymph or caddis to the stream bed and keep it there so that its movement is controlled, is necessarily heavy. The nymph must be brought to the bottom in as near a static position as possible and only then can it be given the natural movement. It is very difficult to slow down or adequately control an already moving imitation but the static nymph can be twitched, stripped, jerked or lifted as required. The heavy rig doesn't provide the most aesthetic fly fishing but it is productive.

The first way of achieving the deep presentation is relatively easy but not very subtle. It works well on all water types, from fast riffles, moderate and slow-moving pools and the calmer flats. A floating line is satisfactory with a fast-sink braided leader and a heavily-weighted fly. Alternatively a fast-sinking line may be used with a short leader. The leader weight and length varies with the type of water to be fished. The riffles need the shortest total leader length of about five feet, and the slowest water the longest leader, perhaps twelve to fourteen feet. If crawling nymphs are to be imitated you have to keep the fly on the bottom and the length of leader and any additional weighting to achieve this must reflect the current pace. The cast is made across and downstream and the sinking leader and nymph should get to the bottom by the time the line is facing straight down the river. Resting on the stream bed the nymph can now be retrieved in a natural manner giving it a movement appropriate to the pattern. The angle of retrieve is determined by the type of fly line and leader. A fast-sinking

Hans van Klinken takes a grayling on a deep-sunk bug from a small chalk stream carrier.

line and leader will give movement to the nymph on a nearer to horizontal level than when using any leader on a floating line.

Perhaps all stonefly and upwinged species except the burrowing nymphs move upstream to some extent. Even the cased caddis inches its way against the current, the free-living caddis species crawl or pull themselves back upstream on to the bottom after being suspended on their threads in the current. Shrimps rapidly dart in all directions. Each must be fished with a natural movement: the shrimps in short, fast draws with pauses between; the crawling stonefly and upwinged nymphs in a slow, steady retrieve; the cased caddis inches back very slowly. It is doubtful whether any upwinged or stonefly nymphs (except the largest species of the latter) can move upstream in a current speed greater than one and a half feet per second (about a mile per hour) which is fairly slow. Many need much slower water. It should be remembered though that the couple of inches of water above the stream bed is significantly slower than that at the surface. The rougher the bottom the deeper the calmer zone just above it. A riffle over fine gravel produces an inch or two of tolerable current; over golf ball size stones the habitable zone might extend to four inches.

The type of stream bed, whether chalk gravel, pebbles, larger stones, solid rock, moss, weed, sand or mud will give clues as to the type of nymph to be fished. Many species only inhabit specific areas. The pattern type has to be correct because it is being fished right in its natural environment. One of the biggest drawbacks with this style of fishing is that rocks, weed and debris on the stream bed are easily snagged. The simplest way of minimizing this is to weight the nymph so that it fishes upside down with the hook point uppermost.

A useful pattern for this presentation is the Leadhead Nymph which can be fished fast or slowly. If pushed, I'll admit I fish it because it is a pattern that proves an exception to the rules and can be fished over any river bed with a moderate to fast current. I don't really know what trout and grayling take it for but sometimes they need it in a dead-drift or if that fails

Fig 38   The live-nymph technique.

High summer, low water and bright sunlight contrive to make fly fishing difficult. There is a steady glide towards the far bank where trout will be lying deep. Often a pattern like a small weighted stone-clinger or olive nymph fished deep will work.

it is retrieved with quick six-inch pulls. No insect of this size and colouring moves in this way but trout and grayling love it. Something about it makes me question its right to a legitimate place in the tradition of river fly-fishing and I certainly don't think it should be used for wild browns on a clear chalk stream or anywhere where a more subtle approach should be used, but it does have its place on other rivers. When it is fished with quick draws I'm afraid it moves into the lure category and is no longer a 'nymph'. It can be an excellent pattern for bottom-hugging trout and grayling.

Swimming nymphs can be represented with the live nymph technique. They won't be able to swim upstream in water moving in excess of about a mile an hour and so the faster water should be avoided and the imitations should be restricted to moderate and slower-paced sections. The agile-darting and, to a lesser extent, moss-clinging species all swim close to the stream bed and in midwater in slower weedy streams. The retrieve should be in quick short pulls or with longer draws in what Gary Borger calls the 'strip-tease technique'. Imagine a nymph swimming upstream. It darts forward three to nine inches depending upon the current against it. It pauses before darting again. As it pauses it doesn't maintain its position relative to the stream bed but it is carried downstream momentarily in a dead-drift; a three steps forward, one step backwards progression upstream. The stronger the current, the slower its progress. This movement is easily imitated in the retrieve when between each pull the line is allowed to dead-drift downstream for just a second or two. Many agile darters in only a slowish current move upstream in a constant wiggle without a pause and this progression is easy to simulate. The problem is that agile-darters are very small and fishing a weighted imitation close to the bottom is only possible in a slow current.

The rate of any retrieve should be carefully monitored. One day they will take at one speed, another much faster or more slowly. Usually it is a case of experimenting to discover what is acceptable. Sometimes I have cast into a deep pool and let the line lie there for a minute or two. Tugs are felt as the nymph or caddis hangs on the dangle just above the stream bed, gently fluttering in the currents. Often it is in the first two slow pulls that the takes come.

Two factors should be considered in assessing the imparted movement. As a general principle the retrieve should be in inverse proportion to the current speed, i.e. fast current, slow pulls; slow current, quicker retrieve. Certainly nothing moves upstream fast in swift water. The second consideration is the type of imitation being fished. How does the natural behave? The deep live nymph technique can be retrieved in a figure-of-eight working of the line hand. It may need three twists a minute or fifty a minute. It might take one long draw every thirty seconds or a continuous steady retrieve without breaks. Experiment but be aware of the current speed and the pattern being fished.

Crawling nymphs and swimming nymphs particularly don't just move up and downstream but they also move across the currents, or more often, down in the drift and across in a swimming action. The old wet-fly methods, often dismissed as merely raking the stream are not as unnatural as we have sometimes been told. When weighted patterns are fished with sinking leaders across and downstream they well represent the crawling and swimming nymphs caught up in the drift and swimming to the side in a general downstream arc. There is often nothing quite so tantalizing as a nymph swimming away from the nose of a trout.

THE ROLLING NYMPH

The name given to this technique originated with Neil Patterson who named the style after using it very successfully for stubborn trout in the Kennet. The action of a deeply-sunk nymph rolling or dragging along the bottom is not new; indeed, some of the techniques described on the previous pages are designed to do just this. What prompted Neil Patterson to experiment with the method was that trout in high summer were staying down deep and he needed something acceptable and effective that conformed to an unwritten chalk-stream code. In water deeper than the two feet down to which a copper-wired Pheasant Tail Nymph was normally successful something heavier had to be used. He came up with a heavily weighted imitation and a presentation technique to match.

As in the best chalk-stream tradition the technique should ideally be used to visible fish as in this method there is rarely any indication on the line or leader when a trout or grayling has taken. A floating line is used with a mono leader treated to sink, with a tippet of four to five feet of the finest diameter you can feel confident with. After the three essential calculations of trout depth, current speed and nymph sinking rate are computed the cast is made upstream or up and across stream so that the fly fishes on the bottom about a foot upstream of the target trout. Drag should be avoided by mending the line or by making the type of cast necessary to provide enough slack line to be taken up before the fishing zone is reached.

As the nymph closes down on the trout through that last foot or so it should be scraping the gravel on the bottom. Just before it reaches the fish twitch or draw it to one side.

115

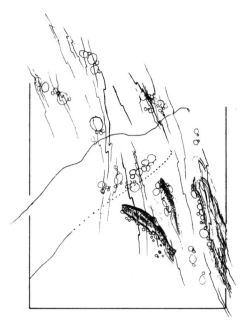

Fig 39   The rolling nymph.

The nymph shouldn't be lifted, but moved sideways. It is this horizontal movement which sometimes is so effective as the nymph moves diagonally across the trout or grayling's nose. The dragged or rolled nymph which moves horizontally away from the fish behaves in a manner guaranteed to arouse trout and grayling. When the dead-drift fails and the induced-take doesn't induce this is a presentation technique that offers another chance of success.

The trout must be watched for any indication of a take. It may only be an inch or two of movement or it could be a couple of feet as it follows the nymph to one side. If the nymph can be clearly seen the moment of the take is easily tracked. If not, it is a question of estimation of the nymph's position and tightening on any movement from the trout. Fortunately, the clear streams on which the technique can only be applied often have areas of gravel bottom against which both fish and fly can be seen more easily.

Fig 40

116

MINOR TACTICS FOR MAINTAINING THE DEEP PRESENTATION

In addition to the use of a heavily weighted nymph, possibly with a sinking line if that is what you enjoy, with or without a sinking braided leader presented in a manner that ensures it fishes just an inch or so above the bottom, there are the further considerations of keeping it there for as long as possible and of maximizing the trout-taking opportunities. Some of the presentation techniques referred to have described just how this can be achieved. Other tactics involve the weighting of the fly and leader in conjunction with one of the presentation methods.

Putting additional weight on the leader usually involves one or more split-shot or wrap-around lead strips. Just how much additional weight is required to fish the nymph on the bottom depends of course on the weight of the nymph, sinking speed of the line or leader, water depth, current speed and the time available for it to sink (determined in combination with the presentation technique) before it reaches the fishing zone. It will be trial and error until the correct mix of weight, fly and technique are found.

On no occasion now do I find it necessary to fish with additional weight on the leader because of the versatility of the braided leader. With a wholly mono leader I have been known occasionally to include extra weight and I am aware that this is unacceptable to some fly fishers; it breaks an unwritten code that for some reason proscribes additional sinking aids. Is their logic questionable? The same fly fishers will soak their dry flies with every new liquid, grease or aerosol spray to keep them afloat. If they strive so enthusiastically to maintain their flies above the surface by artificial means why deprecate and deplore the use of another aid to ensure the nymph sinks effectively? The tenet of their argument is that the fly may be weighted or tampered with to float or sink but to include anything else on the line or leader is simply no longer fly fishing in the traditional and long accepted sense. Fishing a small nymph close to the river bed is often impractical as little weight can be added to the dressing so other ways of achieving depth have to be used. Incidentally, when fished upstream, an unweighted nymph below a weight on the leader will behave more naturally in the currents than a very heavy one. By putting weight eighteen inches above an unweighted nymph the depth is achieved and the nymph responds in the currents just above the stream bed.

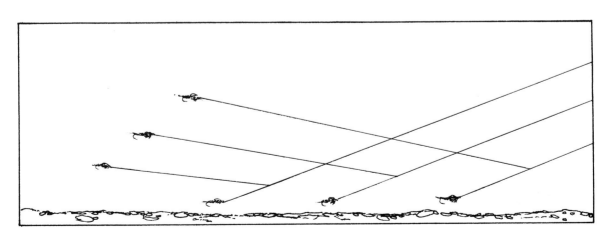

Fig 41   This illustrates what is possible when using a heavily weighted dropper with a point fly of various weights. The length of the leader to the point fly and the length of the dropper have some influence on the depth at which the point nymph is presented. The strength of the current also has an influence; the slower the speed, the higher the point nymph fishes.

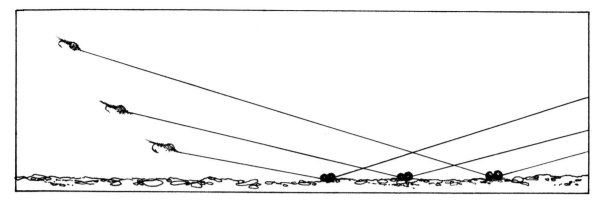

Fig 42   Adding split-shot to the leader may ensure it sinks to the bottom. Nymphs of different weights or the varying placement of the weight on the leader enables a variation in the fishing depth. The lowest nymph is the heaviest one and on the shortest line below the weight. The highest nymph is the lightest with the longest line.

Whether you place additional split-shot on the leader or on a dropper there is another alternative. Not only does it answer the criticism of the anti-additional weighting adherents it also provides, even doubles the chances of taking fish. Doubling the trout-taking opportunities ought not to be lightly discounted. Instead of weighting the mono or dropper use a weighted nymph on a dropper the same weight as any additional split-shot that would have been used. This has the same effect of sinking the leader and it gives the chance to fish a different nymph pattern. Giving a choice of food increases the catch rate. Care must be taken so that the two patterns are of a type that can be fished in a similar style and movement. A fast-moving cased caddis in hot pursuit of a shrimp will arouse some suspicion! If the split-shot or weighted dropper is heavier than the point fly, then the nearer the two are the deeper the point fly will fish. The greater the distance between the two the shallower it fishes (*see* Figs 41 and 42).

PATTERNS FOR THE DEEP PRESENTATION

In addition to the nymphs listed here, caddis imitations will be found in chapter three and other dressings in chapter twelve.

Montana Stone (Brooks)
In its largest sizes this nymph represents the *Pteronarcys* genus of North America stoneflies. It is equally as acceptable in its smaller sizes for the larger British and European species. It should be weighted as desired with turns of lead wire or lead foil being built up on the back. The latter method allows the hook to fish point-up and reduce snagging on the river bed. The colours below are those recommended by Charlie Brooks but they can be amended to suit different species. After the body has been wound on and ribbed, tie in together the two hackles with the fibres on one side stripped away. These are wound in a single turn at the rear and front of the thorax with about a quarter of an inch between the turns. The ostrich herl is wound at the bases of the hackle.

Hook   4 4X long-shank to 8 2½X long-shank Code D4A, H1A or CS2BL
Thread   Black
Tail   Six fibres of crow or raven primary tied in a V
Rib   Oval copper tinsel or brown flat mono
Body   Black fuzzy yarn, four strand
Hackles   One grizzly saddle and one grizzly dyed dark brown
Gills   Light grey or white ostrich herl
Head   Large varnished tying thread

Woolly Worm

In its various sizes and colours this simple yet stunningly effective pattern represents stonefly and upwinged nymphs, dragonflies, damselflies and caddis larvae. It is a standby pattern on many western American streams and in its middle and smaller sizes is a good but undervalued European fly. Although it is not one of Brooks's own dressings it is tied 'in the round' which may, with its life suggesting palmered hackle, account for its success.

Hook 4–14 2X to 4X long-shank Code D4A or H1A, weighted as necessary
Thread To match the body colour
Body Black, brown or olive chenille or other natural or synthetic yarn
Rib Silver or copper wire
Hackle Five to seven turns of palmered hackle: grizzle is the usual choice but badger, black, ginger and olive are used depending on body colour and species being represented.

Leadhead Nymph

I have caught hundreds of trout and grayling on this pattern devised by Hans van Klinken. It can be fished in any of the dead-drift presentations or with up and across stream movement; the latter more in the manner of a lure. I cannot offer a convincing explanation of what fish take it for, except to comment that they go for it very enthusiastically. One suggestion is that in the dead-drift presentation it is taken for a cased caddis tied in reverse, the green butt representing the larva and the partridge fibres its legs.

I have watched Hans catching big fish with it on freestone and chalk streams in Britain and Europe and catching fish at the ratio of 4:1 compared with other highly experienced anglers using other patterns. I'm sure that a large part of its success is that its weight ensures that it fishes right on the bottom. It is not a pattern that suits everyone's tastes and I confess that after a season or two of its use I've

Hans van Klinken with a grayling caught from the river Costa on a Leadhead.

begun to question its use as the manner in which it fishes can so easily turn it into a lure.

I have used the Leadhead in all types of streams and from big Scandinavian rivers to small North Country streams and I have invariably caught fish. I could recount story after story of how this fly has consistently outfished other patterns on the bottom. Some of the English fly fishing team came to the River Ure needing some practice on its river type for bottom-hugging grayling in anticipation of a forthcoming world championship. It wasn't very long before the Leadhead Nymph caught its first few grayling and for the rest of the weekend this became virtually the only pattern that caught fish on a high and very difficult river.

It can be fished in any of the deep presentations on a floating or sinking line. I watched it being fished in its creator's hands through some fast ripples where I doubted fish could make a lie. As Hans allowed it to drift downstream and across and then retrieved with short pulls of the line he was taking fish after fish. I was delighted, as any host should be when a guest catches fish but Hans was catching fish from places where I said he shouldn't bother fishing. My fourteen years' experience on this short stretch of river had to be re-evaluated thanks to the Leadhead.

The weighted head ensures the fly gets down quickly. It also has three further benefits. The position of the weight makes it fish with the hook point uppermost; this minimizes snagging on the bottom, allows the nymph to be presented head down like something grubbing along the riverbed, and offers the likelihood of a firm hook-hold when a trout takes it.

Hook 8–14 long-shank Code H1A or G3A
Thread Brown
Tail Brown Partridge tail fibres wound as a collar between the butt and the body
Butt Fluorescent green flexibody or fluorescent lime green wool or floss
Body Shaggy brown fur well picked out
Head Lead substitute shot strongly bound in on a looped piece of mono (the split towards the eye)

Brown Stonefly Nymph (Fogg)
I have used this nymph for about seven seasons since reading about it in Roger Fogg's excellent book *The Art of the Wet Fly*. I fish it on a single fly leader or on the point of a three-fly cast and as a search fly when there is nothing hatching or without a sign of a moving fish. It has been invaluable on rivers where the larger stoneflies can be expected. I have also done well with it with the Leisenring Lift method on clear streams which have never seen a stonefly of this size. I dress it the manner described below with lead foil built up on top of the shank so that it fishes point uppermost. It can be dressed without the varnished back and with an untrimmed hackle to produce a nymph 'in the round' for rougher waters.

Hook 8–14 Code CS7, G3A or H1A (2½X long-shank) weighted as required
Thread Brown
Tail The butts of two cock pheasant tail fibres tied in a V
Body Various shades of brown seal's fur or substitute and built up at the thorax
Hackle Palmered brown hen to match the body colour, over the abdomen only, with the upper and lower fibres trimmed away. The thorax back is clear-varnished
Rib Clear nylon mono through the hackle, finishing behind the thorax

NYMPHING THE BOTTOM: A SUMMARY

1. Measured over a season the stream bed is the main feeding area on most rivers. During some days it may be the only feeding area.
2. Nymphs, shrimps and caddis larvae permanently inhabit the substrata of the stream beds.
3. On the substrata all nymphs, shrimps and caddis larvae move downstream and across the flow at various times. They also occasionally move upstream.
4. The current speed at the stream bed is slower than at the surface. The rougher the bed, the larger the slower zone.
5. Successful deep presentation will require

The large stonefly nymph, *Perla bipuncta*.

either weight in the nymph, on the leader, a sinking braided leader or the use of a sinking-line, or perhaps two or more of these in combination.

6. Patterns of exaggerated size are more likely to succeed when fished close to the river bed than when fished elsewhere. To quote Charlie Brooks, the deep water expert, 'I'm a firm believer that unless the fish are definitely feeding on a certain insect type, a fly representing the largest of the indigenous naturals is the best to produce worthwhile trout.'

8 Midwater Nymphing

'It is well to remember that angling is only a recreation, not a profession. We usually find that men of the greatest experience are most liberal and least dogmatic . . . It is often the man of limited experience who is most confident.'

Theodore Gordon

On most rivers midwater is not a major trout feeding area. In a stream that is relatively free of weed there is no ready source of food midwater. The only time nymphs and pupae appear here is as they traverse the zone as quickly as possible on their ascent to the surface prior to emerging. Some trout will follow their rise from bottom to top and intercept food on the way up but midwater is not an area trout hold position in because there is no food continuing on this drift level. Nymphs are moving vertically and not horizontally. Trout adopt positions where food comes easiest. In a stream without weedbeds these lies are on the bottom, or during a hatch near the surface.

If the stream is weedy, and this is typically true of chalk streams, spring creeks, some limestone streams and isolated pockets of freestone rivers, then midwater feeding is a much stronger probability. The nymphs, shrimps and larvae that abound in the weed are either inadvertently caught up in the current or nymphs more willingly enter the drift to move downstream from weedbed to weedbed. In a slow to medium paced weedy river there is always the chance of trout holding midwater because of the food drift at this level. If trout expect food on this level it becomes an important fishing zone.

THE SAWYER METHOD

The greatest exponent of midwater nymphing was Frank Sawyer. Whereas the chalk stream nymph fishers of Skues's generation concentrated on the inert nymph just below the film Sawyer took nymph imitation and presentation a step further and deeper. Neither Skues or Sawyer was wholly a nymph fisherman; rather one method supplemented the other as they moved from nymph to dry fly and back again as the trout's behaviour changed. Their ideal was that neither would cast to non-visible fish. It was deemed unethical. I confess it's a code that doesn't normally suit me. But on the clear chalk streams fish-spotting isn't too difficult.

Sawyer was a naturalist as well as a fisherman. His job as a river-keeper on the clear waters of the River Avon enabled him to study the fish and fauna of the stream over many seasons. It wasn't just a case of noting trout and fly behaviour but he researched and recorded in detail what he found. He was an amateur scientist whose observations and findings were of considerable value to professional entomologists. His style of nymph fishing and his patterns have left their mark on trout fishing the world over. Even though, in theory, his methods might be limited to a small number of chalk streams like the upper Avon on which his styles were developed, in effect he initiated a fishing style and a handful of patterns that have been adopted widely in Europe and North America. Whether or not you will ever fish an English chalk stream, Sawyer's book *Nymphs and the Trout* (1958, revised 1970) is essential reading for anyone with any interest in learning about trout attitudes towards nymphs.

The essence of his now-named Netheravon method is that one finds a trout in a clear stream resting midwater. Observe it taking nymphs. Cast an imitation some few feet upstream; allow the nymph to drift, drag-free, to within an inch or two of the fish; raise the rod tip causing the nymph to rise just six inches from the trout, and then as it takes the nymph, tighten before the fly is rejected. With clear water a trout has as good a view out of the water as the angler has into it. A poor stalk or a bad cast and all could be betrayed. It requires a calculation of sinking speed of the nymph, water speed and an assessment of the trout's depth; a high degree of accuracy and precision in casting; a delicate presentation over a clear and relatively slow calm surface; skill in line control; the eyes of a hawk to detect the take and the reactions of an Olympic sprinter on the starting blocks to set the hook. Sawyer took many of his trout and grayling this way and he was extremely good at it. Few anglers will ever achieve his skill at this particular technique. Have you heard the story? You are lost deep in a forest. You have a choice of whose help you enlist to find the way out: a pink elephant, a bad nymph fisher or a good nymph fisher. Answer: choose the bad nymph fisher; the other two are figments of your imagination.

I tell the story only in relation to Sawyer's methods on his type of stream. Some other nymphing techniques are easier but that certainly does not imply that easier methods or other river-types are more enjoyable because they are less demanding. The opposite is true. The satisfaction derived from a difficult job successfully completed is far greater than when using a less skillful style. The problems and difficulties that arise with Sawyer's methods are easy to imagine. Not least is the extremely taxing task of either keeping a visual sighting of the nymph or monitoring the trout's reaction when you think your nymph should be going past its nose end. If failure is the biggest incentive to success there should be a lot of highly motivated nymph fishers, of which I'm just one. I would just like to make one further comment which applies equally to almost any other fly fishing style:

what you have never tried or are new to sometimes appears very difficult, or in the case of the Netheravon style is shrouded in mystique. Master the basics and the subtleties will soon follow. To be competent in this style needs no more skill than that required when upstream nymphing to unsighted trout on freestone rivers. Each requires different skills.

The directly upstream cast is possible but the diagonally upstream or across the stream approach prevents both line and leader from passing above the trout. The other difficulty with a cast from directly below is that the nymph and the trout's reaction are harder to see. Very often the decision of which way to fish is beyond your control and is determined by the circumstances of the lie. Sawyer's techniques are best employed on visible trout but they can be put with good use to unsighted

Frank Sawyer: a legend in his own lifetime; seen here using a figure-of-eight retrieve.

Never before had one man studied a single river so intimately over such a long period. Sawyer distilled his knowledge into a fishing style, a totally new method of tying nymphs and two classic fishing books.

fish. The leader is well-greased to float after allowing sufficient leader untreated to sink to the fishing depth. Movement of the leader will be the only clue to the take. The drawback is that only a proportion of the takes ever register in such a way.

Frank Sawyer took a radical approach to nymph imitation. He maintained, quite rightly, that the agile-darting nymphs that predominate in the chalk streams swim with their legs folded underneath them and hence there is no need for their representation in an artificial. His four best-known patterns (three nymphs and one bug) make no concession to leg imitation. Their key feature is the body. His nymphs are characteristic in that apart from the copper wire underbody they use just a single material for the tails, abdomen, thorax and wing cases, and do not use tying thread.

They were designed with an economy of dexterity, complexity and materials; three sure signs that guarantee if a pattern works it will be popular. The absence of a hackle enables a quick entry through the surface film and the layers of copper wire that weight the nymph ensure that it sinks to midwater in a moderate or slow current. The slim profile is an excellent imitation of the small agile-darting species.

The basic design of Sawyer's nymphs is the same in each of his patterns, providing a slim profile with a single colour throughout the dressing. His Pheasant Tail Nymph is the best known and most widely used of his patterns. It was used by Sawyer mainly to represent the nymphs of the olives and iron blues. The basic colour of the pheasant tail herls would not seem to be the ideal to copy these naturals. Very few agile-darting nymphs are deep-brown-coloured; indeed most are shades of greenish-yellow olive but olive nymphs they do represent although I cannot say why. My guess is that it is as much in the way they are fished, i.e. with some induced movement at a critical time, that makes them so attractive. The Grey Goose Nymph was Sawyer's solution to copying the lighter coloured nymphs of the pale watery (*Baetis fuscatus*) and spurwings (*Centroptilum luteolum, C. pennulatum*). Sawyer staked a great deal on these two patterns and on his ability for accurate casting, nymph control and seeing and reacting to trout takes. He once wrote this: 'Both artificials have proved to be effective throughout the season. Range in hook sizes can take care of the actual sizes of the naturals. Often when one fails to attract, the other is successful. But when no response to either is obtained I consider myself beaten.' That's confidence.

Sawyer's Pheasant Tail Nymph
Hook   12–16 Partridge A, G3A, H1A or CS7

Thread   None
Tail   Three cock pheasant tail fibres, the tips of the body herls
Underbody   Fine copper wire with a hump at the thorax
Overbody   Pheasant tail fibres wound with the copper wire and tied slightly fatter at the thorax
Wing-case   Pheasant tail fibres doubled and redoubled

Sawyer's Grey Goose Nymph
Hook   12–16 Partridge A, G3A or CS7
Thread   None
Tail   Grey goose fibres, the tips of the body herls
Underbody   Fine copper wire with a hump at the thorax
Overbody   Grey goose fibres wound with the copper wire and tied slightly fatter at the thorax
Wing-case   Body fibres doubled and redoubled

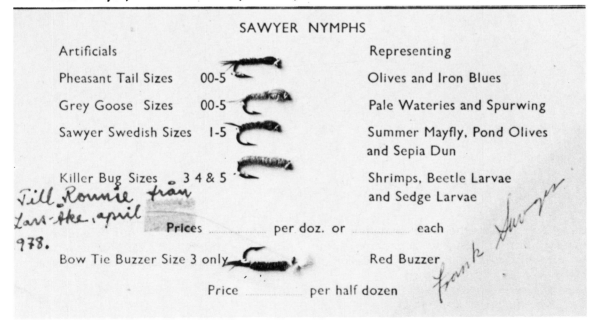

Five examples of nymphs actually tied by Frank Sawyer.

As well as having been designed for quick entry into the water, Sawyer made sure his nymphs sank quickly by using a variation of the tuck cast or what he called 'pitching' a nymph.

One last thought about Frank Sawyer's techniques: after catching his first trout of the day Sawyer would smear slime from the trout's body on to his nymph. He believed its taste was made more acceptable to another trout and delayed its instant rejection. Isn't such a practice a step towards bait fishing? Fly fishing is about the imitation of the natural insect and its behaviour and not about making the fly taste. I'm not taking a swipe at a fishing folk hero, merely raising an eyebrow.

The Induced Take

Frank Sawyer and his protégé Oliver Kite emphasized that it isn't just the size, shape and colour of the natural nymph that have to be replicated in the artificial but it must also behave like a natural. In the clear slow-moving waters of a chalk stream trout have adequate time for inspection of a nymph bear-

ing down on them. One feature that will convince fish of the authenticity of a nymph is its natural behaviour. If a trout is only half persuaded by an artificial its fears can be allayed by the spontaneous movement of the nymph just inches in front of its nose. Its genuineness is confirmed. Even if a trout sees the artificial in a dead-drift and is convinced it is a real one, it may not want to feed for a number of reasons. However the sudden upward swimming motion less than a half second's drift away triggers a Pavlovian response. This, more than any other, factor was the key to Sawyer's and Kite's success.

The level of presentation should be either in line with the trout or more ideally, slightly below it. As the nymph approaches the last foot before the fish the rod tip is lifted causing the nymph also to rise through the water in a single smooth movement just inches in front of the trout. About a foot of movement is adequate. This simulates the darting motion of the natural or its ascension to the surface.

A hundred examples of the success of the method could be related but this one will serve its purpose. A few years ago I fished the River

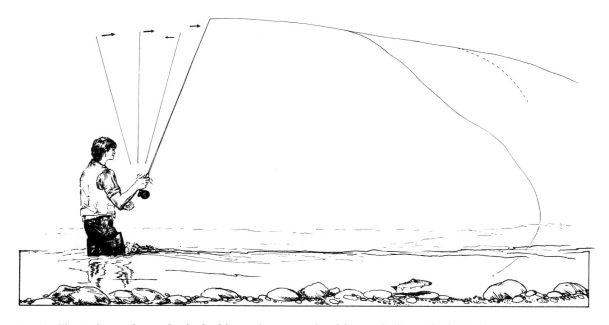

Fig 43   The pitch or tuck cast. On the final forward power stroke of the cast the line is checked so that the nymph tucks under the leader and enters the water first.

Oliver Kite on the Foston Beck, East Yorkshire.

Kyll in Germany. It is one of the best trout and grayling streams in that country, flowing through the beautiful countryside of the Eifel area. I had joined some Dutch friends in the hope of some good grayling fishing. We certainly had that and no shortage of brown trout. One of the memories of that week was of a trout ensconced six feet out from the bank on which I stood some five feet above the water. The fish lay about eighteen inches below the surface resting in a slight depression on the bottom. The water was slow and clear and the surface smooth. It saw me as soon as I saw it and I wondered whether it was worth the effort casting, surely it would disappear with the first wave of the rod. It was rising occasionally to something invisible on the surface and also taking something small

near the bottom. In full view I cast a number of dry flies, some of which it looked at and refused before I moved on to Sawyer's Pheasant Tail Nymph. This fish was remarkably tolerant of my presence and the unsatisfactory flies or presentation I was offering. It continued feeding knowing that I was there trying to fool it. It was as though it was saying 'Show me whatever you want but I can sort out the food from the rubbish you're offering.' I picked up the gauntlet.

The clear water ensured that I could watch both trout and nymph and suffer the humiliation of coaxing not the slightest interest. After half a dozen dead-drifts I gave the nymph a lift of about six inches. The intention was to continue the draw for rather longer but the trout intercepted. I tightened but didn't

An attractive glide on the river Kyll, Germany. Hans van Klinken puts one of his patterns to the test.

Superb holding water for trout and grayling and excellent clear freestone nymph fishing.

Slow water nymphing in the clear water of the River Test.

Flies in order from top to bottom: Original E.R. Hewitt nymph, one of the fathers of American nymph fishing; Box Canyon Nymph; Casual Dress tied by Polly Rosborough; Unnamed nymph (a little worse for wear) believed to have been tied by Charles Brooks; Whitlock Nymph; Kaufmann's Brown Stonefly Nymph tied by Randall Kaufmann.

Flies in order from left to right, top to bottom: Mating Shrimp tied by John Goddard; Grayling or Killer Bug; Dove Bug; Goldhead; Edwards' Shrimp tied by Oliver Edwards; Leadhead Nymph tied by Hans van Klinken; Gold-Ribbed Hare's Ear.

Flies in order from left to right, top to bottom: Swanny Nymph tied by Hans van Klinken; Caseless Caddis tied by Hans van Klinken; Klinken Nymph tied by Hans van Klinken; Mono Sedge; Hatching Sedge Pupa (Roberts); Emergent Sparkle Pupa tied by Gary LaFontaine; Edwards' Ascending Sedge tied by Oliver Edwards; Klinken Nymph tied by Hans van Klinken; Klinkhamer Special tied by Hans van Klinken.

Flies in order from left to right, top to bottom: Sawyer's Pheasant Tail Nymph; Spurwing Nymph tied by Tom Waites; Sawyer's Grey Goose Nymph; Spurwing Nymph tied by Oliver Edwards; Sunk Spinner tied by Charles Jardine; Ecdyonurus/Heptagenia Nymph tied by Oliver Edwards; Large Dark Olive Nymph tied by Oliver Edwards; Blue-winged Olive Nymph tied by Oliver Edwards; Mayfly Nymph (Walker); Post Ovipositing Female Sedge tied by Oliver Edwards.

Flies in order from left to right, top to bottom: A.D. Buoyant tied by Charles Jardine; Jardine's Emerger tied by Charles Jardine; Halo Emerger tied by Gary LaFontaine; Yellow May Dun Emerger tied by Oliver Edwards; Suspender Midge Pupa tied by John Goddard; Suspender Olive Nymph; Nymphing Emerger tied by Hans van Klinken; Once and Away tied by Hans van Klinken; Emerger Nymph tied by Hans van Klinken.

Flies in order from left to right, top to bottom: Swisher & Richards' Wet Emerger; Mottram's Smut (variation); Orange Dotterel (golden plover); Waterhen Bloa; Soft-hackle Emerger (USA); Partridge & Orange; Hare's Lug & Plover; Roman Moser's Emerger tied by Charles Jardine; Yellow Sally.

The author netting a nymph-caught trout on the River Test.

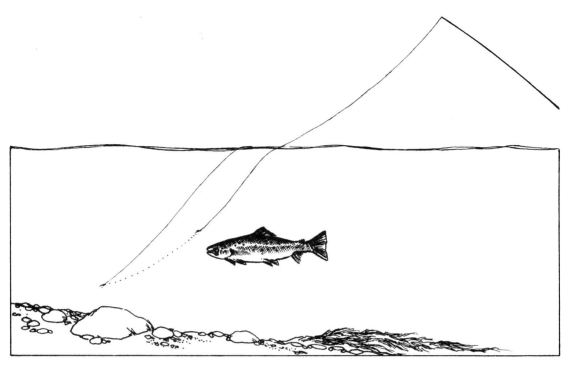

Fig 43   The induced take.

connect. A moral victory to me, perhaps. It continued feeding unperturbed. A couple of minutes later I put the nymph in a dead-drift without any reaction. The next cast I concentrated harder and lifted the rod tip. He was on and I'd won a battle of wits against the witless. I'm not sure what the incident proves except here was a trout that was prepared to ignore an angler in favour of feeding and that whilst the pattern was satisfactory but unacceptable it had to be presented in a specific way for the illusion to be complete.

Don't be restricted to using the induced take only on visible fish. When fishing out likely lies it pays to employ the method even when the exact position of a fish isn't known. I would go so far as to suggest that almost half of my trout caught when fishing blind upstream have been drawn into taking after I've lifted the nymph. The less generous reader might describe this as no more than a variation of sink-and-draw. I prefer to think that it's the application of water-reading skills in conjunction with the induced take to dupe a trout that

I could reasonably expect to be found where I'm fishing.

The Advance Lift

The advance lift is a variation on the induced take and is particularly useful when trout are nymphing with plenty of food to choose from. A moderately heavy nymph or shrimp is essential as it has to sink to the trout's level a few feet upstream of it. The rise of the nymph is performed three or four feet in front of the trout, after which it must sink to the fish's level before it passes by. The movement ensures that this nymph is the one that catches the fish's eye and maintains the trout's attention over any others drifting in the flow. Early on in the drift it has been singled out from the natural nymphs. No attempted inducement, whether advance, lateral or on its nose end is guaranteed to succeed but it usually ensures that the nymph receives an inspection at the very least and of the trout that do inspect a proportion will be duped.

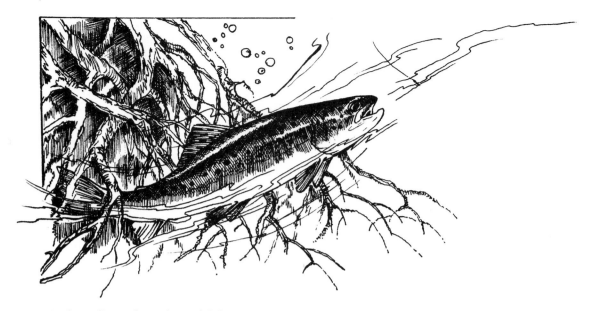

Fig 44 A 'plopped' nymph can draw a fish from cover.

The Lateral Lift

The lateral lift is the induced take applied on one side of the fish and at the same depth. A feeding fish is much more likely to move to food to one side of its drift lane than one steadfastly ignoring food. The latter can be enticed in this way but I'd sooner put a nymph into its mouth than ask it move half a yard to intercept food. I usually confine the lateral lift to occasions when because of my casting inability or the geography of the lie I am prevented from putting a nymph directly in line with a fish. Unless a fish is hungry and moves laterally for the dead-drift nymph the lift should be applied slightly upstream of a ninety degree angle to the trout. The great thrill is the second of travel as the fish moves to inspect or intercept the nymph. The self-control is commendable too as the temptation is to anticipate the take and whip the nymph out of the closing jaws of the trout.

The 'Plopped' Nymph

This is a technique more for use on non-feeding fish patiently waiting for some major nymph activity. It is also a useful ploy for fish sheltering under cover where it is impossible to cast a nymph or dry fly directly to them. Fish under the bank or low hanging branches can be attacked in this way. Falling terrestrial insects will enter the water in this way so there is some element of imitation in the style of fishing. The intention is to cast the nymph or shrimp so that it enters the water with a 'plop' that attracts attention. The weight of the artificial should be sufficient to guarantee a disturbance. Small nymphs are not very effective and it is better to use a shrimp pattern that will take some lead underbody. Using a larger nymph is a tactic that shocks but fails to elicit the required response. Most trout in these circumstances are made more wary by too big a nymph. It is far better to use a shrimp which can be of a reasonable size and hide a lot of weight without causing a trout to think less in terms of food but of an intruder competing for its lie.

Of course the 'plopped' imitation works very well on recently stocked trout. For most of its life the hatchery trout saw food entering the water in this way. Even with trout that have been in the river some months I wouldn't be surprised if the 'plop' triggered a feeding mechanism deep within its memory. On some fisheries I visit I can drop small stones from a bridge or parapet and up to half a dozen trout converge on the stone for inspection. Some will mouth it out of interest but usually only once. These are certainly not wild fish and I've no doubt what they are taking it for. Far be it from me to recommend such underhand tactics when *fly* fishing but I just want to make clear why a 'plopped' nymph or shrimp sometimes works so devastatingly well.

The Leisenring Lift

In his little book *The Art of Tying the Wet Fly*, originally published in 1941 Jim Leisenring described his method of inducing a trout to take. Despite the book's title it has been this one nymph fishing technique that has survived half a century. Fifty years on it seems to

get more and more popular. The Leisenring Lift is a technique that its creator employed either to sighted fish or those whose lie was known. Accurate presentation is essential and the imitation should be of a natural that could be reasonably expected. Because the nymph is caused to make an upward lift it is particularly useful just before and during a hatch situation. However it isn't only during a hatch that it takes fish; a drifting nymph that suddenly lifts to the surface in the manner of an upward swim a foot in front of the trout is liable to be found between its jaws pretty quickly. The movement is the inducement to feed. It may be a reasoned act by the fish; 'Is this a nymph coming my way? It must be, the little beggar is making a break for it.' Bang! Or the trout makes an automatic and unconsidered reaction; the nymph rises and the feeding

This is a long run of moderately-paced water between 2–4 feet deep. Fish were found all along its length. Gary LaFontaine fishes with a swinging caddis pupa.

131

mechanism is triggered. Many sub-surface methods involve a planned or unintentional lift of the fly and trout often take at this point.

The cast is made across and upstream of the fish taking into account current speed, depth and fly sinking rate. The progress of the nymph must be assessed so that it reaches its fishing zone in a dead-drift on the same level or below the trout and six to twenty inches in front of it. This may involve some mending of the line to remove the downstream belly in the floating line. When it reaches the target zone there should be no slack line and the rod which has been held low is raised high. This causes the artificial to lift in the manner of an upwinged nymph or caddis pupa on its way to the surface. The nymph lifts and simultaneously begins to swing to the side. It is a deadly method for a feeding fish and even if the trout has shown no signs of feeding the enticing behaviour of the nymph just inches in front of its nose is often irresistible. The swinging lift can be in a single continuous movement or with a very small and slow

jiggling action imparted by the rod tip to simulate different nymph actions.

A handsome brown trout which later pulled the scales down at three pounds nine ounces was clearly visible just a few inches off the gravel bottom in about two-and-a-half feet of water in a clear chalk stream. It was a yard upstream and about eight feet out from my bank. I cast from the cover of a bush. From this position I offered it all sorts of things; some of which it had a close look at and one it had mouthed and rejected before my eyes had told my brain to tell my right hand to do anything about it. I gave it a rest for five minutes; this needed working out carefully. It would probably be my best trout of the season and I was rapidly working through my fly box with unseemly haste. I squatted behind the bush peering through the leaves with my pulse pounding and my heart in my mouth as I examined the alternatives. There was a small rubber-legged Girdle Bug in the fly box . . . should I? . . . I very nearly did I'll tell you. I'm not sure whether it was my conscience or the

Fig 45   The Leisenring Lift.

fear of the keeper or my host emerging from the distance whilst the fish was being played that stopped me. I came to my senses and realized that a different presentation was the answer rather than a pattern change. I rested the fish for a full ten minutes. The hands on my watch went backwards. There were a hundred and eighteen rooks in the trees across the field. Then the trout moved. A half-inch at the most. Its mouth opened and shut with speed of a camera shutter. It was feeding again. I edged round the bush and now four or five yards upstream of the fish I gently cast out the Grayling Bug. It was going to be a good day after all. The bug drifted down to the trout's level and about two feet upstream, I stuck out my rod arm to give it a bit more drag-free drift, then three inches in front of it the drift stopped. I was lucky. That first cast was perfect and the drift judged to a millimetre. It was the cast Jesus would have told Peter to make. I raised the rod slightly, the bug lifted and the rest, as they say, is history.

I don't think the choice of pattern was as important in this instance but it was the stimulation of its movement that was the trigger. Dozens of upwinged nymph species and caddis pupae rise in this manner and such natural behaviour is bound to dupe fish.

All presentations are most effective when they are made to visible fish but the Leisenring Lift can be used on unsighted fish in pools and lies known to hold trout. The takes are felt through the tightening line or are seen as line movement. If the lift is continued and a take comes just below the surface the swirl of water displacemet may be seen. Setting the hook is simply a matter of lifting the rod higher whilst pulling the line down with the other hand. It is an excellent method for fishing the riffles which are a main area for emergence for many nymphs and caddis pupae.

A variation on the technique when fishing blind is that after completing a fruitless lift drop the rod tip and recover the slack line. Lift the rod again and repeat the procedure. This imitates the nymph or pupa rising to the surface. In anything faster than a slow current the behaviour is unnatural; no insect swims diagonally against the current to emerge. Despite this the method works.

Charlie Brooks had a similar tactic for fish lying slightly deeper. He called it the Rising-to-the-Surface Method and used full sinking or sink tip lines and short leaders to achieve some depth. The cast is made across or across and downstream. When the fly has sunk to near the bottom the slack line is taken in and the rod tip is lifted in a single movement from a low position to about eleven o'clock. The rod tip is dropped again while at the same time retrieving the slack line. The intention is not to allow the nymph to sink so there is a steady rise to the top. The rod tip is raised and the procedure repeated until the leader reaches the rod tip. Before a couple of lifts are completed the cast will have swung directly downstream but the sequence should continue until the cast is fished out even though there is a directly upstream retrieve. I have not fished the technique, though to be effective it sounds as if a long initial cast has to be made. The artificial's behaviour is not very natural as the rising nymph or pupa moves against the current. There are times when trout are prepared to ignore the upstream movement and are satisfied with a suitable imitation coupled with the trigger of the rising action. Brooks commented that the technique works best when some sort of insect activity is taking place – I've yet to try a method that doesn't work best then.

The wet-fly methods across and downstream receive a measure of success for reasons discussed elsewhere in this book. Unweighted flies with a floating line have a practical fishing depth of little beyond the upper layers. Weight is required, either in the flies or leader to enable them to be presented midwater.

9 Nymphing Below the Film

'You can imitate the nymph, but you cannot imitate the wriggle.'
G.S. Marryat

Much of the writing of Skues relates to nymphing in the uppermost layers of the stream, where the nymphs are ending one era of their life and about to begin another. Skues did not discover that this was a main feeding area for trout; that is as old as fly fishing itself. He applied the logic of his legally trained brain and stated his case for sub-surface fly fishing. He popularized and made it an acceptable way of fishing on the English chalk streams.

Until the dry-fly era began, fly fishing just below the surface or in the film was well established on the chalk streams, only to disappear under the weight of the dry-fly dogma. Skues argued passionately and convincingly for the ethical acceptance of casting a single fly to a trout feeding below the surface. These fish were invariably in the top few inches of water. What the chalk stream fisher had missed out on for a whole generation had continued unabated on the freestone rivers of Britain. Fishing flies awash in the film or just below it was the principle style of fly fishing for the rest of the country. Chalk stream fishers had a lot to learn and Skues was their sage.

Before Skues, anything below the surface had been known as wet-fly fishing. But all that changed as the style of a single fly cast upstream to a single fish evolved on the Itchen. Taking all that he had learned of the North Country style of flies and fishing, and building on his growing knowledge of entomology, Skues devised his own patterns specifically to represent the nymphs of the upwinged duns he observed the Itchen trout to be taking. He put his own invention of the marrow spoon to good use and tied patterns to match the natural nymphs he discovered in trout stomachs.

Who could argue against his logic of matching the hatch below the surface? George Edward MacKenzie Skues has world-wide recognition as being the father of modern nymph fishing. It is only proper that in a book on the same subject that I reiterate it. Even though his books deal with a limited style of fishing on one type of stream, of which there are very few, they are of immense value because they were a watershed from which evolved many of the nymph techniques today.

It is equally true that some of our current methods and patterns came in a direct line from nineteenth-century fly fishers and bypassed that incestuous little corner of southern England. Some nymphing styles I use in Yorkshire have very little to do with what has gone on in the last one hundred years in Hampshire and Wiltshire. Some of the American soft-hackled nymphs and emergers owe far more to T.E. Pritt, W.C. Stewart, John Jackson and Michael Theakston than they ever did to Skues. Examine the patterns and methods within this book and draw your own conclusion. What is irrefutable is that fishing a fly in or just below the surface film is highly successful and has been so for centuries. The names given to the differing presentational styles and fly designs may vary wherever they are used but whether you call it wet-fly fishing or nymphing or fishing the emerger, spider, flymph or floating nymph, the truth is that for the majority of the time it is a nymph or metamorphosing nymph/dun in the upper layers that is being imitated. I accept that some of the spider patterns well represent drowned duns and spinners but they are also excellent emerger imitations.

W.H. Lawrie's little book of 1947, *The Book of the Rough Stream Nymph* is a work of practical fishing instruction soundly based upon entomological observation. Although his comments are confined largely to Scottish rivers the principles of nymphing on any freestone river remain the same. Perhaps the most outstanding section of its mere 103 pages is the one headed 'Surface Fishing of Nymphs'. In it he recommends methods and patterns for the emerging nymph and emphasizes its importance to the fly fisher who would usually think in terms only of dry-fly or wet-fly fishing. The two complementary skills are combined in nymphing the film. Spider patterns in the film were an established tactic but Lawrie tied nymphs to represent specific species on the point of emergence.

Fishing the upper layers where fish are more likely to be visible to the angler provides some very entertaining fly fishing. In fact, the surface film is the most exciting inch in fly fishing. So much happens at the air/water interface that within a couple of inches a wide variation in pattern-type has been devised to copy a particular stage in an insect's life.

Upstream and slightly across with a small nymph imitation just below the surface. This is nymphing in Skues style on his length of the Itchen at Abbotts Barton which because of his pioneering work became one of the most historically important rivers in fly fishing.

135

The river Gim, Sweden. The shallow stickles on the right of the stones are never more than knee depth but they hold trout and grayling.

Nymph, emerger and dun, or pupa, emerger and adult are three stages within inches and seconds of each other.

Trout follow the migration of mature nymphs to the surface. They feed on them as they begin their ascent as the first few become more active and leave the safety of their habitat. If a major hatch is about to begin the trickle becomes a surge and trout quickly progress to taking nymphs below the surface prior to feeding on the adults. In the early stages of the hatch it is the nymph fished just below the surface that is often the most successful. Trout are not yet concentrated on the duns and they have been taking the ascending nymphs, so the nymph imitation just below the film works well. It may be that the nymphs do not hatch at this stage; they have reached maturity and are agitated awaiting emergence conditions. They travel to the surface and back again and trout feed on them at all levels. When they do

so just below the surface it looks as though a hatch should be imminent but the nymph and trout activity dies as quickly as it arose. In most nymph migrations to the surface a hatch develops. Fish move from feeding solely on the nymphs to both nymphs and duns and then possibly exclusively on the duns. Sometimes, even though there are plenty of duns on the surface trout ignore them and concentrate on the nymph or emerger. This is particularly so in the case of the March Brown and Late March Brown when though the duns appear in large numbers they are almost wholly overlooked in favour of the nymph. Fly fishing evolution confirms this; for every imitation of these duns devised at least half a dozen sub-surface patterns have been created.

The emerging stage of the half-nymph, half-dun is very attractive to trout. Insects are particularly vulnerable here as they shed one lifestyle to adopt another. I mentioned earlier that some species seem to suffer a higher mortality rate than others at this point, and also that the surface of some rivers makes the break through the meniscus very difficult. If there are relatively few duns on the surface and there are obvious signs of trout feeding in or just below the film it is probably the suspended nymphs or struggling emergers they are taking. Quite a range of patterns have been developed to take these fish feeding in the film. Some of the patterns are definitely wet for fishing wholly below the surface, others merely damp for use in the film, and more are primarily floaters with just a part of them in the film.

Even when trout are feeding confidently on duns the artificial emerger often succeeds. Never is it more useful than when, during a hatch, trout won't look at the artificial dry fly and failure is staring you in the face. All trout see of the duns when they are still in the area of the surface we call the mirror is the light pattern of tiny indentations made by their six feet. Until the fly gets into the trout's window trout see nothing of the fly itself. When there are plenty of duns to feed on, the light pattern is barely any feeding stimulus at all. But the struggling emerger is clearly seen in the mirror with its abdomen and perhaps its thorax below the surface. Trout can see this and are alerted to its presence much earlier than to a dun on the surface. Its interest in it as food is stimulated.

A number of studies confirm the trouts' preference for emergers. For his extremely comprehensive book, *Mayflies, the Angler, and the Trout* (1980), Fred L. Arbona, Jr studied the stomach contents of approximately 1,000 trout over an eight-year period. The fly species that hatched most densely caused fish to become more selective than the less profuse species. This is as would be expected. However, the interesting feature was that they became selective towards the emerging insect and not the duns. In many instances during the majority of hatch periods the stomach contents contained only specimens of the emerging insect.

Gary LaFontaine produced some interesting figures for *The Dry Fly – New Angles*. He and a team of friends monitored trout stomach contents on a single river over a number of weeks. On calm days the stomach contents featured 44 per cent duns and 56 per cent emerging nymphs. On windy days the figure for duns was 27 per cent and emerging nymphs rose to 73 per cent. In quoting statistics like these I never suggest that they can be duplicated on trout streams the world over but they ought to make me more aware of what might be happening on my rivers and at least alerting me to some of the preferences trout are known to make elsewhere.

I've often found the rougher parts of freestone rivers provide some of the best nymphing of the upper layers. This is especially so when there is a dense hatch of duns over a short period on restricted parts of the river. I'm not referring to a general hatch of fly over the whole river or a moderate hatch in a confined area but a very good hatch over just a few yards of water for perhaps up to fifteen minutes. This will attract a lot of trout attention because they assemble where food is most plentiful and available. Such places are usually the necks of pools or riffles where the concentration of some nymphs (and caddis) is high. Fish take swimming nymphs in the upper water, wriggling nymphs below the film and hatching nymphs below and within the film in preference to the duns. A mass migration to the surface makes easy feeding.

Fig 46

137

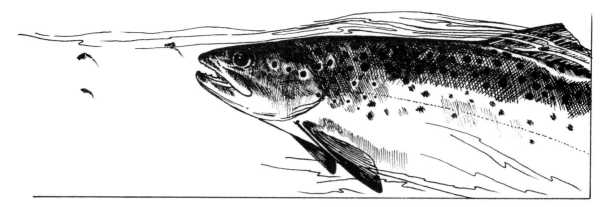

Fig 47

A carrier on the Abbotts Barton length of the Itchen where Skues spent most of his fishing life.

138

In a riffle the disturbance made by trout feeding in this way may mislead the fly fisher into thinking the duns are being taken. Only by close observation or by the failure of the dry fly will the truth be revealed. The old North Country spider patterns fished upstream in the surface were and still are excellent emerger imitations.

THE SKUES METHOD

The Skues method, so called in deference to his pioneering work, is relatively simple in its theory and practice. The idea is to imitate the mature nymph a few inches below the surface. The cast is made up and across the stream with the intention of presenting a small artificial nymph, usually a size 16 or 18 to a visible trout. There are five important ingredients to the Skues method; the upstream cast, the size of the artificial, the dressing which imitates an indigenous species, and the cast just upstream of a visible fish – searching the water was forbidden. I'm not making judgements, merely laying out the facts. The fifth requirement is that the presentation is a natural drift with no induced takes or additional movement imparted. All in all, it is a very similar technique to the traditional

A fine 3lb brown trout was the reward for the first cast of the day for Lars-Åke Olsson.

upstream dry fly except the imitation is a few inches lower in the water. The presentation, drag-free drift and strike are virtually the same as those in dry-fly fishing; the level at which the artificial drifts has simply been lowered. Just as dry-fly fishing in its basic form is straightforward, so is nymphing just below the surface. Skues fished the method in the pre-hatch period and then moved on to the dry fly as trout took the duns. It required very little change in technique. Three-quarters of a century later we can be forgiven for wondering what all the fuss was about when Skues decided to fish his imitations slightly deeper than on the surface. The depths of depravity were reckoned to be about a couple of inches.

The Skues method is tailor-made for bulging fish and often works on non-feeders just below the surface. An accurate cast can put the nymph upstream of the visible trout and the reaction can be followed even if the nymph itself cannot be tracked. It is an exciting form of fishing but it isn't necessarily all easy. A duff cast, too big a fly or sight of the line or shadow can spell disaster if it's a wild or wise trout you are after. Hatchery fish will be much more tolerant. I also use the Skues method minus one ingredient; I search the water. It is not the most productive searching technique but in certain conditions it is the most appropriate. I use it thus on two occasions. The first is on the small streams or becks that flow off the North Yorkshire moors. In summer months the trout look to the surface for much of their food. In low water a dry fly doesn't have much appeal but just below the surface a nymph does. I can spend a whole day with such a technique, working my way upstream on a beck between six and fifteen feet wide. Each cast has to be almost directly upstream. A less-than-perfect cast produces the wake of three or four fish tearing for cover. As a second search method I use it on the bigger rivers when I anticipate a hatch through my knowledge of the river and its fly life. Because I have regularly fished some rivers for a number of seasons sometimes I can have an educated guess at what should be happening on a particular evening. If the duns haven't started yet it is likely that the mature nymphs are active and may even be making preliminary ascents to the surface. The most likely food is those nymphs and it would be illogical to fish an imitation of anything else. I cannot see the fish I'm casting to so I have to rely on other indications of the take.

I suppose one can only call it the Skues method if all the aspects of his methods are complied with, but the techniques described above are often used with patterns other than those that would have found favour with Skues. Patterns representing sedge and midge pupae can both be used with the same method. I discuss fishing these imitations in this way in the chapter on caddis and in the midge section later in this chapter. Simple spider patterns are also fished up or across the stream to bulging trout and may be presented inertly in the film or upper layers. These are not nymphs by some definitions but in my view we are talking semantics and not fishing practice. I believe that for most of the time trout see spider patterns as emerging nymphs (and sometimes as drowned duns) but if fish see them thus I'm not arguing about what fly fishermen should call them.

If you are fishing to visible trout there is really no need for surface indications of the take; you can monitor a trout's behaviour. But when searching the water the leader is the key guide. If the nymph is in the film or within the upper inch or so there is almost bound to be a visible sign of the fish itself, but if it is within the next six or eight inches no rise-form or other clue may be given except a leader movement. Sometimes a good-sized fish feeding even a foot or more below the surface will produce an upwelling on the surface. When trout feed in the upper layers there is no place for strike indicators of garishly coloured foam or wool. Any trout worthy of capture will disappear the moment such a leader hits the water. Indicators may have a place when fishing the faster riffles, in poor light or when fishing a few feet down but on a calm surface they should be avoided and certainly avoided for nymphing the upper layers where a clear sign of a take is usually given.

The only indicator one can successfully use near the surface is the leader itself which

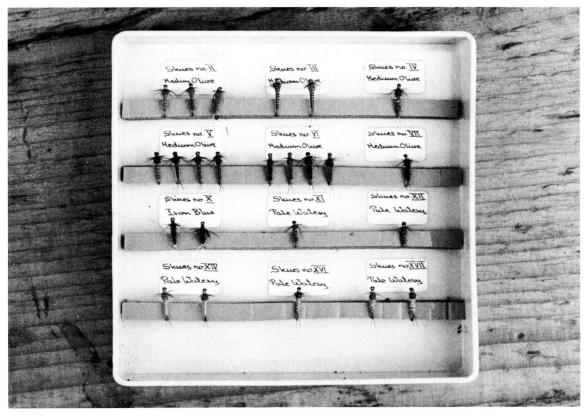

A collection of reproduction Skues nymphs tied in his style with the exact materials by Danish fly dresser Henrich Thomsen.

should be thoroughly greased to float. The grease doesn't seem to deter fish unduly just a couple of feet away, unless on the smoothest slow sections where the leader should be most carefully greased with the minimum amount to make the nylon float. The pause in the leader's drift, a dart upstream or, in a slow current and calm surface, a sliding disappearance down the hole where it enters the meniscus, are all sure signs a fish has taken. At the very shallow depth being fished it is almost bound to be the sign of a take. There is none of the frustration experienced when fishing deep of fouling weed or the stream bed with the inherent uncertainty of never knowing whether the leader indications are trout takes being missed.

The pattern-types described in the rest of this chapter are principally ephemeroptera

imitations, with the addition of a few midge and smuts. However, the surface film is a main area for feeding on caddis pupae and emerging adults. Imitations of these can be found on pages 49–51 and in chapter twelve.

THE WET FLY IN THE FILM

Winged wet flies have been catching fish for centuries. On first thoughts this strikes the thinking fly fisher as odd; with the exception of a handful of North American species very few ephemeroptera hatch from nymph to winged adult near the stream bed or midwater. Few do complete this process on a rock or stone just inches from the surface but as a rule the only winged fly below the surface is a drowned dun or an egg-laying *Baetis* spinner

141

or one of the minority of caddis species that oviposit under water. Surely the winged artificial hasn't been so successful imitating just these? Well, what are the alternatives? Just what do the winged wets like the Greenwells, March Browns and Butchers represent?

Some of them will be taken for a winged adult below the surface, particularly an ovipositing caddis, but remember that such flies appear as an extremely minor part of the diet. Some of the more sombre-coloured patterns may be taken as nymphs (despite the presence of wings) because the manner in which they are fished in the across and downstream style sometimes gives a fair imitation of a nymph swimming to the surface. The wings are compressed against the body by the current and many (even most) feeding fish seeing something fairly suggestive of what they are eating are duped. Most fish approach the artificial fly from below and never see the wings on its upper side. On a windy day or in rough water it may be that quite a few flies fail to make a successful transition from nymph to flying adult and the wind or turbulent water ensures that wings become waterlogged and the helpless fly is swept below the surface. Here is an opportunity for the winged fly to be imitated below the surface but in practice the artificial winged wet fly rarely succeeds in doing this. Most winged wet flies are fished across and downstream. The drowned adult drifts exactly in accordance with the current; any other movement is unnatural. If the winged wet fly is fished in a totally drag-free drift then an imitation is being achieved. But if, as is often the case, the fly is being fished in a downstream arc or with any hint of drag it is behaving as no drowned adult could ever behave. Winged wet flies are undoubtedly successful but they are certainly inaccurate imitations of any natural upwinged, stonefly nymph or caddis pupa. I very, very rarely fish with them in rivers. The only time they are of real value is during late evening when patterns like the Invicta, Grouse and Green, and Grouse and Yellow are taken for emerging adults or egg-laying females.

The other reason for the winged wet fly's success is that because it is often retrieved, or fished with some movement or held steady in a moderate current (which in a trout's eyes equates to the same thing), it represents fauna other than an insect. Shrimps and tiny fry move in such ways and these flies are very fair imitations if that is what trout want to see in them. A winged wet March Brown could pass for an emerging natural March Brown in the film in a March Brown hatch or a shrimp when fished at the bottom with the appropriate movement and a small minnow or fry which abound in most trout rivers.

Winged wet artificials are very poor imitations of nymphs and my recommendation is that if you want to represent the natural nymph you should choose a more specific imitation.

FLOATING AND EMERGING NYMPHS

I'm not too sure whether a floating artificial nymph is dry-fly fishing or not, and if it is, whether I should be including it in a book on this subject. However, it is nymphs that I'm writing about and it just so happens that some of them float. The natural live floating nymph hangs in the meniscus with the upperside of its thorax and the bursting wing pads touching the underside of the meniscus. I do not think it possible for a nymph to be actually on the surface and floating; only the winged adults break through the film. I've never seen a nymph that is genuinely *on* the surface. Floating nymphs are suspended or buoyant in the film. Here we come to the extremely fine line between what is a floating nymph and an emerger or a trapped stillborn, and so vague is the demarcation line that one merges into the other in a blur. Only at the two extremes – suspended nymph and a trapped winged adult are the naturals and artificials clearly different. Those in the middle can often be both one and the other. Most suspended nymphs will be alive and showing some signs of movement as the adult encased within its nymphal skin prepares to escape.

The appropriate paragraphs on pages 24–8 confirm just what is happening in the process

Fishing with a spider pattern directly upstream is a well-proven tactic when fish are taking emergers.

of emergence and how the translucence of the natural is a key feature.

It is very possible to represent the floating nymphs with a standard nymphal imitation of the species and present it correctly in the film. By tying on light wire hooks and using buoyant materials and greasing the nymph a satisfactory imitation is achieved. One of the key features of the first signs of emergence from the nymphal shuck is the thorax, head and wings of the adult, and many floating nymph patterns incorporate the first developments of the wings or an exaggerated thorax. In some cases the patterns make use of highly buoyant materials for the wing clumps, ensuring that the imitations float exactly as the natural with the minimum amount of flotant or grease on the fly and leader. In practice it is better to grease only the wing clump, ensuring that the abdomen sinks more naturally

within the film. Because there is a very grey area whether some patterns are either a nymph, emerger or dry fly I have had to make a decision as to which patterns to include in a book about sub-surface fishing. I have decided, rightly or wrongly, that in this instance if the body of the fly is in the film or below it I can include it. If the body floats on the surface or is supported above it I am calling it a dry fly.

Ephemeralla Floating Nymph (Nori and Tada Tashiro)

From the vice of Japanese fly fishers, Nori and Tada Tashiro, comes this wonderfully impressionistic and buoyant floating nymph. Although it is tied with the American ephemeralla species in mind it is suggestive of a number of other nymphs and the styrofoam wing clumps can be used for other imitations.

143

Fig 48   A presentation made to a trout feeding in the shadow of overhanging branches. A slack line cast is made so the nymph drifts drag-free over the trout.

Hook 12–14 Tiemco 2487 or Partridge L4A or E1A
Thread Olive
Tail Olive-dyed pheasant tail
Abdomen Fly-Rite polypropylene dubbing #34 (Quill Gordon)
Wing clump White Styrofoam bound down lengthwise over the top
Legs Olive-dyed partridge

Floating Nymph

This is a composite dressing from a number of sources which differ in small aspects only. It should be colour and sized-matched to the naturals. Of the two styles described below my most successful is the one with a parachute hackle. It balances better in the water and floats very well with the wing clump supported out of the water by the hackle.

Hook 12–16 Fine wire Partridge Code L4A or E1A
Thread To match the body colour
Tail A few hackle fibres, partridge or wood duck fibres or Microfibetts
Abdomen and thorax Fly-Rite polypropylene dubbing or fine fur dubbing, tapering to the rear
Wing clump Poly dubbing or fine fur dubbing piled on top, or Poly Wing to colour match the natural's unfolding wings
Legs Hen hackle or natural or dyed speckled partridge as a throat hackle or a cock hackle wound round the base of the wing clump

Floating Nymph (Arbona)

Fred Arbona describes this imitation for the smaller *Baetis* nymphs. The principal difference between this and the last dressing is the inclusion of legs at the base of the wing clump which act as outriggers and help keep the fly balanced. The body material is a blend which Arbona believes gives optimum translucency: a third seal's fur, a third acrylic Orlon wool, a third soft natural fur.

Hook 14–16 Partridge Code L4A or E1A
Thread To match the abdomen colour
Tail Four to six hackle fibres in a fan horizontal with the shank

Abdomen Dubbed mixed fur, as above
Wing clump A mixed fur ball, colour-matched for the natural's wing
Legs Four or five cock hackle fibres tied in each side of the wing clump and cemented for durability
Thorax The same dubbing as for the abdomen wound a couple of times behind and in front of the wing ball

Suspender Nymph

Using a stub of cork as a means of suspending a fly in the film was first suggested by J.C. Mottram in his book *Fly Fishing: Some New Arts and Mysteries* (1915). Theodore Rogowski first used the ethafoam ball in a stocking mesh which was later picked up by Neil Patterson, John Goddard and Brian Clarke. The ethafoam ball held in a nylon stocking mesh holds the nymph high in the film and is a good impression of the bursting thorax and wing pads. Any ephemeroptera nymphs can be copied in this way. The ethafoam can be coloured to match the natural's thorax. Do not use Pantone pens as this destroys the ethafoam. The dressing given here is John Goddard's Suspender Mayfly (*Ephemera danica/vulgata*).

Hook 12 long-shank Partridge Code H1A or E1A
Thread Brown
Tail Three tips of cream-coloured ostrich herl
Abdomen and thorax Mixed white, tan and yellow seal's fur subs (2:1:1) (A ready-made alternative is Fly-Rite #25 cream variant polypropylene dubbing)
Rib Brown monocord or tying thread over the abdomen
Suspender Ball Ethafoam ball or closed-cell foam in a nylon mesh and indelibly coloured brown

Jardine's Emerger

Charles Jardine ties this system nymph to be fished just below the film.

Hook 14–16 fine wire Partridge Code L3A, L4A or E6A

Low water and very little flow make for difficult fishing. Grayling are rising to emergers in the film.

Thread Crimson
Tail Lemon wood duck or light-blue dun fibres
Abdomen and thorax Dubbed mixed rabbit and mole's fur
Rib Stripped quill
Emerging wing Two grey mallard slips tied short and rear-facing either side of the body at the rear of the thorax
Hackle Lemon wood duck tied either side of the thorax only

A.D. Buoyant (Hatching Agile Darter)
This imitation of the emerging agile-darting species is fished motionless in the film. It is devised by Charles Jardine who developed the Jardine Living Nymph hook with Partridge on which this is tied.

Hook 16–20 Code GRS7MMB
Thread Hot orange or olive
Body Mid-olive Antron/hare blend

Abdomen back Flashabou or Lureflash pearl tape
Thorax back Brown or grey Polycelon foam
Hackle Thorax fibres carefully picked out

Walker's Hatching Nymph
This pattern of Richard Walker's represents the nymph body with the erecting wing emerging out of the top of the thorax. It should be fished with the body in the film and the wing dry and visible above the surface. The original dressing used a bunch of cock hackle fibres for the wing but the poly yarn alternative is more durable.

Hook 12–16 Partridge Code L3A or E1A
Thread To match the body colour
Tail Cock hackle fibres in two widely spaced bunches
Abdomen and thorax Dubbed fur, hair or polypropylene
Wing-case Feather fibres on the upper side of

the thorax divided either side of the wing base
Wing A bunch of cock fibres or poly yarn to emerge from the top of the thorax
Hackle Short-fibred throat hackle to match the legs or underside of the natural

Swisher and Richards' Wet Emerger

Doug Swisher and Carl Richards suggest the emergers can be fished from the lowest depths through the upper layers to being dry on the surface. However, it is in the top few inches that this pattern excels. The fly is cast upstream of the fish and allowed to sink to a depth below the trout's level. As the fly closes down on the fish, the fly is made to lift in the water by raising the rod tip. Heavier wire hooks than those recommended below should be used for deeper presentations.

Hook 14–16 Partridge Code E1A, G3A or L3A
Thread Olive or to match the body colour
Tail Barred wood duck fibres
Body Dubbed fur or polypropylene
Wings Dark-grey hen hackle tips, wide and webby, slanting back at about 45 degrees, about two-thirds the body length
Legs (optional) Dyed partridge hackle or wood duck fibres to match the natural

Halo Emerger

Gary LaFontaine devised this ephemeroptera emerger after studying the emerging nymph/dun from below the surface. I have quoted his comments on page 27. The thoracic skin splits and expands outwards beyond the sides of the body and the adult emerges through a circular escape hole. Gary found that the edges of the skin glow with an aura of diffused light which he set about imitating with large-cell closed foam. Olive, brown and cream versions have resulted.

Hook 12–16 Code CS20, L3A, E1A or E6A
Thread Black
Tag Clear Antron wrapped round the bend
Tail Marabou fibres
Body Thinly dubbed seal's fur subs, thicker at the thorax
Halo Large-cell closed foam in two short clumps either side of the thorax

Wing Fluorescent orange dyed deer hair tied sparse, extending over the eye

Nymphing Emerger (van Klinken)

My Dutch friend Hans van Klinken has some remarkable patterns to his credit. This is one of his emergers which has proved extremely successful. Within weeks of Hans showing me this fly I received the manuscript of Gary LaFontaine's book *The Dry Fly – New Angles* in which he describes for the first time the Halo Emerger and what it intended to represent. I think the success of Hans van Klinken's dressing is due partially to the halo effect of the polycelon foam overlapping the body with a similar effect as the Roman Moser Balloon Sedge and the LaFontaine Halo Emerger. The light shining through this produces a diffused aura to imitate a critical stage in the natural. Without realizing exactly why, Hans has hit upon a dressing which emphasizes one of the traits in the natural which trout key into.

Hook 10–16 Partridge K2A
Body Tying thread in a natural colour
Thorax Peacock herl
Wing and Wing-case Polycelon foam in white or natural wing colours

Emerger Nymph (van Klinken)

In a similar style to the previous pattern Hans also ties this dressing with a deer hair wing to represent the struggling with partially erect wings. The deer hair is tied in with the tips towards the rear; wind the thorax; pull forward the deer hair and secure in a forward sloping flare.

Hook 10–16 Code K2A
Body Tying thread in a natural colour
Thorax Two strands of peacock herl
Wing-case and wing Natural deer hair

Once and Away

For many years continental fly fishers have used the cul de cunard feather from a duck's *derrière*. Only in recent years have British fly fishers caught up with the idea. The two drawbacks with the feather are that they are expensive and fragile. Hans van Klinken ties this variation which can be fished dry, damp or wet. It is tied in the manner of the Emerger Nymph.

Hook 10–16 Code K2A
Thread Brown or olive
Body Tying thread, stripped quill or brown horse hair
Thorax Two strands of peacock herl

Wing-case and wing Five feathers from the area around a duck's preen gland

Pheasant Tail Emerger
Another of Hans van Klinken's dressings is this excellent emerger which takes the attributes of the Pheasant Tail nymph which is mainly for use midwater and adds a hackle and wing to produce an emerger pattern

Hans van Klinken on the river Kyll, Germany. He is fishing an emerger downstream in a natural drift in a parallel food lane.

which is highly attractive in medium to fast water. The white polypropylene yarn wing is highly visible.

Hook 12–16 Code E1A or L3A or 22 Code K12ST
Thread Tan
Tail Cock pheasant tail fibres
Abdomen Cock pheasant tail fibres tapering to the rear
Rib Fine gold wire
Thorax Peacock herl
Hackle Natural red-brown cock wound in parachute style round the base of the wing
Wing White poly yarn

Flymphs

There is hardly a more aptly-named pattern than the half-fly, half-nymph design from Vernon S. Hidy. Flymphs should be fished entirely below the surface to represent the active struggling insect. Hidy's choice of materials and tying style evolved around the need for a high degree of translucency in the body material, giving due importance to the choice of the tying thread showing through and in the choice of, and manner of, the application of the dubbing. All Hidy's dressings used natural hair or fur. If there is any translucency at all in a natural nymph it will be with the gas build-up at emergence. When strongly back-lit at the surface and when viewed from below this is most visible. Materials being used to copy naturals in this situation should give due prominence to translucency. Hidy used natural materials for the dubbing which he spun between two strands of thread to produce a delicate tapered body. The resulting bodies were much heavier dubbed than North Country spiders which also use natural fur in a manner to obtain maximum translucency. The rear-sloping hackle provides the correct flexibility to be activated by the current to simulate the living nymph. To this end he used soft-to-medium hen hackles for slow-moving currents and stiffer hackles on rougher water. All his ephemeroptera imitations are tied on long-shank hooks. The example dressing below is an iron blue.

Hook 14–16 long shank Code E1A
Thread Claret or black
Tail Dark-blue-dun hackle fibres
Body Mole's fur tapering to the rear
Hackle Dark-blue-dun hen, starling or coot

THE NORTH COUNTRY SPIDER OR SOFT-HACKLE FLY

Because the emergers, which are neither nymph nor fly are in transit between two stages of their life cycle their appearance is rather confused. The emerger is a dishevelled blur of legs, nymphal skin, abdomen, thorax and wings, some of which may or may not be very clearly visible. The trend in recent years towards tying emerger patterns has been to include some of these features in a very clear way. Carl Richards and Doug Swisher include a trailing nymphal shuck on some of their floating patterns; others have emphasized the swollen thorax and bursting wing pads with the emerging wings. Sometimes trout demand these features in a dressing and I suggest that this is most likely where a critical view of food in the film is possible. The slow-moving chalk streams, spring creeks and slow low-water conditions of freestone rivers all offer such a view and the closer imitation is often required. Elsewhere and particularly in a rippled surface I think the emergers are very well represented by one of the oldest styles of trout flies: the North Country spider or soft-hackle fly which imitates superbly the confused blur of the metamorphosing insect.

The soft-hackle fly consists simply of a body, which may or may not be dubbed with fur and a soft feather hackle. These are the two keys to the success of the dressing. The selection of the feather is important because its soft, mobile fibres give the impression of the blur of legs and emerging thorax and wings. These feathers are taken either from the back, neck or breast of the bird or more usually a marginal or undercovert feather from the shoulder of the wing. The hackle fibres are enlivened by the current moving through

The North Country spider or soft-hackle emerger.

them and so give the lifeless artificial life, the one characteristic so difficult to incorporate into a dressing. You can make a fly move in relation to its surroundings by retrieving or allowing drag but giving the semblance of movement within the fly itself is the most important feature many modern dressings completely miss. Give me three soft-hackle flies of my choice for a season's fishing the film and I don't think I'd be far behind another angler with every floating nymph or emerger in this book.

In Britain we have been writing about soft-hackle flies for centuries and have used them to represent nymphs, drowned duns and emergers of the upwingeds and the pupae and emerging sedges. The writers and fly fishers of the time rarely categorized them so specifically, but that is what they were used for, depending on the timing and manner in which they were fished. Only much later did we define our dressings and styles of fishing

more rigidly. North America rediscovered the soft-hackle fly for nymph and emerger imitations about fifty years ago. Their two most notable authors on the subject, Jim Leisenring with *The Art of Tying the Wet Fly* (1941) and Sylvester Nemes with *The Soft Hackled Fly* (1975) had an impact in their homeland. If Americans had simply read the English classic on North Country methods, *Brook and River Trouting*, by Edmonds and Lee (1916, 1980) they could have learnt as much a generation earlier. What the American fly fisher knows as the soft-hackle emerger is, in reality, the style of the North Country and Border spiders of the last century and beyond.

Tying the Spiders

If the intention is to fish below the surface in the top six inches of water then many of the medium weight hooks are suitable. Even using the heaviest hooks available will not sink the flies down very far in all but the slowest of currents. For imitations being fished in the critical inch or actually in the film then fine wire hooks prevent the fly sinking too far. They also help achieve the light and dainty dressing often required to imitate the emerging upwinged. I firmly believe that planned exaggeration in a dressing has certain advantages in specific circumstances, particularly when it comes to size in patterns for fishing deep. Even for some types of emergers the size exaggeration works well, for example in the Klinkhamer Special, but in the spider-style of fly dressing the underdressed fly is always more attractive than any overdressed or slightly larger fly. Since the earliest publication of the dressings of North Country flies their scant appearance has always been emphasized. Edmonds and Lee repeated the crucial instruction: 'In copying from nature let the imitation err on the small side if anything.' The advice still holds good today.

The body of the spider should be kept short, perhaps only two-thirds of the way down the hook shank level to the point. If the purity of the dressing is to be maintained traditional Pearsalls Gossamer tying silk should be used. More modern threads are also used but the resulting flies are not strictly accurate. If dubbing is required it should be applied sparingly so that the underlying thread is still very visible. Oliver Edwards describes this as a 'misting' in an attempt to convey just how lightly dubbed the fibres should be. The choice of the colour of thread and dubbing is very important as changes in either will alter the reflected and translucent colour of the fly. This combination of thread and fine natural fur dubbing gives the fly body an acceptable degree of translucency. If the body is too thickly dubbed the translucency is lost completely. Some tyers include a small thorax of dubbed fur behind the hackle. This helps to give the nymphal shape and silhouette, and also set the hackle nearer to a right angle to the shank. Some dressings feature a silk or fine wire rib to represent the segmented natural's body. Slim and sparsely dressed are the key features of the spider.

Many gamebirds produce suitable feathers for the hackle and many simple dressings using a few turns of silk, a mere whisper of dubbing and a feather from a partridge, snipe, woodcock, golden plover, moorhen or grouse produce dozens of dressings which have survived the test of centuries of use. Some authorities were quite specific about which feather was the most suitable but none more so than Edmonds and Lee. Part of the great value of their book is that they were so precise. For example, take the Waterhen Bloa, one of the most successful of all North Country flies. The hackle instruction reads 'Hackled with a smoky grey feather from the under coverts of a waterhen's wing. (The darker side of the feather towards the head of the fly).' Between one and two turns of hackle are all that is required. Anything more is deemed to be overdressed. For many years I was guilty of overhackling my spiders and was taken to task by no less an authority than Oliver Edwards. I can fairly claim my catches certainly improved when I halved the hackles. For me, and perhaps for other tyers too, it was a matter of confidence. How can a fly with so few fibres for a hackle ever imitate anything or catch fish? After a little success the reluctance soon disappeared.

Hackle length varies with the particular dressing but about one and a half times the body length is a good guide. When fishing in a dead-drift across the stream or upstream, the hackles are gently worked by the current and give a much better impression of an emerger rather than a nymph. In this situation a lightly dubbed body is preferred so that there is more than just a layer of tying thread for a body.

An exception to the hackling rule is the style of hackling named after W.C. Stewart who wrote one of the most successful ever fishing books, *The Practical Angler*, in 1857. Within its pages lies some of the soundest fishing writing of all time. He was a major advocate of upstream wet-fly fishing and to achieve his success he tied his hackled spiders in a semi-palmer style, extending half way down the body, now known as Stewart-style. The fibre length of these hackles should be no more than the equivalent of the body length. The blur of fibres on such a fly fished in the film gives an excellent impression of an emerger or drowned dun.

Usually the spider-style fly is finished off with the tiniest head of varnished tying thread. Occasionally a head of a couple of turns of peacock or another fine herl is called for and space should be left for this after the hackle has been tied in.

Fishing Methods

As in all fly fishing, the choice is not simply a case of fly design and specific pattern, but also of presentation. Soft-hackle flies have to be fished in a specific way if they are to represent emerging nymphs near the surface, caddis pupae or drowned duns. Understand first of all, that whether the fly is fished upstream, downstream or across the stream, if it is fished in a natural drift it behaves the same way in each case, with the current flow affecting the hackle fibres in the same manner.

A dead-drift presentation that is slightly downstream of the angler will mean the fly will drift without drag at first, then it will start to track across the current. Now the hackles shape like a very shallow umbrella. For the fibres to cling to the body in a bold nymphal shape it would take an unbelievably strong current. To suggest that the fibres are swept into a nymphal shape with the tips meeting to represent the natural's tail is incorrect, although for many years I believed this to be so. The truth is that a size 14 fly has not enough frontal area to produce the laminar flow to achieve this.

An upstream presentation makes the hackle work in a slightly different way. If the fly drifts naturally in the current, i.e. in a dead-drift, the fibres will be gently moved as water flows through them. Again the fly is not so much giving the impression of a nymph but the fuzzy blur of an emerger or drowned dun. Flies tied with Stewart-style semi-palmered hackles are best fished upstream or across the stream in a natural drift so that the hackles

move as the current flows through. If they are fished with drag downstream and held steady against the current or retrieved, their bulk makes them less effective.

My preferred technique is to fish more or less across the stream casting the fly upstream of the fishing zone which is in an area a few yards up and downstream directly across from my position. The intervening currents ensure that some line mending is necessary for the flies to be fishing drag-free; perhaps a mend as the line hits the water or half-way through the drift. Often a take comes just after the mend as the twitch given to the flies attracts a trout. Casting with an upstream curve in the line or with a reach cast and then a lean to extend the drift is equally effective. As the fly or team of flies drifts downstream any

Lars-Åke Olsson on the water he controls on the river Gim, northern Sweden. He is a great believer in the North Country spiders and uses them with much success in Scandinavia.

River Kyll. Excellent water on a long glide of fairly even depth between one and a half and two feet.

slack line can be retrieved by the non-casting hand or the rod can be lifted to take up the slack. Takes are detected by swirls or movement of the leader or fly line. After fishing through the cast it is a choice of moving up or down a yard before making the next cast. I will work my way up or downstream as the river circumstances demand. I've no fixed ideas about whether it is better to move one way or the other. As the fishing area is more or less directly across the current it probably makes no difference.

Spiders are traditionally fished in a team, usually of three flies. The point and mid-dropper patterns may be swimming nymph or caddis imitations and the top dropper more specifically an emerger. When the team is cast up and across the stream and they drift back into the fishing zone a slack-free line may be maintained to ensure take detection. In stick-les and riffles it is also possible for the top dropper to be kept in the film and as a minor tactic, even worked or twitched by raising the rod tip. Because the top fly is being moved slightly to keep in the film and to act out its role as an emerger so the two flies lower down the team move. The resulting short spurt or steady draw gives a marvellous simulation of the natural nymph or pupa swimming on the final leg of its migration. The intention of working the top dropper often produces excellent results with the point fly. The control of the line as it drifts downstream will determine, as in all fly fishing, how effectively the flies are presented, how they are worked, whether takes will be registered and whether those takes are converted into firm hookings.

It is possible to catch quite a lot of fish simply by casting the team downstream and across the current and letting them arc round

Mid-March on the river Lune. Arthur Oglesby nets the first trout of the season by fishing a trio of North Country spiders across the current.

below. The behaviour of these flies so close to the surface is unnatural. If the presentation was on the bottom it might be different but no nymphs or emergers arc across the stream inches below the surface. Some anglers even twitch their flies back. I don't know what they imitate but they catch fish. They get many more plucks than firm hookings as fish fail to take hold but it is a method that sometimes works well. There is little skill to it and about as much logic.

A more natural downstream technique is to cast the fly or team of flies from a position directly upstream or across and up from the fishing zone. The flies should then be allowed to drift drag-free into the target area by shaking slack line through the rod tip on to the water or by using a cast that produces slack line on the water. I have found this to be an excellent method for fishing the film in all types of water conditions but particularly so in low water and at the tail of a pool as it shallows off. At the tail it is often very difficult to fish

upstream from the faster water in the next riffle, and a downstream approach is necessary. Because the water is low fish scare easily and a far-off, long leader approach is required. The cast is made far enough upstream so that the fish do not see the cast landing on the water and the fly drifts into the fishing zone with all the angler's senses attuned to the different ways takes are registered.

The fly fisher's familiar reluctance to fish upstream or up and across with a team of flies on a fairly fast flowing freestone river probably lies in all the arm work required in the frequent casting, mending, retrieving and re-casting to keep control of the flies. Takes are often missed with many more going unnoticed by the unpractised angler who misses the slight swirl or fails to keep a close contact with the line and leader. It is simply a matter of practice. The pleasure in fishing a fly back inches below the surface in a natural drift is that much more than when arcing a team downstream. It is an even greater pleasure

Fig 49 Upstream with a team of flies. Sometimes takes come as the team is lifted off the surface to recast. The action of the fly rising in the water is the feeding trigger.

when you've tightened on a fish and in the midst of playing it you ask yourself why you actually struck. You cannot remember a swirl, flash or a line or leader movement and you realize that perhaps now you are getting somewhere like a proficient upstreamer when you strike subconsciously on something that can't be described.

In addition to the difficulties of line control and take detection the other major detraction when fishing directly upstream is that fish may be spooked by the line passing over them. The answer is to fish with the shortest practical length of line. Using a very short line is only possible when approaching from behind. By remaining within the blind zone of the trout's vision and with careful wading that doesn't create bow waves or footfall vibrations it is possible to stalk fish to within a good short casting distance of twenty-five feet. The short line means a minimum of false-casting and line mending, a much closer control over the fly's presentation and easier take detection and hooking. Why, except when the circumstances of the lie demand it, is there ever a need for the long upstream cast?

The best short line techniques are an extremely exciting way of fishing because all the action is so close at hand. The cast is made upstream. An angle across the current is acceptable but the emphasis is up rather than across, unless on very rippled water. A long rod is preferred – just how long depends upon the distance to the fishing zone. Spider patterns will sink no more than a few inches. The Stewart-style of hackling is well suited to being fished in this way. As I discussed fishing methods with friends in the preparation of this book it was strongly suggested to me that the principally upstream approach is out of date and more theoretical rather than in current practice. I admit it is not often I see the short line upstream style used but I fish in this way.

Once the close zones have been fished through with short casts it may be impractical to do anything other than fish the rest of the river with much longer casts. All the fly fisher's attention should be channelled into presenting the flies in a natural manner, which in most instances means a dead-drift, maintaining close controlled contact through the line and recognizing the takes.

MIDGES (CHIRONOMIDS)

Perhaps midges are the most numerous aquatic flies. On stillwater there is little doubt that they are the major trout food source throughout the season. In rivers they are often overlooked by the fly fisherman probably because the adult midges are so small the hatches go almost unnoticed. But as larvae, pupae and adults they figure highly in the trout diet. When other fly species are disappearing because of poor water quality the midges become more important. They can tolerate polluted water and appear in the smallest pools and garden water tubs. They have a preference for slow moving or still water and it is in the slower parts of the river that trout concentrate on them. My comments about midge behaviour and fishing with an imitation relate only to rivers. They are worthy of much greater study on stillwaters where their behaviour and imitation is a much bigger subject.

The wormlike midge larvae live in the soft mud, weed beds and pebbly crevices of the river bed. They stay close within their microhabitat but trout feed on them especially if they are abundant or other food is scarce. The imitation of the tiny wriggling larvae close to the bottom is almost impossible to present satisfactorily on a moving river. It is at the pupal and adult stages that the fly fisher's interest is awakened. The larva pupates on the riverbed and within a few days ascends to the surface where it pauses, hanging vertically, perhaps for as long as a minute or so before emerging as a winged adult. It is as pupae hanging extremely vulnerably from the surface for a relatively long time that trout feed upon them so avidly and dramatically. Bulge rise-forms or head and tailing trout with their backs exposed above the surface are often signs of pupae being taken. A few authorities suggest that the dimple rise is a sign that pupae and midge emergers are being taken but I've found that this is usually not the case. Fishing the hatching pupa usually means you are fishing to visible trout, or at least the rise-form is visible. There is no mistaking the take and a bulge or break in the surface results.

The size of pupa on rivers is generally smaller than on stillwaters. 2–5mm is the commonest size range. If you consider that a length of 5mm can be represented by a standard hook size 22 you can understand the problem. A few pupae are larger. Because of the size of imitations we actually use it is the larger flies we copy, whether or not they are actually in evidence.

The pupal characteristics are a tapered abdomen of nine segments from the last of which come tail gill filaments. The head and thorax appear to merge into one. Hanging from each side of the thorax are the folded wings and legs of the adult. At the top of the head are gill filaments larger than those at the tail. Their body colouring varies with species but shades of green, black, brown and orange are common.

The ascent of the pupae to the surface is in a single continuous motion being carried as any current takes them. Upon reaching the surface if the current is slow they may also move in a horizontal plane. Consequently any unintentional drag of the artificial may be overlooked by trout. The back of the pupal skin splits and the adult climbs out onto the surface. After a few moments erecting the two wings, to be folded flat across the back, the adult takes flight. Adult midges rarely show up in any quantity in trout stomach contents. When they do they are usually in a considerable minority against the pupae. The colour of the pupae varies and the best way of determining their colour is to capture a winged adult and examine it. Its principal body colour will also be that of the pupa.

I find fishing the pupal imitation on rivers a real challenge. I claim no great expertise in the methods; indeed it is only in the last few seasons that I've come to realize just how significant the naturals are and how they can be copied. I'd always ignored them as a river fly and restricted their use to stillwaters. It took other angling writers to open my eyes to a blind spot. Despite this I'd found adult midge imitations very successful but perhaps this is because of the fact they are also taken for small terrestrial flies. I regard a Knotted Midge as an excellent general summer fly. It was John Goddard's use of pupal imitations on the chalk streams that impressed me and provoked me into trying them for myself. I have used his Suspender Midge Pupa with success on chalk and freestone streams. I don't claim any great competence in these circumstances and too often the magnificent sight of head and tailing trout has been as frustrating as it was exhilarating.

Although drag in the midge pupa imitation is sometimes tolerated by trout my intention is always to fish in a dead drift. No matter how good a fly fisher I am I will always end up with some drag somewhere along the drift so I don't go out of my way to copy something I've spent most of my life trying to eliminate.

Because midges prefer slow-moving water the hatches there are greater than elsewhere. In calm water trout behave rather differently from those in faster water – they are less likely to be static, waiting for food to come to them. Rather they adopt a cruising circuit around an area, almost as though on patrol. This might actually be a true circuit or simply moving sideways across the stream trying to watch as much of the surface drift as possible.

Most of the imitations are small, certainly a size 14 would be the maximum for any river midge pupa in Britain and a fairly fine tippet is needed for the best drift in an area where trout vision seems to be critical. I use soft nylon which allows most free drift in combination with a cast that obscures as much of the leader as possible. The across or downstream presentation is the one that I have the most success with. When fishing with small flies, perhaps down to size 22 it is likely that the presentation is as much at fault as the pattern and spooking fish should be avoided. Takes come when the trout breaks the surface or there is water displacement where the fly should be.

Suspender Midge Pupa

This is John Goddard's pattern for the pupa hanging in the film. The buoyant Ethafoam

Suspender midge pupa.

where the palmered hackle appears as little more than a blur to give the impression of the emerging fly. The contrasting two-coloured grizzle hackle helps imitate the light and dark features of the natural emerger. It makes no concession to the natural's body hanging below the film.

Hook   16–28 Partridge L3A, L4A, E6A or K1A
Thread   Black Sparton Micro
Body   Peacock herl
Hackle   Very short-fibred grizzle palmered down the body

Schmidge

This is a pattern of my own, devised in 1985 to represent some of the smaller aquatic flies. I was aware of the many tiny flies in the film that trout and grayling can become so occupied with. It was inevitable that any artificial so small would have to be a very basic one to tie if I was to make them. What resulted is a suggestion of many different foods depending upon the colour of the tying thread and the hackle. Its use has convinced me that in various colours it has been taken for hatching midges, emerging micro-caddis species, emerging upwingeds, aphids and other terrestrials. The hackle should be thoroughly treated to float and the body rests in or under the film. You can argue with me whether it should be in a book on sub-surface fishing.

Hook   16–24 Partridge L3A, L4A or K1A
Thread   Coloured Sparton Micro
Hackle   Generous turns of grey partridge or alternative and trimmed to size

SMUTS (SIMULIUM)

Reed smuts are members of the Diptera order of flat-winged flies. They can be expected throughout the spring, summer and autumn on all types of rivers but they are more important to the fly fisher on weedy streams. Trout and grayling feed on the tiny black emerging adults and again when they oviposit. The adults average about 3–4mm and their small size is the main hindrance to a suitable decep-

ensures the fly stays suspended from the meniscus. It also incorporates the abdomen tied round the bend of the hook to copy the wriggling pupa or its curved abdomen. It really is a very good pattern.

Hook   16–20 Partridge L2A, CS20, L3A or A
Thread   Fine midge thread
Tail (optional)   White nylon filaments or white fluorescent wool, tied slightly round the bend
Body   Black, brown, red or green seal's fur subs or marabou
Rib   Narrow silver lurex
Thorax   Brown dyed turkey herl or bronze peacock herl
Head   A ball of white Ethafoam enclosed in a fine nylon mesh

Griffith's Gnat

This American imitation is becoming better known in the UK. I've used it to good effect on Yorkshire rivers. It is fished awash in the film

High summer on the river Wharfe where a small fly in the film is often a trout's downfall.

tion. The ascending pupae are also targets for fish and these can be imitated by the fly fisher.

The small wormlike larvae live on weed and vegetation and are prominent in trout diets. Their size and habitat make them impossible to imitate. At maturity the larva spins a cocoon in which it will pupate. Towards the end of pupation gas builds up within the pupal sheath to surround the adult fly. Eventually the pupal skin splits and black adult fly rises to the surface encapsulated in the gas bubble. The bubble is the means by which it ascends to the surface and it keeps the winged adult totally dry. At the meniscus the adult forces its way through the film to emerge dry and take flight fairly quickly. On the rare occasions I have seen the adults hanging below the film the highly reflective air sac was as prominent a feature as the fly itself.

The imitation is best fished in a dead drift just below the surface or in the film. With all small flies a fine tippet of soft nylon is required to aid a drag-free presentation. In the absence of a specific pattern sometimes any small black fly will work but those that have been tied to give some impression of the air bubble are more likely to succeed. Two artificials have become quite well known. The first is J.C. Mottram's pattern which I have dared to tamper with by including a small silver tinsel or lurex tip at the rear of the body to give a suggestion of the air bubble. This is the only imitation I use and I've had considerable success with it on smutting trout and grayling. It is fished in the film or never deeper than about an inch.

The second pattern comes from no less a vice than that of the Dane, Preben Torp Jacobsen. I've not used it because I've been happy with the first dressing and Jacobsen's body material isn't very common. One interesting feature is that the body should be well soaked in silicone so that when it is immersed in water air bubbles adhere to it. Perhaps an amended dressing with more accessible materials could use the appropriate colour Antron dubbing which also allows air bubbles to adhere.

Smut (Mottram)
Hook 14–18 Partridge E6A, CS20, L2A or L3A
Body Black floss as a thorax only
Tip (optional) Silver tinsel or lurex
Hackle One turn of a small starling breast feather

Smut (Jacobsen)
Hook 14 silvered wide-gape Mustad 72500
Thread Brown
Body Blood-red cow's hair over a base of thin copper wire, tied in the middle of the shank for about a third of its length and soaked in silicone liquid. Give 4 or 5 turns of fine silver wire (0.15mm) at both ends of the body

NYMPHING THE FILM: A SUMMARY

1. On all streams the top six inches of the stream is a main feeding area.
2. On many streams, particularly slow-moving rivers with a thicker surface film there is often difficulty for the emerging adult to penetrate the meniscus. The chances of fish feeding on emergers is higher.
3. With some fly species trout express a preference for the emergers over the adult fly.
4. On windy days emergers are taken in preference to duns.
5. In the early stages of any upwinged hatch, trout feed on the ascending nymphs near the surface.
6. During a hatch of fly there is as much chance of success with an emerger in the film as with a floating dun. Even in a heavy hatch where trout have many adults to choose from the nymph in the film or an emerger often works better than a floater. The struggling nymph is too much of an easy target for trout to pass by.
7. The dead-drift is the movement of most natural nymphs and pupae in the film. Each nymph and pupa is active as it emerges.

Whether you fish up, down or across the stream the aim is to present the imitation in the exact drift lane as the fish is lying. Trout regularly feeding at the top adopt a position just below the surface but they only do so when there is a steady supply of food. They have a narrow window of vision and are usually unwilling to move very far to either side of their window to feed. They are rather more willing to move to a nymph or pupa hanging below the surface than they are a floating fly. The latter shows itself on the mirrored underside of the surface beyond the trout's window only as a dimpled light pattern but the insect below the surface is clearly visible and is the more tempting. Even though there is hope for a misaligned drift the intention should be to present the fly in line with the fish. In a good fly hatch all trout need do is take up position in the food lane and wait for food to come to them.

10 Lines and Leaders

'Is it fine enough to fool fish? Is it long enough to fool fish? Is it strong enough to hold him?'
Lee Wulff on leaders

A great deal has been written about fly lines in recent years with almost every manufacturer claiming revolutionary developments for their particular manufacturing process or line composition and coating. I'm not prepared to recommend any particular brand of line simply because most of them work pretty well and changes are happening so quickly. Some are better than others. Generally speaking, the higher the price the better quality the line. The improved performance of an expensive line over a cheaper one is noticeable. But line A at three times the price of line B will not cast three times further or enable you to catch three times the number of trout. It might improve your casting by a yard or two; the line memory may be less or it may not lose its floating properties quite so easily. In most circumstances a £10 line works very well but when I can afford the £30 line I buy it because good equipment can sometimes make up the deficiencies in my presentation. For the first ten years of my fly fishing I used only mill-end (imperfect) lines and never paid more than £5 for any of them. They were not as smooth or so pleasurable to use as the more expensive lines but I doubt if I've caught many more fish simply because of the better line. For example, less than one per cent of my fishing is done at the limit of my casting distance so why do I need a line that will extend it a few feet? I fish fairly regularly and because much of my fishing time is spent casting I now prefer to use the lines that give me the most pleasure, have a minimum of memory and float high, despite the cost.

I'm not concerned here with the different brands of line, rather the different types of line and their suitability for river nymph fishing. My comments on tackle do not apply to still-water nymphing.

The choice of line is primarily one between a floating or sinking line. The sink-tip line has been superseded by the sinking braided leader which is more versatile, more effective and easier to cast. Forget the sink-tip.

The second choice is whether to use double taper or a weight-forward line. The benefits of the former are that it is a more uniform taper and is marginally easier to cast and it can be reversed when one end wears out. It is also easier to lift off the water at long range than a weight-forward line. Because the weight-forward line has a heavier front end, less line is required to make the rod work. For relatively short casting distances it has some value. It also can be cast further than the double taper should the need arise. The lines are not reversible. The Cortland Nymph Tip line which has a fluorescent red tip is only available as a weight-forward.

Despite the references I've made in this book to sinking fly lines which were made in relation to techniques that were developed before sinking braided leaders were invented, I'm going to suggest that the only fly line needed for ninety-nine per cent of river trout fishing is a floating one. Many anglers will need only a floating line. The sinking line is obsolete except for very specific circumstances. For many summer nymph fishers this has always been so but on big freestone rivers at spring or winter levels when grayling fishing, the sinking line was an alternative. I fished with fast-sinking lines using the Brooks method with much success for early season bottom-hugging trout and depths-of-winter grayling. Those days are past. The introduction of braided leaders of varying sinking rates has almost completely cancelled the need for a sinking line. Almost everything the sinking line does the braided leader can do with improved performance.

Braided leaders are available in a wide range of densities from a floater through to the densest which is claimed plummets at a staggering rate of thirteen inches every second. The range of choice of sinking rates offers much more scope than when using different sinking lines. Keeping a few braided leaders of different densities is very much cheaper than stocking different fly lines on spare spools. They are also much quicker to change. The Airflo brand of leaders is manufactured to sink tip first. This means that the end of the leader nearest the nymph sinks fastest producing more accurate depth presentation and

control. Even the top of the fastest-sinking leader is fine and because of its density, i.e. its weight for volume, it cuts through the water very quickly.

When fishing midwater and above the floating line is the only line for the job. When required, weight in the nymph or in the braided leader ensures it fishes at the correct depth. The question of which line to use when fishing on the bottom depends upon water speed and depth. Only in the fast, deep water will it ever be necessary to consider a sinking fly line and having considered it I would reject it in favour of the benefits of a floating line with a weighted fly and/or sinking braided leader.

For small stream fishing I use a leader made entirely of monofilament. On larger streams and rivers I usually use a braided leader of about four feet between the floating fly line and the tapering mono of nine to ten feet onto

Hans van Klinken takes a fish on a nymph drifted under the tree branches on the river Dove, North Yorkshire.

Roy Shaw holding a fine 2lb grayling which fell to a deep-sunk bug.

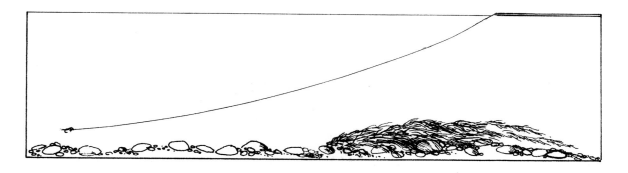

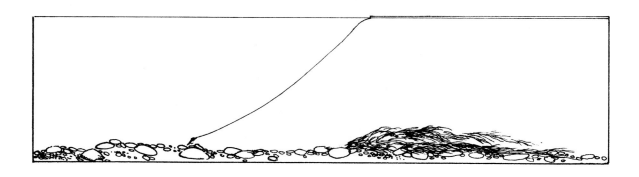

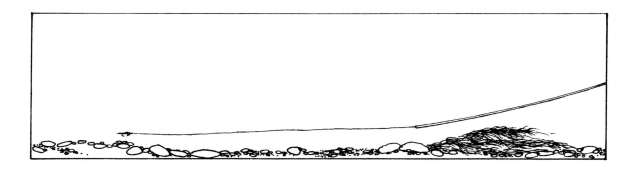

Fig 50   Upper illustration: weighted nymph, monofilament leader and floating line. Middle illustration: weighted nymph, sinking braided leader and floating line. Lower illustration: weighted nymph, monofilament leader and sinking line. These illustrations are based upon the most favourable current conditions and do not take into account the influence of a strong current broadside to the line which would have the most detrimental effect on the sinking line. The floating line offers the most control.

which there may be one or two droppers. If I'm fishing a single fly with a sinking braided leader I use a longer braided section of between five and seven feet with four feet of mono tippet. I find these three leader compositions very satisfactory for almost all my nymph fishing situations.

When fishing deep with a well-weighted nymph attached to monofilament and to a floating line, or to a braided leader and floating line, it will sink at least as quickly and often quicker than when attached to mono and a sinking fly line. On a moving river most sinking lines actually slow down the sinking rate of a weighted nymph. The nymph sinks faster simply suspended by mono from the floating line. The speed of the current midwater is faster than that at the bottom so the current is pushing the leader and/or line that is above the nymph. The diameter of the sinking fly line means that it is more easily dragged by the current than the finer mono and braided tippet which readily cuts through the water. A sinking fly line is more likely to give unnatural drag to a nymph. When using a floating line and a braided leader the sinking speed of the nymph depends upon the density of the leader and the weight of the fly. It is less affected by the horizontal push of the current than when using a bulky sinking fly line, all of which is under the surface. Nymph fishing is about accurate control of the nymph. The sinking line offers poor control. The floating line and monofilament with or without a sinking braided leader offers much more control.

I have yet to come across a situation where I've needed to use the fastest-sinking braided leaders. Should you do so be aware that they will drag down the tip of a floating line and so the most buoyant floating line should be used to minimize this. It is possible to use medium weight fly lines (AFTM 5–6) with the fastest-sinking leaders but it is easier to cast these leaders on heavier lines which require a rod not normally associated with river fishing.

Whatever method is used to get a nymph down to the bottom in very fast, deep water a rod capable of handling the heavier line is required, whether you use the Brooks method with a sinking line or a floating line with a fast-sinking braided leader.

Once the nymph has sunk to the required fishing depth its direction of imparted movement, i.e. other than where the current takes it, is determined by the type of line and leader. If a floating line is used with a monofilament leader or a floating braided leader then the direction of movement of the nymph will be broadly upwards and towards the angler. If a fast-sinking line or a fast-sinking braided leader is used with a heavy nymph the direction of retrieve will be much nearer to horizontal with a small angle of lift. The direction of the movement is a theoretical rough guide as the current pull and the distance the nymph has sunk both affect the direction of imparted movement. Leaders and lines in a range of sinking speeds between the floater and the one lying on the bottom will produce varying angles of retrieve. If a nymph is to be presented with the Live Nymph method on the bottom (page 111) then this is one of the rare occasions when a sinking line might be preferred. The nymph is retrieved along the bottom and a line and leader that will be retrieved at an angle as near as parallel to the stream bed are required. The sinking line is probably the only solution.

In choosing a line and leader remember that *the speed at which a nymph sinks depends upon the weight of the nymph and its leader.* A sinking fly line has very little influence on the sinking rate of a nymph unless attached by a very short leader. The angle of angler-imparted movement of the nymph depends on the type of line and leader. A fast-sinking line with a short leader or a sinking braided leader produces movement of the nymph nearer the horizontal plane. A floating line imparts movement nearer the vertical.

11 Considerations in Nymph Design

'Success is what we're after, but it's the failures that keep us coming back.'
Charles Brooks

Over the last century nymph design has developed along different lines with a number of basic pattern-types evolving. Each is soundly based on good theories of imitation, practical tying methods and successful fishing experience and yet the resulting nymphs differ considerably. 'Polly' Rosborough stresses the fuzziness of nymph bodies; Frank Sawyer and Oliver Kite produced sharply silhouetted nymphs and denied the need for legs; Charles Brooks insisted on tying 'in the round' and stressed the importance of legs. The trend in fishing emergers is to tie clear nymph-shaped bodies and yet I find on the rivers I fish the light silhouette of the soft-hackled spider is equally and often more effective. Every one is different; not one is wrong.

There are a number of schools of imitation in fly dressing. Perhaps four concepts are easiest to define in nymph design.

1. **Suggestive** A nondescript pattern that represents no one species in particular or even one order of flies, but its simple dressing clearly makes it food-like. For example the basic Gold-Ribbed Hare's Ear.
2. **Impressionistic** This style more clearly conveys a representation of a nymph-type or food form. Examples would be general imitations of stonefly nymphs, stone-clinging nymphs, agile-darting nymphs, shrimps etc. Size, shape and colour are major features.
3. **Realistic** These nymphs incorporate the major physical characteristics of the nymph-type or species to be copied; wing-cases, the number of tails, abdomen segments, gills, all

in correct proportion, size, shape and colour. Some dressings make use of a hook with an upward bend to the shank to represent a wiggling swimming action.
4. **Exact** This is nymph replication taken to its finest extreme, down to the to scale inclusion of the features of the natural nymph, including pattern markings on the body, antennae, jointed legs, feathered gills and eyes. Taken to its inevitable end these 'flies' become models. Some of them take hours to make. They look incredibly lifelike and I daresay, some even catch fish, although I guess that many are made to attract anglers more than trout. They are superb copies but I have neither the fly dressing skill nor the inclination to make them. No trout is more likely to be convinced simply by the inclusion of the additional features. Some aspects, such as the rigidity of these dressings actually deter fish rather than attract them.

I confess I've never fished with a nymph from the final category, although this point could be argued strongly; any imitation that has duped a fish must have succeeded in being an exact replication of a natural. Why else would the trout have taken it? All my fishing is done with nymphs (and dry flies) in the first three groups. My preferences are constantly changing from season to season and from day to day to meet the needs of trout and grayling in the rivers I'm fishing. I'm probably right in saying that ninety-eight per cent of my sub-surface fishing is with patterns in the suggestive and impressionistic categories, with occasional resort to a pattern with a more realistic tying. The closer to the real insect the artificial is, the less likely the imitation is to succeed when trout feed on another nymph species, therefore the more patterns you end up having to carry. By tying more specifically you might find yourself changing fly every five minutes!

I believe there are seven principal aspects to tying a nymph imitation. I tried to list them in some order of priority and although I can confirm the first two I could not with any conviction list the last five in order. Strong arguments could be made for any of the five as having precedence over each other in certain circumstances.

1. **Size** Overall size, in terms of length, breadth and depth of a nymph is important, with length being the most significant. *The smaller the natural nymph the more accurate the size of the imitation must be because with smaller imitations just a hook size difference may mean a major size discrepancy*. With small sizes length is the most important factor; with larger flies width and thickness should be taken into account.

2. **Colour** The overall colouring of the imitation must match the principal colour in the natural insect. It should be remembered that the colour of the artificial when wet may be two to four times darker than when dry in the tying vice. Modern synthetic dubbings have far more colour reliability than fur when wet. Specific body patterns, changes in colour, for instance at the thorax, or other variations on the natural may be included in the imitation but how far this is taken depends upon which school of imitation you subscribe to. The colour of the same species of insect may vary from month to month and from river to river so exact colour duplication is almost impossible.

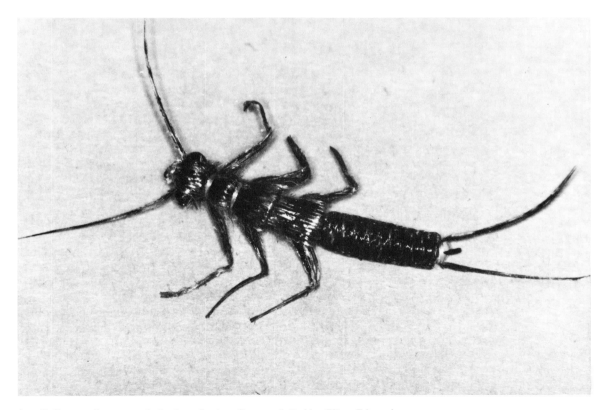

A realistic or perhaps exact imitation of a stonefly nymph tied by Oliver Edwards.

3. **Shape** The shape or silhouette of the artificial should match that of the natural. Again it depends upon how specific an imitation you want to tie. The closer you match the tapering body, bursting wingpads or the flattened shape of the stone-clingers the poorer imitation it will be of species that don't have these characteristics. The suggestive or impressionist designs of nymph are so generally shaped as to represent the widest range of aquatic food.

4. **Action** The *movement* of an imitation through the water depends upon how it is being fished in relation to the current and what degree of imparted movement or drag the angler directs or permits. The *action* of the artificial refers to the mobility of the materials used in the dressing and to what extent water passing through or over those materials produces movement within the nymph to imitate the body movements of the natural i.e. the tail, legs, gill filaments and abdominal wiggle.

5. **Translucency** When strongly back-lit some nymphs, pupae and emergers are part-translucent. The closer to the surface the imitation is designed to be fished the more important is the inclusion of translucent materials and the style of tying to maximize this effect. Notwithstanding the translucency of the actual fibres of the dubbing, a more translucent effect is produced by minimizing the amount of material being used. When in doubt use less body dubbing rather than more.

6. **Reflectivity** At the point of emergence nymphs and pupae have a fine layer of air beneath their outer skin. This mirror-like layer of air is highly reflective. Materials that trap air in their fibres are thus very effective in making emerger patterns. Antron's high degree of reflectivity and its air entrapment properties make it ideal for imitations where these features are important.

7. **Texture** Once a trout takes hold of an artificial the texture of it plays some part in how long it holds on to the fly before rejecting it. The larger the fly the greater care needs to be given to texture. There is always the insurmountable problem of a rigid hook bend and sharp point but in addition to these detrac-

tions there is some evidence that fish will reject a pattern if it is too hard or rigid; it is simply too unnatural. I am inclined to think that a very soft texture doesn't alert a fish but the more alarming hardness does.

The pluralism in nymph design has happened simply because all fly fishermen and fly tyers continually experiment with designs and materials particularly after periods of frustration with existing fly patterns. Inevitably certain features have been singled out for emphasis by different authorities at different times for specific circumstances. What we are left with are a number of designs that have been proved effective. Though often created for particular water types they are, nonetheless accepted by trout the world over. For example Sawyer created his Pheasant Tail nymph to give a general impression of some of the agile-darting nymphs of the upper Avon; Brooks did the same with his stonefly monsters for the big rivers of western America; LaFontaine produced the Sparkle Pupa for the mid-west American caddis; Goddard tied the Suspender midge for the slow chalk streams; van Klinken, the Leadhead and Klinkhamer Special for Scandinavian grayling; anon, the Goldhead for Austrian trout and Edwards' Ecdyonurus nymph for North Country rivers. The list is endless. Although each was designed for a specific circumstance, like most other patterns each of these will work wherever the natural nymph or caddis is to be found. I have used Skues' patterns in North America; North Country spiders in Scandinavia; Brooks' nymphs in Yorkshire; Sparkle Pupae everywhere and the permutations are endless. Each is successful because each is representing a food source found world-wide to a common species of fish that recognizes a nymph for what it is whether it's in the Test Valley, Montana, Lapland or the Chilean plains.

Sometimes trout may demand a pattern with fuzziness, other times with translucency. They might take any pattern so long as it's small, dark and darting fast or conversely, only if it's two inches long and almost static on the stream bed. Occasionally they'll take

Excellent nymph and dry-fly water. Hans van Klinken fishing the river Kyll.

almost anything, when they choose to ignore our conflicting theories of imitation. Perhaps the answer to the problem of their erratic pattern acceptance is that trout sometimes demand a particular feature at a certain time and that aspect of the natural or the imitation is the trigger to its acceptance. The answer is to know what trout are feeding on, how the key features of the natural can be incorporated in an imitation and to be prepared to carry a range of patterns to match the likely fishing situations. Many good fly fishermen could use a single pattern-type all season and catch a creditable number of trout but if you fish widely or there is a range of aquatic flies in your river you need patterns to match each stage of their life cycle. Inevitably the fly-box fills up.

This book is not concerned primarily with tying methods for sub-surface flies; that subject alone provides sufficient material for a whole book. I have mentioned in passing the style of the soft-hackle or spider fly and in addition I want to mention briefly the different ways of tying the nymph body. I believe this is the most important feature of the natural insect and therefore is the most critical in the imitation. I don't want to merely repeat information that is far better and more fully expressed in other excellent books (*see* the bibliography) but the important body tying methods warrant explanation. One book I thoroughly recommend is *Imitative Fly-Tying*, written and illustrated by Oliver Edwards and to be published shortly. I've been able to see some of the text and artwork and it is packed with information on natural and artificial flies and how a more accurate imitation can be tied. It will prove to be of immense value.

THE NYMPH BODY

In addition to the many different natural furs, hairs and herls, there are now very many synthetic materials or blends of natural and synthetic materials to choose from. All published dressings will specify certain materials but my own view is that unless there is an overriding reason why one particular herl, fur or synthetic is mentioned a close substitute usually makes no difference. I will be criticized for diluting the purity of the dressing but I'd like to justify myself a little and say that in my writings I have always strived to publish the accurate original tying of a pattern but what happens in my own fishing practice might be different. The materials may alter but the effect will be the same. For this reason I often describe the recipes for my own patterns in the widest terms, eg 'any mottled brown feather' or 'a long-fibred light-brown fur'.

Wound feather fibre herls make very acceptable nymph bodies. They are cheap, mostly easily obtainable and are simple to work with. The hundreds of barbules on each wound herl produce an effect not unlike the gills along the natural's abdomen. Some herls, most noticeably cock pheasant tail, are not a single colour but a broken mixture of colours and shades, part matt and part shiny and reflective to copy the mixed colours of the natural nymph. Pheasant tail offers no translucency but other herls with longer barbules create a hazy edge to the nymph body which may give the impression of translucency.

Originally all flies were made with entirely natural materials. Dubbed hair and fur bodies for nymph and wet flies are very effective. Some are translucent. Over the last two decades the use of synthetic fibres has increased, either as a substitute for the natural materials or as a mixture to provide the finished blend with the best attributes of both materials. Just a glance at a couple of fly-tying catalogues reveals twenty synthetic body dubbings,

blends or yarns suitable for nymphs. With most of these synthetics being available in a wide variety of colours, as many as fifty in one range, one can be forgiven for pausing before choosing.

The properties of these materials varies. Each one offers more of one and less of another. Features such as colour reflection when wet, translucency, air entrapment, texture, fuzziness and mobility are needed to a greater or lesser extent depending upon the natural insect being represented and where it is being fished.

Natural Hair and Fur

Angora Goat   Good substitute for seal's fur; offers similar features as seal except water-repellency; Orvis supply thirty colours.

Beaver   Grey-brown but mainly brown, water-repellent, glossy, some translucency.

Hare/Rabbit   Mask and ear; mixed speckled black, brown, tan, creamy and pale yellow fur; mixed soft and stiff fibres; produces fuzzy or shaggy bodies. Rabbit underfur: blue fibres.

Muskrat   Speckled grey; fine dubbing; some translucency; water-repellent.

Mole   A short-fibred soft, fine dubbing; dark blue-grey colour but can be bleached and dyed; excellent for lightly-dubbed bodies.

Australian Opossum   Various shades between cream, grey, red-brown; easy to dub.

Otter   Mid to dark brown; water-repellent; underfur best for dubbing.

Red Fox   Fine, easy to dub.

Seal   Natural fur is creamy and brown but is widely dyed; translucent; water-repellent; soft, baby seal's fur is easiest to dub; some types offer coarse crinkly underfur; becoming scarce as it is no longer imported.

Wool (sheep)   Natural and dyed colours; various fibre lengths; fine, soft, crinkly fibres are easiest to dub; absorbs water; good air entrapment.

Natural and Synthetic Blends

Orvis Antron/Hare blend   75 per cent Antron and 25 per cent hare's fur; natural qualities of hare plus additional benefits of

170

Antron; easy to dub; fourteen colours; recommended.

Synthetic Body Materials

Antron   Fibres are square in cross-section with excellent air entrapment; translucent; good sparkle when wet; wide range of colours; good nymph and caddis pupa material.
Body Glass/Polyband   Fine 'D' shape vinyl strip wound as a ribbed body; stretches for tapered bodies: some colours are translucent; range of colours.
Chenille   Water-absorbent; buggy and only suitable for largest bug-type patterns e.g. Wooly Worm.
Furry Foam/Body Gills   To be cut into strips and wound like a yarn to produce a fuzzy body; provides good representation of the natural's gills; thirteen colours.
Flexibody or Flexiform (Piscatoria)   A translucent (some colours), stretchy polyurethane to be cut into strips for winding; over twenty colours.
Furry Lead   Fine lead wire covered with synthetic fur and tinsel; good for heavyweight patterns but the tinsel can be a distraction; ten colours.
Larva Lace   A hollow vinyl; translucent in some colours; stretches; can be wound or threaded over the shank; twelve colours.
Latex   Stretchy, translucent, rubbery material for winding ribbed bodies.
Ligas dubbing   A soft, easy to dub material; translucent; seems to combine the benefits of Antron and polypropylene; wide range of natural colours.
Polypropylene dubbing   Very fine dubbing; easy to work with; specific gravity less than water; good for emergers or floating nymphs; forty colours.
Sparkle Yarn/dubbing   This should be a mixture of coloured and clear Antron but often coloured Antron is described as this. The clear fibres add extra sparkle in addition to other Antron properties.
Swannundaze   A stretchy vinyl material for winding bodies; 'D' shaped, one side flat, the other rounded; some colours translucent, also transparent available.

My own preference in the imitation of any natural fly, whether as a nymph, pupa or adult is for a body of natural or synthetic dubbing. Furry Foam or Body Gills have their limited uses but the wound vinyls I find much more restricting and in most patterns much less effective. Dubbing should be applied in such a way so that all the potential benefits of the material are maximized. In most nymph and pupae patterns the aim should be to produce a tapering body in which there are a few fibres sticking out and tied so that when worked in water the material responds with its own mobility as the current flows over it.

The simplest way of applying dubbing is to take a small amount in the hand and spread it thinly on the taut waxed tying thread. Twist it around the thread between the thumb and the first finger in a single direction. Don't twist it both ways or you'll be working against yourself. Continue to roll it until the dubbing surrounds and clings to the thread. Add more material further down the thread and repeat as necessary. When tying tapering bodies don't thicken the dubbing on the thread but wind in more turns of the uniformly dubbed fibres. I don't really think that it matters too much whether the fur is dubbed onto the thread in a clockwise or anti-clockwise direction, although both schools have their diehard adherents. The only time it is of any significant consequence is if the tying thread used is a multi-strand type in a spiral weave. In this case it is better to dub in a direction following the direction of the strands of the thread. To dub the opposite way would be to loosen the thread fibres. I hasten to add that this is rather theoretical as I know of excellent fly dressers who dub the opposite way.

Two further methods of producing nymph bodies are worthy of mention. With the thread wound to the rear of the shank, make a loop of the thread with one side waxed. Spread the fur of dubbing along the waxed length; close the loop and add a weight to the bottom and spin clockwise. The weight at the bottom may be heavy hackle pliers or a purpose-made dubbing whirl. The fur is now ready for winding. If longer-fibred materials are used and the fibres are laid along the thread a corded,

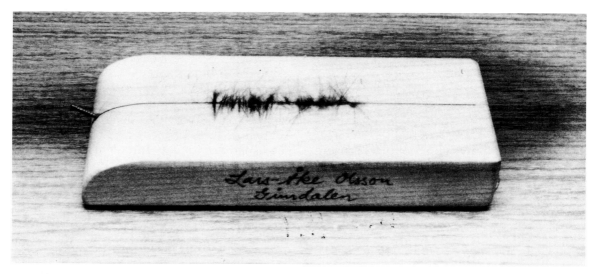

A spinning block; useful for creating fuzzy bodies with longer-fibred materials.

segmented body is produced that is neat and durable. If stiff, short-fibred materials are used and are laid across the thread a spiky, fairly fuzzy body results.

The second method is for longer-fibred materials when a shaggy, fuzzy body is required. Because longer fibres are difficult to lay across the thread without them falling away, a spinning block is used to enable the fibres to be evenly spaced out in a more manageable way. These loops are made independently of the fly being tied. A number can be spun at one sitting and stored on strong cardboard until needed. The longer fibres produce bodies that give the impression of a blur of legs, gills, tails and antennae. They also allow air to be trapped and give the impression of mobility.

The commonest fault of a dubbing on small patterns is that it is often not sparse enough and rather heavily applied. If there is any translucency in the material the colour of the thread can be seen through the dubbing. This was a common and important feature in the North Country spider patterns and it is an aspect of body dubbing often overlooked. With smaller patterns I suggest it is a feature well worth incorporating. W.H. Lawrie went so far as to write of dubbed nymph bodies that: 'It is better that the colour of the dubbing

be wrong than that the colour of the silk be incorrect.' In big nymph imitations there is so much body bulk that the colour of the underlying thread may be lost completely unless the body is built up from many turns of thinly-dubbed thread.

After any dubbing has been wound on it can be tampered with to produce a better effect. Where required, longer fibres can be picked out for legs or a greater fuzziness or the side fibres picked out to represent the gills; the body may be trimmed for neatness or some fibres pulled away if it is too heavily dubbed. In addition to a dubbing needle one of the most useful and effective body improvers is a small piece of Velcro glued on the end of an ice-lolly stick or similar. It is an easy way of quickly roughing up the body.

WEIGHTING NYMPHS

The only effective way of fishing midwater and deeper is by using a weighted nymph in conjunction with an appropriate style of presentation. Just how you weight the nymph determines how fast it sinks; what sort of angle it adopts in the drift; whether it fishes upside down or not and how much influence the current has on its movement. To a greater or lesser extent each of these factors should be considered when weighting. Some weighted patterns need to behave differently from others. Also you should be aware that a heavily weighted nymph drifts more in a straight line in the current than an unweighted one. Because of this the course and directional movement of a weighted pattern is more controllable than one without weight. Conversely the unweighted nymph is more likely to be taken where the current wills it and because it is nearer the actual weight of the natural nymph it moves more naturally in a dead-drift.

Frank Sawyer and others have used copper wire as the main weighting medium and this is fine for patterns to be fished midwater. If you want to achieve depth quickly lead wire or foil is a better choice. My preference is for lead wire as it is easier to work with and more readily obtainable than foil. However in the case of small imitations where bulk is to be avoided foil is more effective as it can be tied flatter than wire.

The position of the weight on the shank affects the angle of the nymph in the water. Of course the tension from the leader affects the angle but in a free drift a nymph with all the additional weight at the thorax will have a head-down position only if a long-shank hook is used. A thorax-weighted normal shank length hook still drifts on the level or even head-up because of the influence of the leader. A more even weight distribution on a long-shank hook will mean a broadly horizontal attitude and a rear-weighted nymph (only practical on larger patterns) permits a head-up drift. In choosing the method of weighting there are three primary considerations. How does the natural behave? In using a chosen presentation technique and weighted leader, if required, how much lead is needed to get the fly to where the fish are? If the nymph is to be fished close to a stream bed which has a lot of snags would it be easier if the nymph fished point uppermost?

There are additional weights in the form of appendages to the nymph e.g. a split-shot as used on the Leadhead or a gold bead on the Goldhead. These need no further weighting.

My own preference when using a largish weighted nymph on the bottom is to apply the weight so it fishes upside down and point uppermost. On the North Country rivers a large stonefly nymph has proved very effective and I dress this with the lead wire bound on top of the shank. When this is tied the hook is reversed in the vice and the rest of the dressing tied in upside down. If the waters to be fished are fast and turbulent there is little point in dressing a nymph with a clear upper and undersides as the artificial spins and twists in the current. Tying in the round is a better prospect. In more moderate currents an imitation with features specific to the dorsal and ventral sides is acceptable.

When imitating some of the stone-clingers I like to represent their broadening body and thorax by the shape of the lead wire. After winding the wire in over the front half of the shank it can be flattened with a pair of pliers. Not only does this provide a more realistic shape to the artificial but it also behaves more naturally. As a natural stone-clinger swims to the surface or is caught in the current above the stream bed the varying speeds of the water moving over stones etc on the bottom has much more of an influence on its behaviour than on a slim agile-darting nymph. It is jostled and rocked as its broad body is affected by the currents. They ascend to the surface in a slight side-to-side wobble. When the shape of the imitation is also matched in this way it helps it to match the natural's behaviour. When describing agile-darting nymphs, George Marryat is attributed with: 'You can imitate the nymph, but you cannot imitate the wiggle.' That may be so but at least with the stone-clingers you can imitate the wobble.

NYMPH HOOKS

Apart from the obvious suitability of the shank length for the pattern the other main consideration is that of weight. If the aim is to present the fly in the film or thereabouts, lighter weight hooks are an advantage. Similarly, heavy hooks are useful for when fishing deeper.

Hook or shank shape is also a variable factor although most patterns are tied on a straight horizontal shank. There are a few alternatives on offer for specific dressings. Natural shrimps and caddis pupae are frequently curved and to aid their imitation Partridge hooks K2B, K4A and K12ST are very useful. Partridge also produce the H3ST hook for tying the flat bodies of the stone-clinging nymphs. One of their recent developments is the MM3B Jardine Live Nymph hook suitable for tying patterns with gently curving body. Some hook manufacturers produce long-shank nymph hooks with a pronounced up or downward bend imparted to the front half of the shank. A well-tied nymph tied on these looks very impressive and I've no doubt the bent body well imitates the swimming motion of some naturals. My experience of their use, however, is that they catch no more fish than straight-bodied imitations and in slow water I'm inclined to believe that the unnaturally permanently bent body might even detract fish with a clear view of the fly. If you wish to tie on such hooks I recommend that a long-shank hook is placed firmly in the vice and you bend the hook yourself to the position you want.

12 A Selection of Nymphs and Sub-Surface Flies

'It isn't the least bit necessary to be able to identify the naturals; just find out what's crawling around or drifting with the current and match it for colour and size as best you can.'

Al MacClane *The Practical Fly Fisherman* (1953)

AGILE-DARTING NYMPHS

Bare Hook Nymph

Oliver Kite would fish this pattern to prove that it wasn't so much the detailed imitation of the nymph itself that mattered but the convincing factor would be its natural movement. When fished with a lift through the water in the manner of a nymph rising to the surface the Bare Hook Nymph worked. The trigger for the fish is its movement. There's little else it could be; certainly not translucency.

Hook   14–16 Code A, G3A or CS7
Thread   None
Thorax   Copper wire built up to shape

An agile-darting nymph. Note the hairy tails, gills along the abdomen and the mature wing-cases.

Greenwell Nymph

This is as good a general olive nymph imitation as you could need. Based on the original Greenwell's Glory it has been adapted into a nymph design. It carries no weight and is only suitable for fishing in the upper layers. When waxing the tying thread dark cobblers wax should be used and not clear wax.

Hook 12–18 Code A, G3A, CS7 or 18–20 GRS7MMB
Thread Well waxed primrose or yellow
Tail Greenwell (ginger/black) hackle fibres
Abdomen Waxed yellow thread
Rib Very fine gold wire
Thorax Grey or blue-grey fur
Wing-case Grouse hackle fibres with the ends turned under as legs

Iron Blue Nymph

A number of similar dressings to this one have been devised. One particular feature is the claret tying thread and tip. Nowhere on the natural nymph or dun does this colour appear, or at least not to the human eye. However it is a colour in the female spinner. Sometimes key colours in the female spinners are worth including in nymph and dun imitations either in the tying thread underbody or as another feature. The general body colour of this imitation is nearer that of the natural dun and not the nymph and yet the body colour works and has done for centuries.

Hook 14–16 Code G3A, L2A, CS7 or 18–20 GRS7MMB
Thread Claret
Tail White cock fibres
Body Mole's fur with a tip of tying thread exposed at the rear
Thorax Mole's fur
Wing-case Black crow or moorhen wing
Legs Wing-case fibres tied beneath the body

Gimriver Nymph

Lars-Åke Olsson created this *Baetis* nymph for his local river. Needless to say it catches wherever *Baetis* species abound. The fly is part of a series, nine of which Lars and Ronnie Eriksson devised for the Gim, a beautiful grayling and trout stream in mid-Sweden. The capercaillie feather used is much harder to obtain in the UK and could easily be substituted with the slightly lighter dark brown partridge.

Hook 12–16 Code L2A or GRS2A
Thread Olive
Tail 2–4 mottled brown feather fibres from a marginal covert capercaillie wing
Body Olive-dyed hare or beaver's fur, tapering to the rear
Legs 3–4 capercaillie fibres, as for the tail, on each side, between the thorax and the wing-case
Wing-case The butt of the same feather used for the legs folded forward over the legs

Large Dark Olive Nymph (Price)

This can represent any olive nymph although Taff Price tied it with *Baetis rhodani* in mind.

Hook 12–14 Code G3A, L2A, CS7 or 18–20 GRS7MMB
Thread Yellow
Tail Dark-olive hackle fibres
Abdomen Mixed olive seal's fur subs and hare's ear fur
Rib Fine gold wire
Thorax Brown seal's fur subs
Wing-case Dark-olive swan or goose fibres
Legs Tips of the wing-case fibres or olive cock fibres

Large Dark Olive Nymph (Edwards)

This excellent imitation from Oliver Edwards is very realistic. It is slim and translucent; it has dark wing-cases just like the mature nymph. But unlike many replicas this one has mobility in its legs and has a fuzzy thorax. Some of Oliver's patterns require a high level of tying skill but the additional effort will prove time well spent. Additional weight can be added under the thorax.

Hook 18 long-shank Code H1A or 18–20 GRS7MMB
Thread White, which after winding is coloured dull orange
Tail Badger hair dyed medium-olive

Abdomen Olive flexibody or olive-dyed polythene strip in overlapping turns
Wing-case Dark turkey feather fibres with a narrow strip of abdomen material down the centre
Legs Small speckled partridge feather dyed or coloured medium-dark olive, laid flat on a smear of varnish over the thorax before wing-cases are bound over
Thorax Olive-brown hare's belly fur

Spurwing Nymph (Edwards)
This is the same style of tying as the previous pattern.

Hook 18–22 2X long-shank, nickel-plated if possible
Thread Danvilles Spiderweb
Underbody A tiny amount of lead foil under the thorax
Tails Five or six lemon wood duck fibres or dyed mallard flank/breast feather fibres
Abdomen Very pale, almost colourless olive Flexibody or Flexiform (Piscatoria) in 8–9 quarter overlapping turns
Thorax Very pale yellow-olive fine synthetic dubbing
Legs Grey partridge hackle dyed pale yellow-olive, tips only about 3mm long
Thorax cover Flexibody, as for the abdomen
Wing buds Any black feather fibres, 2 clumps
Head Thorax cover folded back
Eyes The wing bud material trapped in the thorax wing cover folded back and trimmed

Spurwing Nymph (Waites)
The spurwing nymphs are probably the fastest of all the agile-darters. As Frank Sawyer pointed out, fast-moving darting nymphs always have their legs compressed tight against the body and so there is no need for their imitation. Tony Waites, head-keeper to the Driffield Angler's Club devised this pattern.

Hook 14–18 Code L2A or G3A
Thread Grey
Tail Three natural grey heron herl tips
Body Fine silver fuse-wire covered with three natural heron herls built up at the thorax

Rib Very fine silver wire
Wing-case (optional) Natural heron herl

STONE-CLINGING NYMPHS

Flat-Body Nymph (Roberts)
Many of the rivers I fish in the North of England have most species of stone-clinging nymphs in considerable numbers. Sometimes an imitation that specifically represents their characteristic flat broad shape does better than the usual cylindrical shape of most artificials. I fish this weighted pattern deep on the bottom as a general searching nymph and again in its smallest size just under the surface in a hatch. The hook used is the Partridge H3ST which was designed to imitate the stone-clinging nymphs. The hollow body of these double-shanked hooks can be packed with fine lead wire without having to include extra bulk above the shank which would eliminate the flat shape.

Hook 16 long-shank Code H3ST
Thread Olive
Tail Three olive Micro-fibbets marked with indelible pen, or brown partridge fibres
Abdomen Dark-olive or brown ostrich herl over a weighted shank
Rib Fine gold wire

A stone-clinging *Ecdyonurus* nymph.

Thorax Dark-olive rabbit's fur with fibres picked out; upper and lower dubbing trimmed flat
Wing-case Mottled brown quill or pheasant tail fibres
Legs Speckled brown partridge feather laid flat on a smear of varnish before wing-case is bound over

Yellow May Dun Emerger (Edwards)
There is a suspicion that some flies hatch out just under the surface rather than actually at the surface and the yellow May dun is one such species. Oliver Edwards devised this dressing when he discovered trout taking the emerging nymphs just showing the first signs of the wings.

Hook 16 Code H1A
Thread Pre-waxed yellow
Tail Grey partridge dyed pale sulphur-yellow
Abdomen Natural or synthetic fur dyed pale sulphur-yellow, covered by overlapping turns of 2mm-wide clear polythene strip
Thorax Same fur as the abdomen
Thorax cover and legs Grey partridge dyed pale sulphur-yellow
Emerging wings Light-brown Raffene trimmed to shape and size
Head Varnished yellow thread
Eyes (optional) Black head cement

August Dun Nymph (Roberts)
This is my own nymph of this species which is prolific on one of my local streams.

Hook 16 Code H3ST or 18 CRS7MMB
Thread Yellow
Tail Yellow guinea-fowl fibres
Underbody (optional) Lead wire packed between the split-shank
Body Mixed brown and pale-yellow seal's fur substitute with a few fibres picked out through the rib
Rib Fine gold wire
Wing-case Any dark mottled feather fibres
Legs Sparse turns of golden plover (ash-coloured feather with yellow tips) over the front of the thorax

March Brown Nymph (Roberts)
This is a pattern of my own devising which I've found very useful early season even on rivers that never see a March Brown hatch. It is probably suggestive of all the dark bronze stone-clingers. Even though the Draper Flat-Bodied Nymph hook, code H3ST produces quite a large imitation I'm of the opinion that when fishing deep in the early season a slight exaggeration in nymph size can be a help rather than a detraction. The leg hackle is laid flat on the thorax on a narrow strip of varnish before the wingcase is tied over.

Hook 14–16 Code H3ST, H1A, E1A, CS7 or 18 GRS7MMB
Thread Brown
Tail Three widely-spaced cock pheasant tail fibres
Body Cock pheasant tail over a lead wire underbody
Rib Gold wire
Thorax Hare's ear fur with the upper and lower fibres trimmed flat
Wing-case Woodcock wing feather fibres or any mottled brown substitute
Legs Small brown speckled partridge hackle laid flat

Ecdyonurus/Heptagenidae Nymph (Edwards)
Although Oliver Edwards tied this dressing with the *Ecdyonurus* species in mind it serves equally well to represent the *Rhithrogena* and *Heptagena* species common in all stony rivers. All of Oliver's patterns are extremely impressive to look at in the vice. They are equally as effective in fishing practice. The size and colouring can be amended to represent all stone-clinging species. When the tying is finished the abdomen back is darkened with a dark brown Pantone pen.

Hook 14–18 long-shank Code H1A
Thread Danvilles Spiderweb
Tail Three widely-spaced moose mane hairs or stout guard hairs of elk, skunk or moose dyed brown-olive
Underbody Fine copper or lead wire tied in a short broad head and flattened

Abdomen Yellow-olive Flexibody or Flexiform (Piscatoria) in 5 or 6 quarter overlapping turns
Abdominal gills Wound yellow-olive ostrich herl trimmed top and bottom
Thorax Yellow-olive Ligas dubbing
Wing buds Grouse hackle tip pulled forward
Legs Guinea fowl under cover dyed yellow-olive
Head Light-brown Raffene with optional black eyes coated with nail varnish

BURROWERS

Mayfly Nymph (Walker)
The only British species of burrowing nymphs are the *Ephemera danica*, *E. vulgata* and the very much rarer *E. lineata*. No trout can tell them apart. In the days before emergence they are active in the water. I'm sure that some of the success of the artificial is that such a large nymph is too much of a mouthful to let pass by. Richard Walker produced the most effective dressing thus far. Except for an emerger there is no need for any other.

Hook 10–14 long-shank Code H1A or GRS7MMB
Thread Brown
Tail Pheasant tail fibres
Abdomen Light yellow-buff angora wool with an optional lead foil underbody, and two bands of pheasant tails fibres near the rear
Rib Brown nylon thread over the abdomen
Thorax As for the abdomen, well picked out
Wing-case Pheasant tail fibres, with the ends turned down for legs

MOSS-CREEPERS AND SILT-CRAWLERS

Blue-Winged Olive Nymph (Edwards)
The nymph is inactive except at emergence. This is another highly realistic and effective dressing from Oliver Edwards.

Hook 18–20 Code L2A
Thread Orange

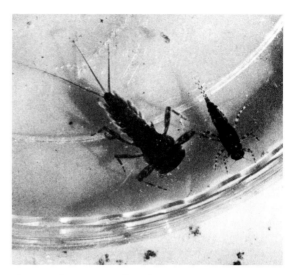

A stone-clinging nymph and a moss-creeping blue-winged olive (*Ephemerella ignita*).

Tail Dark mottled partridge tail
Abdomen and thorax Sandy hare's ear fur
Rib Finest gold wire on the abdomen
Legs Dark partridge hackle
Wing-case Dark partridge tail fibres in two clumps with a clear divide between
Head Dubbed sandy hare's ear fur, smeared with varnish, tightened into a spindle and wound on

Caenis Nymph (Carnill)
Bob Carnill's imitation is as fine a *Caenis* imitation as I've seen. It was devised for stillwater fishing but there's no reason for its use to be so restricted.

Hook 16 Code G3A
Thread Brown
Tail Three widely-spaced brown partridge hackle or tail fibres
Body Drab-brown swan, goose or heron herl
Rib Stripped peacock quill
Thorax Hare's ear fur
Wing-case and thorax cover Biot quills from the narrow side of a heron primary feather, the quills are tied in with the broad ends facing rear over the body, and trimmed and rounded so they extend halfway down the body
Legs Speckled partridge fibres

SHRIMPS AND BUGS

Red Spot Shrimp

This is Neil Patterson's dressing that incorporates an imitation of the orangey-red blob seen on some natural shrimps. As an alternative to the original body material I use Ligas dubbing which is claimed to be ultra-translucent, an important feature in shrimp imitations.

Hook   10–14 Code A or K2B
Thread   Waxed olive
Underbody   Fine lead wire
Body   Mixed olive seal's fur substitute and olive mohair, dubbed either side of a round tuft of fluorescent red wool which is trimmed to leave a red blob on either side
Rib   Gold wire
Back   Double layer of clear plastic
Legs   Body fibres picked out

Edwards' Shrimp

Most of the shrimps in my local streams are very pale olive or grey but very few patterns are tied with grey as the principal colour. This excellent dressing from Oliver Edwards also includes head and tail appendages.

Hook   10–14 Code G3A or CS7SHW
Thread   Grey
Underbody   Lead wire or foil bound onto the top of the shank in a hump
Tail and head appendages   Pale olive dyed or natural grey partridge fibres
Back   Clear polythene
Body   Dubbed mixture of very pale olive-dyed fine fur and grey partridge fibres with the fibres picked out for legs
Rib   Nylon mono in a neutral colour, about 4lb breaking strain

Mating Shrimp (Goddard)
Hook   Wide-gape 10–12 Code A or K4A
Thread   Olive
Underbody   Fine lead strips built into a hump on top of the shank
Body   Mixed seal's fur substitute olive, dark brown and fluorescent pink (6:3:1)
Rib   Oval silver wire
Back   Clear PVC or polythene

Killer or Grayling Bug

Frank Sawyer's excellent grayling bug also works well on trout and on rivers other than the chalk streams for which it was devised. Few flies can be so easy to tie, nor many so effective. The only clue to the reason for its success is that it excels in waters where shrimp abound.

Hook   10–16 Code G3A or CS7
Thread   None
Body   An underbody of fine lead wire overlaid with beige darning wool in a cigar shape, and fine copper wire is used to tie in and finish off the materials

Dove Bug

This is my own bug devised for grayling but with a number of very good trout to its credit. It should be fished deep, as close to the bottom as possible and fished in a dead-drift or with an occasional lift. It is probably taken for a sedge pupae drifting along the bottom prior to ascending, or a shrimp. My intention was simply to make it edible. The colours I use vary slightly and now I use one with green fur rather than orange and pink.

Hook   10–12 Code G3A or CS7
Thread   Brown
Body   An underbody of lead or copper wire covered with mixed seal's fur substitute; rear half, orange and pink; front half orange and brown
Rib   Fine gold tinsel, gold or copper wire

SOFT-HACKLE OR SPIDER FLIES

If tyers want to maintain the purity of their dressings and use silk instead of the modern synthetic threads I have quoted the relevant Pearsall's silk references if the dressing was given by Edmonds and Lee.

Hare's Lug & Plover
I've found this to be an excellent general olive imitation and when wound with a semi-palmered hackle it becomes a very successful

Frank Sawyer fishing the upper Avon for grayling.

emerger when allowed to drift drag-free in the film.

Hook 14–16 Code A, G3A or L2A
Thread Waxed primrose or silk
Tip (optional) Gold tinsel tied very small
Body Thinly dubbed hare's ear fur tapering to the rear
Rib Fine gold wire
Hackle Golden plover marginal covert feather (pale-brown or dark ash feather with yellow tips)

Partridge Series

Bare thread or silk, perhaps a rib of wire and a couple of turns of hackle combine to make some of the easiest flies to tie and some of the most effective. By changing the body colour a whole range of nymphs are represented. Black, blue, yellow and orange are the commonest. All use the speckled brown partridge feather except the yellow version which uses the grey feather. The Partridge and Orange is perhaps the most versatile of North Country flies as it works throughout the trout and grayling seasons.

Partridge and Orange

Hook 12–16 Code A, G3A or L2A
Thread Orange, Pearsall's No. 6A silk
Rib (optional) Gold wire or fine oval tinsel
Hackle Brown partridge

Partridge and Blue

Hook 12–16 Code A, G3A or L2A
Body Dark blue thread or silk, lightly dubbed with lead-coloured lamb's wool
Hackle Brown partridge

Woodcock Series

This series of soft-hackled flies share the same well-marked woodcock hackle with the varia-

North country fly fishing a team of flies on the river Ure.

tion of the colour of the body. They are taken for a range of nymphs, emergers and caddis pupae. Other body colours include orange, brown and yellow.

Hook 12–16 Code G3A, L2A or A
Thread Green
Body Green thread or silk thinly dubbed with seal's fur substitute
Hackle Woodcock marginal covert feather

Snipe and Purple

A good imitation when the iron blues are about but also a pretty good early and end of season pattern.

Hook 14–16 Code L2A, G3A or A
Body Purple thread, Pearsall's No. 8
Hackle Dark snipe marginal covert feather, preferably spoon-shaped and sparsely tied

Dotterel Series

In the same way that the partridge and wood-cock series can be varied by their body colour so can this one. They are taken for various nymphs and emergers. The Stewart-style hackle improves the emerging imitation. The dotterel is now a very rare and protected species but the golden plover marginal covert feather is a suitable replacement.

Hook 12–16 Code A, G3A or L2A
Body Coloured thread or silk
Hackle Small golden plover, pale-brown or dark ash with yellow tips

Waterhen Bloa

This is a superb fly that most North Country fly fishers would not wish to be without. It can be used throughout the season as a general olive imitation or more specifically as an imitation of the iron blue. It is one of my favourite top dropper patterns for northern rivers. The wax used on the tying thread should be dark cobbler's wax.

Hook 14–16 Code A, G3A or L2A
Thread Yellow thread or unwaxed Pearsall's No. 4 silk
Body Tying thread thinly dubbed with mole

or blue water-rat's fur and sometimes a tip of tying thread is left exposed
Hackle Undercovert or marginal covert feather from a moorhen's (waterhen) wing

Poult Bloa

Hook 14–16 Code A, G3A or L2A
Thread Primrose thread or Pearsall's No. 3 silk
Body Tying thread, optionally dubbed with natural red or ginger fur
Rib (optional) Fine gold wire on the undubbed body
Hackle Slate-blue feather from a young grouse underwing or as a substitute marginal covert of a coot's wing

February Red

This is one of the earliest stoneflies and is often found in the weedy, slower streams more normally associated with plecoptera.

Hook 14 Code L3A, L2A or E6A
Thread Dark-orange
Body Thinly dubbed mixed claret and brown seal's fur substitute
Rib Dark-brown thread
Hackle Two turns of woodcock or semi-palmered over the front third of the body

Dark Spanish Needle

This is Pritt's dressing for the widespread stoneflies commonly known as needle flies. As their name suggests both the adults and nymphs are very slim.

Hook 14–16 Code A, L2A or G3A
Body Orange-brown silk, Pearsall's No. 6B
Hackle Feather from the darkest part of a brown owl's wing or substitute
Head Peacock herl

Yellow Sally

One of the easiest adult stoneflies to recognize is the yellow-bodied and yellow-green winged yellow sally. The adults can be expected from April to August and the nymphs will be actively moving over the substrata towards the margins prior to emergence. This is my own dressing adapted from Pritt's. It has also worked when yellow May duns (*Heptagenia sulphurea*) were emerging, when the nymph and emergers seem more attractive than the adults.

Hook   14–16 Code L2A, G3A or L2A
Thread   Primrose
Body   Dubbed pale yellow fur
Hackle   Golden plover (pale-brown or dark-ash coloured with yellow tips)

MISCELLANEOUS NYMPHS

Hare's Ear

From a long-shank size 8 to a standard size 18 the Hare's Ear in its different guises, with or without a gold rib, is perhaps the most versatile fly pattern devised. It may be leaded to fish deep in the manner of a caddis larva (Lars-Åke Olsson has a copper-ribbed leaded version), nearer the surface as a caddis pupa or a nymph, and in the film as an emerger or a dry fly. Much depends upon the size of the dressing and the manner of its presentation. The dubbing can be applied to produce a fuzzy body, suggestive of a wide range of food.

I've had considerable success with the fly using sizes 16 and 18 as an emerger in or just below the film. When trout take small flies in the film it is often very difficult to work out what they are taking; I've found the nondescript, fuzzy Hare's Ear very acceptable. For some years I fished a suspender version with an ethafoam ball trapped in a stocking mesh. Now I often use an even simpler emerger pattern with a fold of transparent, colourless closed-cell foam as a wing-clump. This keeps the nymph buoyant, gives the impression of crumpled wings and additional translucency. The standard simple dressing takes a lot of beating.

Hook   Long-shank 8 – standard 18 of a shank length and shape to match the natural
Thread   Tan, orange or yellow
Underbody (optional)   Lead wire or foil
Body   Mixed hare's ear fur – the longer fibres may be picked out for legs
Rib (optional)   Fine flat gold tinsel or wire

Colonel's Game Pie Nymph

This nymph has a very 'trouty' look about it and I know from firsthand experience just what a good pattern it is. I first saw it in Michael Leighton's excellent little book *Trout Flies of Shropshire and the Welsh Borderlands* (1987), in which he repeats the comments of its creator, Colonel George Ellis, that it is taken for a shrimp, cased caddis or a hatching sedge. I also suggest it is a true ephemeroptera nymph imitation.

Hook   12 Code L2A, L3A, CS7 or 16–18 GRS7MMB
Thread   Brown
Tail   Bronze mallard fibres
Body   Dark hare's ear fur
Rib   Fine gold wire
Thorax   Mixed rabbit underfur and guard hair, over an optional under thorax of lead wire
Wing-case   Cock pheasant tail fibres
Legs   Brown partridge tied as a beard hackle

Teeny Nymph

An American pattern devised by Jim Teeny – most effective for me when fished in relatively calm, very slow-moving water. I've used still-water tactics retrieving it in with slow pulls in the upper layers. I don't like fishing patterns whose reason for success escapes me. It is probably taken for an agile-darting nymph.

Hook   12 Code CS7 or CS20 or 14–16 long shank H1A
Thread   Black or brown
Body   Cock pheasant tail fibres
Legs   Two bunches of cock pheasant tail fibre points; one at the head, the other halfway along the body

Swanny Nymph

This is Hans van Klinken's dressing. It looks like a midge pupa imitation but it has an extremely translucent abdomen.

Hook   12–14 Code H1A
Thread   Black Sparton micro
Body   Clear Swannundaze held in place with waterproof superglue

Thorax Long-fibred red fox with some fibres well picked out for legs
Wing-case Peacock herl

Fledermaus

This American pattern is extremely popular in its homeland and is becoming better known in the UK. Polly Rosborough claims that a size 8 Fledermaus would be his choice if he was restricted to a single fly whether wet, dry, nymph or streamer. This is the original dressing from Jack Schnieder. Rosborough's dressing has a collar of Australian opossum fur and an underwing of silver mallard side feather and overwing of brown widgeon side feather.

Hook 10–16 long-shank Code H1A or D4A
Thread Brown
Body Muskrat body fur of mixed length fibres tied to be shaggy
Wing Grey squirrel tail

Casual Dress

This is Polly Rosborough's creation epitomizing his fuzzy fly philosophy. He dresses it in a range of sizes from a 12 upto a massive 3X long-shank size 2 and never fishes smaller than a 14 in any pattern.

Hook 10–14 long-shank Code H1A or D4A
Thread Black
Tail, Body and Collar Muskrat back fur, felted in hot soapsuds, rinsed and spun on the shank
Head 3–5 black ostrich herl strands, twisted together and wound

Klinken Nymph

This is a fairly nondescript nymph from Hans van Klinken that has served me well on a variety of waters. Although it is a round nymph and not designed with the flat-bodied species in mind when viewed from above or below it has sufficient bulk to represent these nymphs. It just looks edible. Hans doesn't specify weighting the body but I recommend it is done to ensure it fishes deep where these nymphs are found.

Hook 14–16 long-shank Code H1A
Thread Grey
Tail Pheasant tail fibres
Abdomen Olive-brown ostrich herl wound with clear or translucent olive Swannundaze wound so that the herl shows through to represent the gills
Thorax Grey squirrel tail fibres
Wing-case and legs Pheasant tail fibres

Sunk Spinner

Charles Jardine ties this imitation of the post ovipositing *Baetis* spinners which crawl below the surface to lay their eggs. Inevitably some of the flies are caught up in the drift and trout feed on them. They are not nymphs in any way but the manner of fishing the imitation is similar. Artificials are best fished downstrem of obstacles in the river or other places where spinners are known to crawl below the surface. If fish can be seen feeding in the evening and the obvious nymph patterns fail it might just be the spinners they are taking.

Hook 16–20 Code E6A
Thread Hot orange
Tail Two Microfibetts or nylon paint brush bristles
Body and abdomen Pale yellow Antron/hare mix
Wing Pearlescent Mylar tinsel laid as wing pads
Hackle Smoky pale-blue dun clipped top and bottom

An Afterthought

In *A Summer on the Test* (1924), John Waller Hills found it necessary to write this . . .

'More and more each year does nymph fishing become a part of the modern angler's equipment, and he who does not possess the art is gravely handicapped. And at the same time has come the realization that this art is both difficult and delightful. It demands different qualities and it makes a different appeal, it opens new fields of observation and experiment, and it is as exacting a process as the other, for upon my word I find trout harder to catch under water than on top.'

Upon my word, so do I.

Bibliography

'The shelves of volumes on trout fishing already outstretch the lifetime of the most aged and bookish angler . . . These publications are of two sorts, romantic fiction and science fiction.'

Richard Gordon *Instant Fishing* 1979

Arbona, Fred L. Jr, *Mayflies, the Angler, and the Trout* (Winchester Press, 1980, USA).

Borger, Gary, *Nymphing* (Stackpole, 1979, USA).

Brooks, Charles, *The Trout and the Stream* (Crown, 1974, USA).
Nymph Fishing for Larger Trout (Crown, 1976, USA).

Dunham, Judith, *The Art of the Trout Fly* (Chronicle Books, 1988, USA).

Fogg, Roger, W.S., *The Art of the Wet Fly* (Black, n.d.).
A Handbook of North Country Trout Flies (Old Vicarage Publications, 1988).

Goddard, John, *Trout Fly Recognition* (Black, 1960)
Waterside Guide (Unwin Hyman, 1988).
and Clark, Brian, *The Trout and the Fly* (Benn, 1980).

Edmonds, H.H., and Lee, N.N., *Brook and River Trouting* (Privately printed, 1916), reprinted 1980, Orange Partridge Press).

Elliott, J.M., Humpesch, U.H., Macan, T.T., *Larvae of the British Ephemeroptera* (Freshwater Biological Association, 1988).

Gordon, Sid., *How to Fish from Top to Bottom* (Stackpole, 1955, USA).

Harris, J.R., *An Angler's Entomology* (Collins, 1950).

Humphreys, Joe, *Trout Tactics* (Stackpole, 1981, USA).

Hynes, H.B.N., *A Key to the Adults and Nymphs of the British Stoneflies* (Freshwater Biological Association, revised 1977).

Jorgensen, Paul, *Modern Trout Flies and How to Tie Them* (Nick Lyons/Doubleday, 1979, USA).

Kaufmann, R., *The Fly Tyers Nymph Manual* (Western Fisherman's Press, 1986, USA).

Kite, Oliver, *Nymph Fishing in Theory and Practice* (Jenkins, 1963, 1969).

Koch, Ed., *Fishing the Midge* (Freshet, 1972, USA).

LaFontaine, Gary, *Caddisflies* (Winchester Press, 1981, USA).

Lawrie, W.H., *The Book of the Rough Stream Nymph* (Oliver and Boyd, 1947).
All-Fur Flies and How to Dress Them (Pelham, 1967).

Leisenring, James and Hidy, Vernon, *The Art of Tying the Wet Fly and Fishing the Flymph* (Crown, 1971, USA).

Martin, Darrel, *Fly-Tying Methods* (David and Charles, 1987).

Migel, Michael J., and Wright, Leonard M., *The Masters on the Nymph* (Winchester Press, 1979, USA).

Nemes, Sylvester, *The Soft-Hackled Fly* (Published by the author, 1975, USA).
The Soft-Hackled Fly Addict (Published by the author, 1981, USA).

Overfield, T. Donald, *Famous Flies and their Originators* (Black, 1972).
G.E.M. Skues: The Way of a Man with a Trout (Benn, 1977).

Pritt, T.E., *Yorkshire Trout Flies* (Goodall and Siddick, 1885).

Richards, Carl, Swisher, Doug and Arbona, Fred, *Stoneflies* (Winchester Press, 1980, USA).

Roberts, John *The New Illustrated Dictionary of Trout Flies* (Allen & Unwin, 1986, Unwin Hyman, 1988).
A Guide to River Trout Flies (Crowood Press, 1989).

Rosborough, E.H. 'Polly', *Tying and Fishing the Fuzzy Nymphs* (Stackpole, 1958, 4th ed. 1988, USA).

Sawyer, Frank, *Keeper of the Stream* (Black, 1952).

Nymphs and the Trout (Stanley Paul, 1958, Black, 1970).

Schweibert, Ernest, *Nymphs* (Winchester Press, 1973, USA).

Skues, G.E.M., *Minor Tactics of the Chalk Streams* (Black, 1910).

The Way of a Trout with a Fly (Black, 1921).

Side Lines, Side Lights and Reflections (Seeley Service, 1932).

Nymph Fishing for Chalkstream Trout (Black, 1939).

Silk, Fur and Feather (Fishing Gazette, 1950).

Itchen Memories (Black, 1951).

Stewart, W.C., *The Practical Angler* (Black, 1857).

Swisher, Doug and Richards, Carl, *Fly Fishing Strategy* (Crown, 1975, USA).

Whitlock, Dave, *Dave Whitlock's Guide to Aquatic Trout Foods* (Winchester Press, 1982, USA).

Index